Eckhart Arnold
Explaining Altruism
A Simulation-Based Approach and its Limits

PRACTICAL PHILOSOPHY

Herausgegeben von / Edited by

Herlinde Pauer-Studer • Neil Roughley
Peter Schaber • Ralf Stoecker

Band 11 / Volume 11

The aim of the series is to publish high-quality work
that deals with questions in practical philosophy from
a broadly analytic perspective. These include questions
in meta-ethics, normative ethics and "applied" ethics,
as well as in political philosophy, philosophy of law
and the philosophy of action. Through the publication
of work in both German and English the series aims
to facilitate discussion between
English- and Germanspeaking
practical philosophers.

Eckhart Arnold

Explaining Altruism

A Simulation-Based Approach and its Limits

ontos
verlag

Frankfurt I Paris I Lancaster I New Brunswick

Bibliographic information published by the Deutsche Nationalbibliothek
The Deutsche Nationalbibliothek lists this publication in the Deutsche Nationalbibliographie;
detailed bibliographic data is available in the Internet at http://dnb.ddb.de

North and South America by
Transaction Books
Rutgers University
Piscataway, NJ 08854-8042
trans@transactionpub.com

United Kingdom, Ire, Iceland, Turkey, Malta, Portugal by
Gazelle Books Services Limited
White Cross Mills
Hightown
LANCASTER, LA1 4XS
sales@gazellebooks.co.uk

Livraison pour la France et la Belgique:
Librairie Philosophique J.Vrin
6, place de la Sorbonne ; F-75005 PARIS
Tel. +33 (0)1 43 54 03 47 ; Fax +33 (0)1 43 54 48 18
www.vrin.fr

©2008 ontos verlag
P.O. Box 15 41, D-63133 Heusenstamm nr. Frankfurt
www.ontosverlag.com

ISBN: 978-3-86838-007-1

2008

Printed on acid-free paper
ISO-Norm 970-6
This hardcover binding meets the International Library standard

Printed in Germany
by buch bücher dd ag

Contents

Chapter 1

Introduction

In this book I examine evolutionary explanations of altruism that are based on computer simulations. When speaking of *explanations* of altruism, this means that this book is not primarily a study that tries to explain altruism itself, but a critical examination of how these explanations work. Its aim is twofold: On the one hand, it will expound this type of explanations of altruism, describe its working mechanisms and the results that can be obtained. In this respect this book strongly draws on the simulation based approach to the evolution of altruism that was pioneered by Robert Axelrod and William D. Hamilton (Axelrod and Hamilton, 1981) and made popular through Axelrod's book on "The Evolution of Cooperation" (Axelrod, 1984). However, after the more than twenty years that have passed since the publication of this book, the fact can hardly be ignored that the simulation-based approach to the explanation of altruism did not quite live up to the very expectations and aspirations that it once gave rise to and to the "simulation hype" it caused. Therefore, this book will on the other hand broadly discuss the limits of this approach. My aim is to give a clear diagnosis of this failure, to explain why this approach remained largely unsuccessful and also to point out what lessons regarding the research design of computer simulations can be learned in order to allow a more purposeful employment of computer simulations for scientific explanations in the future.

In this introduction, I first say a few words about the topic and theoretical background that is, about why the evolution of altruism is a topic that interests us, why an evolutionary approach may be suitable to tackle the question of altruism and, finally, how computer simulations come into play here. Then, I briefly explain my method for examining the simulation-based evolutionary explanations of altruism and its alleged failure. Basically, my method consists in conducting some simulations in the common fashion of this approach myself and looking at the corresponding empirical research both in biology and in the social sciences. I also give in this introduction a very brief overview of the main results of my inquiry. Finally, I present the structuring of this book and, in this context, further describe the methodological decisions I have taken.

1.1 The explanation of altruism as a scientific problem

The explanation of altruism poses an intriguing riddle both in biology and in the social sciences. In biology the question is how, if "survival of the fittest" is the rule, altruistic behavioral traits can evolve when altruism means by definition the giving-up of some of an organism's own fitness in order to increase the fitness of another organism. Yet, as ants, honeybees or the behavior of brood care in almost any species testify, altruism does exist in nature. How then, did it arise?

Similarly, while we all believe that humans are moral creatures that can by proper education and appropriate incentives learn to behave as altruists, the question still remains why, if – as we observe in many areas of life – egoism is the road to success, altruistic norms should continue to enjoy a high and general esteem. Should not a lack of secular success of the adherents of altruistic norms mark such norms as unrealistic if not foolish?

Moreover, altruism raises not only important questions in the empirical sciences, but also for moral philosophy and metaphysics. For, when we postulate altruistic moral norms we surely want to know (if we are not pure *Gesinnungsethiker*) whether and to what degree we can realistically expect obedience to these norms. From a metaphysical perspective the question of the viability of altruism links to the old question of whether the world as a whole is good or bad and, if bad, whether it can be made any better or if we will have to cope with the fact that "the realm of virtue is not from this earth" (Schopenhauer, 1977).

Thus, the existence of altruism demands an explanation and the desirability of altruism calls for an understanding of the circumstances under which altruism can flourish. In this book an examination will be made as to what an evolutionary simulation-based approach can contribute to the understanding of altruism.

1.2 Method and central theses

Why use an evolutionary approach for the explanation of altruism? In biology the answer to this question is obvious: Any phenotypic trait of any organism must – according to Darwin's theory of evolution – have evolved through natural selection. If a certain organism or species exposes an altruistic behavioral trait then there must be an evolutionary explanation for it. The situation is different in the social sciences. As is usual in the social sciences there exist many competing paradigms upon which a scientist could draw in order to explain the genesis of social norms, including norms that prescribe altruistic conduct. The evolutionary theory of culture which seeks to apply the principles of the Darwinian theory of evolution (reproduction, variation, selection) to the evolution of cultural traits is a comparatively young contender. Its practical value for the social sciences is still disputed[1] and, due to the fact that there exist many good alternative explanations for cultural developments, it would be too much to expect that the evolutionary theory of culture could repeat in the social sciences the very success that Darwinism had in biology. Yet, there are some good points in favor of it. First of all, the evolutionary theory of culture may prove able to explain things that other theories of cultural developments cannot explain.[2] Then, where it proves able to explain cultural developments, it most probably can provide general patterns of explanation that can be applied both in biology and in social sciences. If the evolutionary theory of culture should prove to be successful then it could be regarded as a great advance in terms of the economy of knowledge. Finally, explanatory patterns that cover different areas of research may profit from synergistic effects, which means that an advancement of modeling or empirical research in one of the fields may carry over to the other fields.

However, there are also downsides to such a generalizing approach. Most notably there is the danger of overlooking peculiarities of the respective areas of research and, as always with generalizing, there is the danger of oversimplification. Ultimately, the choice to use an evolutionary approach to study altruism is – as far as the social sciences are concerned – to some degree a matter of preference and motivated by the desire to find an explanation for altruism as broad as possible.

Given that it has been decided to use an evolutionary approach to study altruism the next question would be why computer simulations should be employed to furnish the evolutionary research on altruism. In

---

[1]See Bryant (Bryant, 2004) for a fundamental criticism of the evolutionary theory of culture.
[2]See Arnold (Arnold, 2002) for some speculations on this topic.

principle, there would be four different alternatives: 1) One could rely on purely verbal reasoning to explain the evolution of altruism. But then, verbal evolutionary explanations tend to be notoriously weak. It is almost always possible to construct some sort of evolutionary story of why some certain trait had to evolve and often it is just as easy to explain on the same level why its opposite should have evolved (even if in fact it did not) if only because it is usually easy to feign some plausible selective conditions under which the trait in question would be advantageous. 2) Another alternative is mathematical modeling. It allows – as one should presume – for a very precise expression of the concepts in question, but it can easily become extremely complicated and tedious, once it rises above the mere expression of the concept of, say, reciprocal altruism to models that can halfway realistically depict a situation in the real world where altruism evolved.[3] 3) The latter problem can potentially be addressed by numerical models, which class includes also the computer simulations of altruism. Computer simulations are an extremely flexible, easy to use and powerful tool. Of course all computer simulations rely on mathematical background theories such as, for example, evolutionary game theory. In this sense there does not really exist an opposition between computer simulations and mathematics but rather a dependency. But with computer simulations it is easily possible to go beyond what can be modeled in purely mathematical terms. Because of their ease and power, computer simulations seem to have been regarded by many as the tool of choice for the study of the evolution of altruism. 4) Last but not least, there is the empirical approach to altruism, which roughly means looking at empirical instances of potentially altruistic behavior and drawing inferences about these by means of common reasoning.

In principle, the empirical approach should not be regarded as an alternative to the theoretical approaches described above. For, any systematic empirical research must be guided by theories or at least theoretical preconceptions about the subject matter. In turn, the models and theories should of course be tested against empirical data. However, in practice there really exist two approaches with quite a different style and flavor to each of them. The empirical approach is a "bottom up" approach, where scientists start with empirical observations and gradually develop more and more complex models to account for them. The the-

---

[3]See Boorman and Levitt (Boorman and Levitt, 1980) for a comprehensive treatment of the mathematical modeling on the genetics of altruism. It seems that Boorman and Levitt received comparatively little attention in the philosophical literature on the evolution of altruism. This may be due the difficulties for most readers to understand the mathematical presentation or to the fact that computer simulations of altruism have become so popular in the meantime.

oretical approach (as opposed to the empirical approach) is what could be called a "top down" approach, where scientists start with theoretical considerations and models and then (hopefully) adjust them to the empirical instances that these are to be applied to. Unfortunately, in the case of the research on altruism there exists a wide gap between the theoretical and the empirical research[4]. From the vast amount of computer simulations on altruism produced, hardly any has been successfully applied in empirical research. Partly, this gap is due to the division of labor in science, where one group of scientists develops the models and another group does the empirical research. But this alone cannot explain why there is such a lasting discrepancy between the computer simulation based theories and the empirical research.[5] The discussion of this problem, the understanding of its causes and the consequences that should be drawn form the central topic of this book.

In the course of this book, I look at both computer simulations and empirical research in order to examine this question. Purely mathematical models of altruism will not be discussed. The reasons for leaving them out are primarily of pragmatic nature. The epistemological questions concerning mathematical models are not exactly the same as those concerning computer simulations, although presumably many of the results about the epistemology of computer simulations arrived at in this book will also hold true for purely mathematical models. Also, the just mentioned problem of a strong discrepancy between theoretical modeling and empirical research in the study of the evolution of altruism seems to be even more glaring in the case of computer simulations if only because the use of computer simulations makes modeling much easier and more powerful so that the mere popularity of this tool has exposed dangers that are already imminent in purely mathematical modeling.

In order to better understand how computer simulations of the evolution of altruism work, several simulations and simulation series in the Axelrod-fashion will be carried through to simulate different kinds of altruism. There are basically three different kinds of altruism: Reciprocal altruism, kin selection and group selection. Most simulations will be done on reciprocal altruism and some on group selection. For the sake of completeness, kin selection will also briefly be discussed but not simulated. Although they are intended to illustrate the use of a certain method rather than to be particularly original, the simulations presented here are new in the sense that they are not merely repetitions of computer simulations that have already been carried out and described in the scientific literature on the subject. It is, however, one

---

[4]See Dugatkin (Dugatkin, 1998) for a discussion of this problem.

[5]See Hammerstein (Hammerstein, 2003a) for a vivid depiction of this discrepancy.

of the main points to be established in this book that *the results of such purely theoretical simulations (be they as new or unique as they may) are typically not of great scientific relevance.*[6]

Just how irrelevant very many of the models of reciprocal altruism are becomes obvious when they are held against the empirical research on altruism. No empirical research has been done specifically for this book. Instead I review some of the empirical research that has been done in biology and in the social sciences, especially in behavioral economics. Not being a specialist in either biology or economics I am quite aware of the dangers involved with reviewing the results of branches of science that one can at best claim to have a laymans knowledge of.[7] The dangers include misunderstanding, misrepresenting, mistaking the inessential for the essential etc. But these are problems that any kind of interdisciplinary research faces. The only secure way to avoid these dangers would be to refrain from interdisciplinary research altogether or to ignore scientific results in philosophy, neither of which can seriously be considered an option. To the extent to which the more recent scientific research in the two above mentioned fields has found its way into textbooks it is still fairly easy to access. Therefore, I have tried as far as possible to rely on this kind of scientific literature. However, the latest research can only be found in articles in scientific journals. As far as these are concerned, I can only say that I have tried to report the content of the articles that I have quoted as faithfully and accurately as I could as a layman.

Having shown by examining the empirical research that computer models of the evolution of cooperation or altruism can tell us only very little about how altruism evolves, this naturally raises the question why they failed to do so. My answer to this question, which is at the same time my central thesis, generalizes from the simulations of the evolution of altruism and states that *the main reason why computer simulations often fail to fulfill their expectations in science is that the epistemological conditions under which they can possibly explain or prove something are not yet well understood.* Computer simulations are still a relatively new tool in science so that "best practices" for their design or employ-

---

[6]The reason why I do not think they are is explained in chapter 4.1.6.

[7]My field of specialization is political science. Regarding political science, however, I seriously doubt that computer simulations of the evolution of cooperation can provide us with any important insights beyond mere trivialities. See Arnold (Arnold, 2005a) for an extensive criticism of this approach, which also contains *in nuce* some of the arguments that have been expounded in greater detail in this book. In this scepticism regarding the value of mathematical models for political science I feel strongly confirmed by the criticism of the rational choice approach as applied to the political sciences by Ian Shapiro and Donald Green (Green and Shapiro, 1994; Shapiro, 2005), which unfortunately I had not been acquainted with at the time of writing this book.

ment are only beginning to emerge. There still seem to exist quite a few insecurities as to how computer simulations can be used properly in the context of scientific explanations. At any rate, the "tradition" of Axelrod-style simulations of the evolution of cooperation seems to have gone astray if the aim really was to explain how cooperation or altruism evolves. That a whole school or "tradition", if I may call it so, of science is going amiss may be due to the fact that the very business of science sometimes proceeds in an astonishingly naive if not narrow-minded way. In this case, Axelrod had set with his computer simulations a seemingly successful new role model for the study of the evolution of cooperation. What could have been more advisory for aspiring scientists in this field than to pick up Axelrod's model, change it here and there a little bit or even challenge it by designing a similar model that would lead to divergent conclusions and thus produce fascinating new results about the evolution of altruism? And it was so easy: One only needed to know a little bit about computer programming and one could do research on "the evolution of cooperation". (Even philosophers could do that!) Now, the naivety with which science sometimes proceeds – and it certainly proceeded too naively in this case – is to some degree to be excused because if one wants to examine some subject matter one cannot for (economical reasons) at the same time occupy oneself too much with the examination of the method of the examination of the same subject matter. But if this is true then it surely is a philosopher's job to make up leeway and to reflect on what science does and whether it does right what it does. Therefore, the final and most important part of this book is dedicated to the discussion of the epistemological conditions under which computer simulations can be used in the context of scientific explanations. Just as we demand from ordinary scientific theories that they be empirically testable before we grant them the honorable status of a "scientific" theory (that is a theory that can potentially explain certain empirical phenomena), *we need criteria for computer simulations that allow us to classify computer simulations into those for which it can (empirically) be decided if they simulate correctly and those for which this cannot be done.* The criteria I am going to propose in this book are those of *empirical adequacy, robustness* and *non triviality.* "Empirical adequacy" means that all causal factors that have a significant impact on the outcome of the simulated process are somewhere represented in the simulation. "Robustness" requires that the output of the simulation is stable within the range of measurement inaccuracy of the input parameters. And "non triviality" simply requires that the output of the simulation gives us some important information about the outcome of the simulated empirical process. (The last criteria may seem trivial or self-evident itself, but unfortunately experience has shown that this is not the case.[8]) These criteria raise the bar for "explanatory simulations" quite high and it will be discussed at some length if such strict criteria are really necessary. But if they are more or less accepted then it follows that the sort of example simulations that have been presented in this book to demonstrate the principle of Axelrod-style simulations, and with them very many of the simulations published in the literature on the evolution of altruism must be rated as insufficient if any explanatory claim would be based on them. This is quite in accordance with the lack of empirical success of the simulation-based approach to altruism mentioned earlier. But with the above mentioned criteria at hand we can better understand just why most of the computer models of the evolution of altruism had to fail.

Once the epistemological conditions for the proper application of computer simulations in an explanatory context are well understood, it is not only possible to soundly criticize the misguided use of computer simulations. It is just as well possible to derive guidelines of how to design and use computer simulations properly. In order to supplement the critical discussion of what I consider to be a failure of computer simulations with a positive outlook for the future, I offer my own proposal for such guidelines in form of a few simple recipes that scientists can follow if they want to be assured that their simulations are epistemically valid.

1.3 On the structure of this book

The book is organized into four parts. In the first part (chapter 2 and chapter 3) I explain why the existence of altruism, which is a fact of the natural as well as the social world, poses a scientific and philosophical problem. Furthermore, I give a definition of altruism that is broad enough for both biology and the social sciences and I justify this definition at some length. The first part closes with an exposition of the "generalized theory of evolution" (Schurz, 2001), which constitutes the greater theoretical context into which the following models of the

---

[8]To me it seems that the sort of computer simulations that Brian Skyrms devised for the study of the "social contract" (Skyrms, 1996) or "social structure" Skyrms (2004) are trivial to a point where they must be regarded as mere toys. It would be very difficult to draw from his simulations any tenable conclusions with regard to the subject matter of political order (social contract) or social structure that they are allegedly related to. (For a criticism of Skyrms see Arnold (Arnold, 2005a).) A similar objection holds for Schüßler's simulations of cooperation on "anonymous markets", only that Schüßler is at least aware of the problem and honest enough to discuss it (Schüßler, 1990, p. 91f.).

evolution of altruism can be integrated.[9] Because the application of evolutionary theory outside the field of biology is a controversial issue, the different flavors of theories of cultural evolution will be discussed at some length.

In the second part (chapter 4) the three basic evolutionary explanations of altruism will be explained and the modeling on the evolution of altruism will be discussed. The presentation of a whole field or branch of science always raises a certain methodological question: Should one rather give an extensive but in its details necessarily sketchy overview over the whole field or should one present and discuss a few select examples "pars pro toto" in all detail. I have taken the second approach and will present a few self-made computer simulations in order to demonstrate how this type of modeling works in detail. Of course, I could also have taken models that were described in articles in scientific journals. But usually the description in journal articles does not present all the details of a simulation, hardly ever is the source code of the simulation software given and often the information is too sketchy to reconstruct the simulation in an unambiguous way. Also, programming simulations on one's own is quite an instructive exercise. It allows one to notice how many ad hoc decisions enter into the construction of a simulation. By presenting the computer simulations and their results in detail it will be possible to point out both the usual working mechanisms of such simulations as well as the common traps and pitfalls of simulations. The description of these (as I hope) paradigmatic example simulations will be supplemented by a review of a selection of the simulations of the evolution of altruism published in the respective literature. The discussion will cover all forms of evolutionary altruism that is, reciprocal altruism, kin selection and group selection. The greatest emphasis is laid on reciprocal altruism as this is the type of altruism for which the method of computer simulations has been used the most excessively. As will become apparent from the discussion of the simulations conducted by myself as well as those published in the literature on the subject, there is an arbitrary large space of logical possibilities that could be explored by simulations while at the same time hardly any generalizable results can be derived from simulations alone. The reason why all three forms of altruism are covered even though reciprocal altruism would arguably have sufficed to prove the point against the method computer simula-

---

[9]Of course the models of the evolution altruism do not necessarily need to be understood in the context of a *generalized* theory of evolution. For example, as long as we only talk about altruism among animals it would suffice to interpret them against the background of the theory of evolution in biology. But as evolutionary explanations of altruism can be given both in biology and in the social sciences a generalized theory of evolution that does not confine itself to genetic evolution alone provides a very suitable paradigmatic background.

tions is that these different forms of altruism do often not appear strictly separated in the empirical literature on the subject (if only because it is often very difficult to tell apart the different forms of altruism in an empirical context) and it would otherwise be difficult to compare the simulation studies with the empirical research.

In the third part (chapter 5) of this book the results of the computer simulations will be contrasted with the empirical research on the evolution of altruism. It is here where it becomes most obvious that a wide gap exists between the simulation research and the assumptions about the evolution of altruism based on it on the one hand and the empirical research on the other hand. Again, when presenting the results of the empirical research on the evolution of altruism, a similar methodological issue as in the case of the presentation of the simulation research arises. Should one rather give a broad overview of the research or should one discuss only a few exemplary studies in detail. I have tried to combine both approaches and therefore give a broad – though for the sheer size of the topic necessarily incomplete – overview of the empirical research (in biology) first. This way the fact can be assessed that cases where empirical researchers could make good use of the results of simulation studies on the evolution of altruism are extremely rare. In order to understand just why they are so rare, I pick out some examples (both from biology and from social sciences) and discuss them in detail. Since I am going to make a case against the simulation based approach, I was careful to pick out examples that could (at the time of their publication) be considered as showcases for the application of the results of simulation based research to empirical problems of the evolution of altruism. If these fail then the simulation based approach in its present form is confronted with a serious problem. And they do fail, as I hope to be able to demonstrate.

Turning from the diagnosis of failure in the third (and partly already the second part) of this book to the explanation of the failure in the fourth part (chapter 6), I propose and discuss the above mentioned criteria for "explanatory simulations". It can easily be seen that hardly any of the simulations on the "evolution of cooperation" meets these criteria. It is more difficult to show that the fulfillment of these criteria is both necessary and sufficient for a computer simulation to claim explanatory power in a scientific context. Since the epistemology of computer simulations is a relatively young field in the philosophy of science with many open questions, I can hardly maintain to have found the definite answer to the question of potentially explanatory qualities of computer simulations. The fourth part therefore has more or less the character of a philosophical discussion that is, I try to defend these criteria as good as possible against conceivable objections. Given that the proposed criteria provide at least a reasonable guidance, I finally turn to practical considerations and try to devise some "recipes" for the proper use of computer simulations in a scientific context.

In a short concluding chapter the results of this book will be summed up. The main results are that the simulation based approach to the study of the evolution of altruism was largely a failure. This failure resulted from a lack of understanding of the epistemological conditions and requirements of the employment of computer simulations in the context of scientific explanations. Yet, if carefully applied, computer simulations can be a very valuable tool of scientific research. Regarding the requirements of "good" computer simulations, I have made a few proposals in the last part of my book. These may or may not prove sufficient and practical in the future, but if I was able to convey a sense for the necessity to take epistemological considerations into account for a proper research design of simulation based research, then my attempts have not been wholly futile.

Chapter 2

The riddle of altruism

In this chapter it will be explained why the existence of altruism poses a philosophical (and scientific) problem. I try to give a precise definition of altruism that (1) matches our intuitions about altruism and is – save for its greater precision – more or less equivalent to the common sense meaning of the word "altruism", (2) is wide enough to be applied to both biological and social contexts, (3) can be used in the context of a Darwinian theory of evolution. In the following chapter (3), I discuss the generalized theory of evolution, which is the theoretical framework into which later the computer models of the evolution of altruism are to be embedded.

2.1   Altruism in a hostile world

It is commonplace that altruism is a highly desirable attitude. Christianity even declares charity, which is altruism in its highest form, the prime virtue of man. At the same time moralists of all epochs and cultures could never help noticing the deplorable lack of altruism, charity and virtuous observance of the others needs among humans. It would not need the constant admonitions of teachears, priests, prophets and philosophers if altruism was so common and natural a gift as becomes a creature that – according to the book of genesis – is the very image of a benevolent god. The book of genesis has an explanation for this unpleasant state of affairs for sure: It was primordial sin that brought evil into this world.

But when we turn from mythology to science we are apt to get the impression that it is not at all the existence of sin that poses a riddle because the sciences almost univocally assume a human nature that is thoroughly egoistic, if not worse. For economists human beings are pure egoists that, given their preferences, employ their gift of reason solely to the end and purpose of maximizing utility for themselves. The same concept of human nature is shared by many sociologists, especially those that endorse the principle of methodological individualism.[1] And if political scientists do not strictly adhere to the picture of humans as rational egoists then only because they allow deviations to the worse. As Machiavelli put it (when giving the reason for his warning that the duke should reign in blood but not touch his subjects wives or fortunes): "For people sooner forget the death of their own father than the loss of their father's heritage" (Machiavelli, 1980, p. 69 (my translation from German, E.A.)). By saying so, Machiavelli merely put into words a premise that most of the more prudent political thinkers do at least tacitly presume. Among the human sciences (*Humanwissenschaften*) it is – as can be expected – at best pedagogics that offers a more optimistic view of human nature and, possibly, also psychology to some degree. The presupposition that man is by nature an egoistic creature becomes even more credible when we turn to biology. For, the theory of evolution is virtually based on the idea that can – albeit coarsely – be described as the "survival of the fittest", a principle that seems to rule out any non egoistic behavioral traits other than those which are directed towards the closest relatives right from the start. It is this (supposed) consequence of evolution that induced T.H. Huxley to coin the equally popular phrase about "nature, red in tooth and claw".[2] Thus, from a scientific point of view the question is not how sin came to this world, but, quite the contrary, how altruism could come into this world and how it had any chance to survive therein.

Of course the picture of man as a dyed-in-the-wool egoist (if not worse) is far too bleak and it may justly be objected that this picture is cynical and contrary to everday experience. But still the question remains if people (sometimes) really are altruistic, how can they afford to be so and, if altruism is desirable, how can people be induced to behave altruistically? It is no answer to this question that altruism provides so much benefit "to all of us". For, altruism is good for anybody but not for the altruist himself or herself. And altruism is best for the egoist that benefits from the altruism of the others but does not give anything in return. So, once again, how can altruism survive in the long run?

---

[1] *Methodological individualism* is the doctrine that social phenomena should be explained as the result of the actions of individuals (Heath, 2005). In order to explain the actions of the individuals in turn, it is convenient to resort to the assumption of utility maximization, i.e. rational egoism.

[2] For the sake of fairness it should be noted that neither Herbart Spencer nor Thomas Huxley fully endorsed the view that evolution rules out altruism. However, they both thought of ethics and evolution as being antagonistic, so that if ethics (that is the Christian ethics of altruism, benevolence and compassion) is to prevail then only because the civilizational process of society can (in the long run) somehow overcome the iron laws of evolution (Spencer, 1993; Huxley, 1993). It is the opposite view that is advocated here: Evolution can by itself produce altruistic ethics.

To answer the question in this general form an evolutionary approach seems quite suited. There is a strong similarity between the question of when and how altruistic behavioral traits can evolve in animals and the question of how altruistic norms can emerge and be sustained in human society. But before any explanation can be given, a clarification of the concept of altruism is necessary. So, what exactly is altruism?

2.2 The definition of altruism

As has to be expected when using words from everyday language, the terms "altruism" and "cooperation" turn out to be somewhat ambiguous upon closer inspection. For example, is any behavior that turns out to be beneficial to somebody else to be called "altruistic" or only when it is done with the intention to benefit the other person? And what if something is done with the honest intention to serve somebody else but only on the premise that the other person will be grateful and eventually return the favor. Is this kind of mutual exchange of benefits to be called altruism? And, if yes, must we then count every instance of a successful business transaction as "altruistic" because, if carried through freely, it is to the mutual benefit of the business partners? Part of these ambiguities of the term "altruism" stem from the fact that the common notion of "altruism" is closely connected with moral questions and certain ideals of moral virtue. To avoid confounding the different meanings and aspects of altruism, an explicit definition of the term "altruism" is needed.

In this section "altruism" will be defined in view of the general theory of evolution that will constitute the framework of this examination. In order to assure that the definition of altruism meets our research interests, the consequences of this definition will be discussed at some length, thereby comparing it with the ordinary language understanding of altruism. The definition of altruism must not only be clear enough to allow the examination of the problem within an evolutionary approach, it is also important that the kind of altruism captured by the following definition is the very altruism for which the "riddle" of how and why it came into this world and whether and under what conditions it has a chance to survive is to be solved.

For the rest of this study the following definition of altruism will be used: A trait or a type of behavior of an individual is called *altruistic* if it benefits another individual at a cost for the individual itself without immediate or equal return. Some behavior is thus *altruistic*,

1. if it is *beneficial* for another individual

2. and if it is *costly* for oneself

3. and if an equal *return is not guaranteed*

4. and if the *altruist chooses* (or, in case of non-intentional animal behavior, simply if it depends on the altruist) whether the transfer of benefits takes place

The definition is abstract enough to be applied both to sociological and biological settings, for it is not required to assume that the individuals can think or even have a consciousness at all. In a biological setting the costs of the individuals would be interpreted as *fitness costs* in the sense of adverse effects on the reproduction rate. Also, the definition is designed to be wide enough to cover both reciprocal altruism and genuine altruism. *Reciprocal altruism* is altruism on the premise that the bestowed benefits will be returned, but with a certain risk that this might not happen. (Only when the latter is excluded, it is, according to the definition, not called "altruism", any more. This would be the case if the return was immediate.) Thus, even when favors are reciprocated we speak of altruism, but we only speak of altruism when there exists an opportunity for cheating.

Genuine altruism on the other hand means that it is sure that the costs for benefiting other individuals will never be returned. In a biological setting a certain behavioral trait of an individual is genuinely altruistic if it helps increasing the reproduction rate of some other individual and at the same time decreases the reproduction rate of itself. That this is indeed possible and that therefore genuine altruism can survive in nature despite the fact that the survival of some phenotypic trait crucially depends on its increasing the reproduction rate of its bearer over his or her competitors, is one of the most astonishing results of group selection that will be discussed in chapter 4.3.

But does the above definition match our common understanding of altruism? The definition is in some respects rather wide so that it might be disputed that all of the possible types of behavior that match the definition can legitimately be called altruism. For example, a carpetbagger investing a high amount of money into some risky business with the hope of getting a multiple of his investment back would – according to the above definition – have to be classified as an altruist, although we probably would not call his financial speculation "altruism" in everydays life. We might even hesitate to speak of "cooperation" in this case. The above definition is indeed counter-intuitive in cases like this one. The problem is not specific to this definition but it is already apparent in the notion of "reciprocal altruism" which for this reason could equally well be called "reciprocal egoism".[3] The main reason that – in spite of these objections – speaks for a wide definition of altruism is that it captures all behavioral traits that lead in some form or another to cooperation. If the less genuine forms of altruism were named "reciprocal egoism" or similar, there would still be the need for a distinction between types of egoism that encourage cooperation and others that do not. Since we want to find out what chances of survival altruism and cooperation have in a competitive world, it is therefore advantageous to draw the line between altruism and egoism in such a way that the realm of altruism more or less matches that of cooperation. In order to avoid too great a confusion with the common usage of words, it might help to think of "reciprocal altruism" as of a diminutive of altruism. "Reciprocal altruism" is then a kind of altruism that is merely reciprocal but not more.

There are also a few other points that have to be noted about the above definition of altruism. Although the questions discussed in this study have a moral connotation as well, the definition above is purely descriptive. The difference this makes can be explained as follows: When speaking of "cooperation" or "altruism" the moral connotation usually suggests that cooperation and altruism are generally good and laudable. But this is not necessarily the case: The (illegal) pre-arrangement of prices by competitors on a market, for example, is certainly not a laudable case of cooperation and it could hardly be labeled "altruism" because – since altruism is commonly considered laudable – the word would not be used in cases of cooperation that seem ethically doubtful in the broader context. The problem that this example exposes is, however, not a problem specific of the above definition of altruism, but a fundamental problem of moral philosophy: Moral philosophy tries to classify human actions and attitudes into categories of good and bad. But even actions that are generally thought of as being morally laudable can, when appropriate circumstances are given, turn out to be morally deplorable. Killing people is generally considered bad and saving lives is good, but for a soldier in war killing people is a virtue. The problem has to do with the contextuality of moral attributes. To avoid false conclusions this kind of contextuality should be borne in mind.

In addition to the fact that altruism is typically considered to be morally laudable, there exists a more specific reason, why the descriptive definition of "altruism" given above is important for the discussion of ethical questions. Even if "altruism" in a descriptive sense can also be applied to cases of illegal or antimoral conspiracy, it is hardly imag-

---

[3]This was suggested by Gerhard Schurz.

inable (except may be for extreme ethical standpoints like Nietzsche's "Herrenmoral" or Ayn Rand's "Objectivism") that there can be such a thing as moral conduct that does not involve altruism in any form. Altruism in a descriptive sense thus seems to be a necessary though not sufficient condition for morality. Moral conduct typically demands from the individual to follow certain norms even though this may be costly and even when no reward is assured. Thus the questions of whether and to what extent morality has a chance to flourish in a competitive world crucially depends on the question of whether altruism in the descriptive sense is possible in a competitive world.

The above definition of altruism does not contain any psychological or teleological elements such as intention (if humans are meant) or functional design (if organisms are concerned) directed towards benefiting the other. This might appear odd at first sight because cases of involuntarily benefiting others or of benefits which are mere side effects do not seem to be excluded (as they should). As an example a tree that casts a shadow during a hot summer day might be taken. The tree's shade is most welcome for humans resting under it. But is the tree's casting a shadow therefore to be called an example of biological altruism? The obvious objection would be that the tree is not designed to provide needful humans or animals with a pleasant shade on a hot summer day. It is designed to catch sunlight for photosynthesis, the shade being an unintended side effect. To call this "altruism" would surely overstretch the meaning of the word. This objection would be valid, but luckily cases like this one are covered by the requirement that altruism should be costly. There are no extra costs for the tree to cast a shadow. Thus casting shadows does not count as altruistic according to our definition. (Biologists sometimes treat this kind of phenomena under the heading of "byproduct mutualism", where "byproduct mutualism" can be regarded as a degenerate case of altruism (Dugatkin, 1997, p. 42).[4]) But if the tree were an apple tree then its growing fruits would legitimately be called altruistic because growing fruits involves a cost for the tree. It does not matter here that the tree is a plant and therefore cannot have intentions. Presumably, the tree's growing fruits is a case of reciprocal altruism, as the humans or animals eating the apples might help the tree to spread its seeds in return.

One might even take this question a step further by arguing that while

---

[4]From an empirical point of view it is quite reasonable to discuss byproduct mutualism in connection with altruism because 1) it is often very hard to distinguish empirically whether some kind of behavior is an instance of, say, reciprocal altruism or merely byproduct mutualism and 2) there is evidence that in many cases byproduct mutualism is a stepping stone in the evolutionary path that leads to the development of altruism. (See chapter 5.1 for the empirical examples in biology, where this question can often be raised.)

merely accidental benefits for others are excluded by the criterion of cost, this leaves open the possibility for altruistic acts that are not bestowed from a benefactor on a beneficiary but reaped from the benefactor by force. An example would be a rabbit that is eaten by a fox. It would not help to reintroduce the notion of functional design into the definition because a rabbit is – in a way – perfectly well designed to serve as fox food. Absurd cases like that of the rabbit that altruistically lends itself to be eaten by a fox or – to take an example from social life – of crime victims that serve as altruistic benefactors to robbers, thieves and burglars are ruled out by the fourth criterion, according to which it must depend on the altruist whether the transfer of benefits takes place. The criterion is wide enough to capture altruistic actions by humans as well as animals. Even though it may not be apparent at first sight, the criterion can also be applied to inborn (or genetically determined) altruistic traits as they occur in mutualisms.[5] In this case "to depend" means two things: 1) that it is a genetically determined trait of the altruist that makes the transfer of benefits possible and 2) the altruist could also exist without this trait.

The choice of costs rather than intentions as a criterion for altruism has the advantage that it is more objective and that it can be applied equally in biological and sociological settings without the need for differentiating between human intentions, animal intentions, mere functional design of primitive organisms that do not have intentions etc. Furthermore, in a sociological setting the assumption is certainly unproblematic that whenever some altruistic act needs a certain effort, it will not be performed without the intention to perform it.

There is, however, also a downside to neglecting intentions in the definition of altruism. In everday life, especially when human relations like friendship and love are concerned, there exists a distinction which is closely connected to the psychological aspects of altruism and which is at the same time crucial for the valuation of altruism: The distinction between real or true altruism on the one hand and false or merely pretended altruism on the other hand. Altruism is commonly regarded as true only if the benefits one person bestows unto another are given for the sake of the other person and not merely out of egoistic motives like prestige or the hope for a reward. In the latter case the kind of altruism displayed would be regarded as merely pretended and not as honest. Such psychological subtleties are not covered by the above definition of altruism, which is designed to be operational in the first place. Still, should the question arise, the definition of altruism can easily be ren-

---

[5]A *mutualism* is an interspecific association of different species to their mutual benefit. An example would be the association of hermit crabs and sea anemones.

dered more precise, especially so, since the distinction between altruism out of friendship and opportunistic altruism also leaves its mark in the outer world: As the psychological findings indicate, the kind of altruism that friendship evokes is reciprocal only on a long term basis and even defies short term reciprocity (Silk, 2003).

As a final remark, it should be noted that there exists a very specifically philosophical question about altruism, which will only be discussed here briefly and in the following be left out completely. It is the question whether true altruism is possible at all. It could be argued that whenever a person behaves altruistically, he or she does so only because he or she derives at least an emotional reward of some kind such as, say, personal satisfaction. But then – as the argument runs – the action would not be truly altruistic any more because it is done for one's own satisfaction. Indeed, it is difficult to believe that anybody can do anything without at least some kind of inner reward. Only a perfect saint might be able to commit the most gracious acts of altruism and charity and at the same time be wholly disgusted by what he is doing. If one insists on speaking of true altruism only where it reaches a level of perfect saintliness then there is no altruism in this world. But as long as it is not deliverance that is sought and the problem of altruism is confined to how and to what extent altruism has a chance to emerge in natural and cultural evolution, it is safe to assume that already levels of altruism below perfect saintliness can be morally satisfactory.

Chapter 3

The generalized theory of evolution as theoretical framework

Having defined altruism, it is now time to discuss the theoretical framework in which the so defined concept of altruism is to be applied. In this book, I discuss altruism in a Darwinian evolutionary framework with special emphasis on the method of computer simulations. The application of Darwinian evolutionary concepts to the evolution of altruism in a cultural context as it is intended by generalized theories of evolution requires some explanation: While evolutionary theory in biology is well established, the application of evolutionary concepts in the social sciences is still the object of much debate. There exist several different approaches to employing evolutionary thinking in the social sciences. None of these attempts goes uncontested and there is of course some dispute whether an "evolutionary theory" based on the concept of selection is of much use in the social sciences at all. Therefore, the questions surrounding the application of evolutionary concepts to cultural developments will be discussed at some length.

In the following, I first define the concepts of "Darwinian evolution" and "evolutionary theory in a Darwinian sense" and I describe how evolutionary explanations work. Then, I discuss in which areas of science we can make use of evolutionary explanations and I also briefly touch the question, how they relate to competing non evolutionary theories. The answer to this question is trivial only in biology, where evolutionary theory remains uncontested and where the explanation for the emergence of any (altruistic) trait must therefore be found in the realm of evolutionary theory. But this is not the case in the social sciences, where the employment of evolutionary explanations requires some justification. This becomes even more important as there exist different brands of evolutionary theories in the social sciences like sociobiology, which relies on genetic evolution, and theories of cultural evolution, which seek to explain the development of culture in analogy to biological evolution but not by the evolution of genes itself. And there exist mixed forms of both theories. I confine myself to the discussion of evolutionary psychology as an example of the genetic brand (section 3.3.1) and the theory of cultural evolution (section 3.3.2), which assumes that the evolution of culture is a process that proceeds largely independently from genetic evolution. Alongside with the presentation of these approaches, I am going to discuss some of the criticism that has been put forward against these theories and point out possible limitations. Finally, I discuss the place that the explanations for altruism based on evolutionary computer simulations have within this theoretical framework (section 3.4).

3.1 The concept of Darwinian evolution

The word "evolution", when taken in its most general meaning, describes a process of change over time which has a determinable direction. In the following, however, when speaking of "evolution" or "evolutionary processes" what is meant is always evolution in a narrower, "Darwinian" sense. Evolution in a Darwinian sense is a process the course of which is determined by the joint effect of three factors ("Darwinian modules"): *reproduction, variation* and, most prominently, *selection*. We assume here that there exist some determinable evolving entities upon which these factors act, resulting in a directed evolutionary process. In more detail these three factors (or "Darwinian modules") can be characterized as follows:[1]

1. *Reproduction*: There is a set of evolving entities (as for example genes in natural evolution or certain cultural traits[2] in cultural evolution) that is reproduced in generational cycles.

2. *Variation*: In every generation there is a certain amount of variation among the evolving entities, that is, they differ according to their respective properties. Even if some types of entities die out after a while, variation may still be kept up by the the spontaneous appearance of new types ("mutations").

3. *Selection*: The reproduction rate of the evolving entities differs dependent on the interaction of the entities' properties with the environment. Thus the environment selects for certain types of entities

---

[1] The characterization of Darwinian evolution follows (Schurz, 2001, p. 329ff.).

[2] I am not, as it is often done, speaking of memes here because it is still doubtful whether memes exist as entities.

that can then be regarded as "better adapted" than other types of entities.

These three factors are the defining characteristics of a "Darwinian evolutionary process". It cannot be assumed that these three factors alone lead to a directed evolutionary process without any further conditions being fullfilled. For example, evolution can only take place in a more or less stable environment (Schurz, 2001, p. 336/336.). Also, there must be a large enough range of variable types of the evolving entity. In the case of the genome, this is certainly true, as there exists an enormous number of possible combinations of the basic building blocks of the DNA. And one could easily think of further conditions. Still we will not make these conditions part of our definition, but we will speak of "Darwinian evolution" if there is a directed evolutionary process and if this process is determined by at least the three factors *reproduction*, *variation* and *selection* plus potentially further conditions. We will not speak of "Darwinian evolution" or "evolution in a strict sense" if one or more of these factors is absent. (To guard oneself against misunderstandings it is important to keep in mind that especially in the social sciences the terms "evolution" and "evolutionary" are usually not used in the strict Darwinian sense. Even where authors assume that they are describing some social or cultural development process in Darwinian terms it may turn out upon closer inspection that they are in fact not doing so, but that they are merely applying some arbitrary selectionist paradigm.)

Having defined the concept of "Darwinian evolution" we can now define what a "Darwinian evolutionary theory" (or just "evolutionary theory") is. An "evolutionary theory" is a theory of a development process that uses the concept of Darwinian evolution for the explanation of this process. Now, this raises the question to what empirical processes theories of Darwinian evolution can reasonably be applied. If we think of evolution in the broadest sense there are basically three strata of evolution which are of philosophical interest to us: 1) The evolution of the universe, 2) the evolution of life (including the evolution of humans), 3) the evolution of culture, i.e. human history. It seems quite obvious that the evolution of the universe is not an instance of Darwinian evolution. One could of course speak of the evolution of galaxies and solar systems, but it is hard to envisage how reproduction and selection come into play here. Therefore, when looking for possible instances of Darwinian evolution, we must confine ourselves to the evolution of life and the evolution of culture. The merits of the Darwinian theory of evolution in the one field and its prospects in the other will be discussed in the following.

3.2   Biological evolution

Only little needs to be said about biological evolution here. The theory of evolution has by now for a long time been firmly established in biology.[3] As is well known it was first put forward by Charles Darwin to account for the origin and the diversity of the existing plant and animal species. Very simply put, one could say it gives answers to three questions: Why is there such a multitude of different species? How did each single one of them come into existence? (And in particular: How did the human race come into existence?) How come that all of the species are so well adapted to their respective environment? The answers that the theory of evolution gives to these question are (last one first): 1) Living beings are so well adapted to their environment because they have evolved through natural selection. Those types that are not well adapted (or less well adapted than other types sharing the same habitat) die out, leaving just types that have a functional design that makes them well adapted to their environment. 2) Each single species came into existence by gradual evolution from (usually) more primitive species. This also explains how man came into being and thus gives an answer to one of the most fundamental philosophical questions. 3) Finally, the variety of species existing in this world is to be explained by the fact that species may split due to spatial separation or other causes and then evolve into different directions, occupying different ecological niches.

But the theory of evolution is not only able to answer such general questions. It also has a direct impact on the explanation of the characteristics and phenotypic traits found in living organisms. In fact the theory of evolution is the only theory that offers an ultimate explanation for why organisms have certain traits. A phenotypic trait can be any characteristic feature of the organism itself or of its behavior (some authors even include the nests and buildings animals construct like spiders webs, rabbit burrows etc. into the phenotype of the respective animal (Dawkins, 1982)). Therefore, behavioral characteristics such as altruistic or egoistic behavior must also be regarded as part of the phenotype of an organism, and their existence must be explained on the basis of the theory of evolution. This means that for any specific trait of any organism it is either true that (1) it is a functional adaptation to a certain aspect of its habitat and it has evolved by natural selection or (2) it is a by-product of other adaptations of the organism to its environment or (3) it is the heritage of an adaptation in the evolutionary history of the

---

[3]Most of the information about the biological theory of evolution that is given in the following is taken from the book of Ernst Mayr (Mayr, 2001).

organism or (4) it is the result of sexual selection.

But why can we be so sure that the explanation of a certain trait must fall into one of these categories or, more broadly speaking, why can we be sure that the explanation for the existence of a phenotypic trait of an organism must be an evolutionary one? The answer to this question has two parts. One part of the answer is that the theory of evolution is an extremely well confirmed theory. A broad range of empirical evidence supports this theory (Mayr, 2001, p. 12ff.). This evidence includes among other things the fossil record, field observations as well as breeding experiments and molecular genetics. The latter is of particular importance because at the time when Darwin invented the theory of evolution, the specific mechanism of inheritance had not yet been found. When the laws of genetics were discovered this not only solved one of the major riddles about evolution, namely whether acquired properties are passed on to the descendants (which is not the case), but it also turned out that genetics and the theory of evolution fit together like one puzzle piece to another. If it is possible to link independently confirmed theories together, as in this case the theory of evolution and the theory of genetics, then this is always a major scientific achievement. One could say that the successful linking of theories strengthens both theories by providing them with additional, *holistic evidence*.

The other part of the answer to the question why the ultimate explanation for any phenotypic trait of an organism can only be an evolutionary one consists in the fact that the theory of evolution is without any competitors. It is the only theory that can explain why organisms are functionally adapted to their environment or, to put it in a more philosophical jargon, why organisms expose a teleological structure. There is no other way to explain this teleological structure of organisms than by the theory of evolution. This does not mean that we can give a precise evolutionary explanation for each single instance of a functional adaptation. But we can always be sure that there exists an evolutionary explanation. And the reason why we can be sure it exists is that (1) it is possible to give precise evolutionary explanations for functional adaptations in many other cases (2) there is no case where the theory of evolution has been falsified (for example by demonstrating that a certain trait exists although it reduces fitness and is at the same time not an artifact of sexual selection) (3) there is, as has just been mentioned, no alternative theory that could possibly offer an explanation. We are therefore entitled to assume that even in those cases where we cannot give a precise account, the ultimate causes must still have been those that are described by the theory of evolution.

I emphasize the point that there exists no rival to the theory of evolution in biology so much because this is one of the major differences between evolutionary theory in biology and evolutionary theory when it is applied to cultural evolution. There exist many theories that account in one way or other for cultural developments and evolutionary processes (in a broad sense) in human history as well as for the functional adaptations or teleological structures we may find in human cultures. We therefore cannot beforehand assume that the explanation for any instance of functional adaptation or any evolutionary process (in the broad sense of "evolution") in human culture must be Darwinian in the above defined sense. Instead, if we want to make the assertion that a certain feature of culture as for example a social norm or a certain technology is the product of a Darwinian evolutionary process then we have to demonstrate that our evolutionary explanation works precisely in this case and we would have to defend it against possible alternative explanations.

Remaining in the field of biology, how does a "precise" evolutionary explanation for a an evolved trait work? Basically, what evolutionary theory asserts is the following: (1) There is a connection between the reproduction rate and the adaptedness of an organism to its environment. (2) All traits that are too complex to have evolved through a single genetic variation must have evolved through a closed sequence of variation and selection cycles with no gaps. These two assertions show, by the way, that the theory of evolution is not, as it is sometimes charged with, tautological because both assertions can in principle fail empirically.[4] (In fact the first assertion does fail in cases where a trait has evolved through sexual selection in contrast to natural selection, but it would lead too far to go into this topic here.) In order to demonstrate that a trait has evolved in the sense of the Darwinian theory of evolution, what must be shown is that organisms that have the trait are better adapted to their environment and do therefore enjoy a higher reproduction rate than members of the same species that do not possess this trait. For more complex traits like specialized organs the evolutionary history must be clarified. The task of proving that a certain trait confers to its bearer an evolutionary advantage is often not as easy as it might at first sight seem. For, in order to give such a proof the net result of all evolutionary forces acting upon the organism because of this trait must be taken into account. The difficulties involved in drawing up an evolutionary explanation for some trait can be explained with the example of the long neck of a giraffe (Dupré, 2003, p. 37-40): It seems

---

[4]Though the second assertion may be difficult to falsify because one can always maintain that the intermediary steps filling an alleged evolutionary gap have not been discovered yet. See also (Schurz, 2001, p. 335) for some remarks about the falsifiability of the theory of evolution.

plausible to assume that the long neck of the giraffe has evolved because it allows the giraffe to eat the leaves of trees high above the ground. But then a long neck is also a very heavy neck and should under this aspect probably be regarded as an evolutionary disadvantage. In order to precisely explain the fact that a giraffe has a long neck on an evolutionary basis it would be necessary to give an accurate account of the possible advantages and disadvantages such a long neck might have. It is obvious that this is quite a difficult thing to do, though not necessarily an impossible one.[5] Of course, we can be sure that the long neck of the giraffe must have evolved for some such reason as the advantage of picking leaves from trees. But then, the only reason why we can assume this is because the theory of evolution has been so well confirmed in other cases, not because we are able to track down the selective forces in this particular case. We will later see that it is precisely the problem of giving a quantitative account of the advantages and disadvantages of certain types of animal behavior, which makes it so difficult to test our theoretical assumptions about the evolution of altruism empirically.[6] At the same time it is, of course, all to easy to invent "evolutionary stories" about why some trait is an adaption to the environment. This kind of evolutionary story telling is a danger that is especially imminent in the application of evolutionary theory to human culture, to which we will turn our attention now.

3.3 Evolutionary theories of culture

Darwinian evolutionary theories of culture come in many different flavors. In a recent overview Kevin N. Laland and Gilian R. Brown discuss human sociobiology, human behavioral ecology, evolutionary psychology, memetics, gene-culture co-evolution (Laland and Brown, 2004). The multitude of different approaches alone shows that there is not one canonical way of applying (Darwinian) evolutionary thinking to human culture. However, all of these different approaches can be traced back to two basic types: Theories that explain human behavior and human culture by the evolved genetic nature of man and theories that assume an autonomous evolutionary process of culture that is not determined by the human genes. The above mentioned approaches fall either in the one or the other of these two categories or can be regarded as a mixed form of both. To simplify matters, I discuss only the two basic types in

---

[5]As Dupré notices (Dupré, 2003, p. 38), this is much less of a problem in the case of specialized organs because here the evolutionary advantage (i.e. the specific purpose of the organ) is quite obvious.
[6]See chapter 5.1.

the following.

It is important not to forget that the Darwinian evolutionary theories of culture constitute only a small fraction among the many theories of cultural evolution or development that exist in the social sciences. For the understanding and explanation of the process of civilization there are – to name just a few arbitrary examples – the theory that civilization is a process of rationalization (Max Weber), the theory that civilization is a process of internalization of external compulsory forces (Norbert Elias), modernization theories according to which progress in one realm, say, technology, necessitates progress in other realms, say, governmental structure, the theory of history as the history of class struggles (Karl Marx), and many more. The social sciences did not wait for Darwinian theories of evolution to arrive in order to explain functionalistic (or "teleological") structures in the realm of human culture. Also, since Darwin's "Origin of Species" (Darwin, 1859) there have been many attempts to apply Darwinian approaches to human culture, none of which had a lasting success so far. This alone does not exclude the possibility that one day one of these theories will prevail, but it should make one suspicious about the bold claims sometimes raised by evolutionary theorists. It is simply not very credible that any Darwinian evolutionary theory of culture will supersede or integrate all the existing Non-Darwinian theories of cultural evolution, many of which will surely remain much better suited to their specific purposes. Besides, a pluralism of paradigms is typical for the social sciences, and it would be very suprising if this changed just now, although some of the proponents of the newer Darwinian evolutionary theories of culture entertain such hopes (Tooby and Cosmides, 1992; Mesoudi et al., 2006).

When, in the following, we confine our focus to Darwinian evolutionary theories of culture, this should therefore be understood as a topical decision and not as presuming that other approaches would not have anything important to say about the evolution of altruism as far as human society is concerned. On the other hand we will not expect the evolutionary theory of culture to afford an overall explanation of altruism if human behavior is concerned. If an evolutionary theory of culture can highlight some aspects of altruistic behavior among humans then this should be considered as sufficient to give it a right to existence among the many rivaling theories in the social sciences that could possibly be consulted for the explanation of human altruism.

3.3.1 Genetic theories of human behavior

One important class of evolutionary theories of human culture is formed by the genetic theories of human behavior. Sociobiology and evolutionary psychology are the most recent and prominent representatives of this class. The genetic approach to human behavior is motivated by the fact that human nature has been formed by evolution just as the nature of any other animal. At the same time the patterns of human behavior are much more flexible and variegated than those of any other animal species and it is hard to deny that this variety must be due to the cultural environment in which a human is raised. But just to what extent our behavior is the result of genetically transmitted properties and to what extent it is a cultural acquisition is subject to debate. In this "nature-nurture" debate sociobiology and evolutionary psychology clearly take the nature stance. As evolutionary psychology can in many respects be regarded as the successor of sociobiology (Dupré, 2001, p. 21), only evolutionary psychology will (briefly) be discussed in the following. It will be discussed under the following four aspects: (1) Its motivation and scientific intention, (2) its basic conception of human nature, in this case specifically of the human mind, (3) its research strategy and major achievements and (4) a critical discussion of the approach with respect to the question of how well it can possibly explain the evolution of altruism in humans.

(1) Motivation and scientific intention

The *locus classicus* of evolutionary psychology is a programmatic manifest by John Tooby and Leda Cosmides on "The Psychological Foundations of Culture" (Tooby and Cosmides, 1992). In this more than a hundred pages long manifest Tooby and Cosmides broadly describe their idea of a new science of culture with evolutionary psychology in its center. In their opinion the existing social sciences have come to a dead end, mainly, because they rest on a set of false assumptions which is called the "standard social science model" by Tooby and Cosmides and at the core of which Tooby and Cosmides suspect the belief that the human mind is essentially a tabula rasa that gets its shape only by childhood education and by the impact of the society an individual grows up in (Tooby and Cosmides, 1992, p. 24ff.). According to Tooby and Cosmides, this model has effectively prevented the social sciences from making rapid progress and also made it difficult to connect them to adjoining human sciences like evolutionary biology or neuro-science, although this would certainly be desirable. Tooby and Cosmides are confident that once the "standard social science model" is given up and replaced by their own more appropriate model, this impasse will be resolved. It will then become possible to integrate the social sciences into a unified field of human sciences and rapid scientific progress will ensue (Tooby and Cosmides, 1992, p. 19ff.). The appeal to the unity of sciences and the emphasis that is laid on the connectivity to other scientific fields is fairly typical for the justification of scientistic approaches in the social sciences. (We will see it recur in the programmatic scriptures of the non-genetic theories of cultural evolution.) But Tooby and Cosmides do not only base their claim on such assumed secondary advantages. They also believe that their own model is simply more adequate when it comes to explaining human psychology.

(2) Basic conceptions

The model that Toby and Cosmides propose as the alternative to the "standard social science model" is named by them "integrated causal model" (Tooby and Cosmides, 1992, p. 23/24). It is primarily a model about the human mind and can best be described by the popular tool-box metaphor. Rather than assuming – as the "standard social science model" tacitly does according to Tooby's and Cosmides' estimate – that the mind is a tabula rasa or a sort of computer that can be programmed in arbitrary ways to solve any sort of problem, they assume that the human mind is a toolbox containing an intricate set of diverse capabilities each of which is highly specialized in order to fulfill a certain task. These context specific capabilities, they reason, must have evolved through natural selection to address specific challenges in the environment of the ancestral humans. Why nature could not have provided humans with a general problem solving brain rather than a toolbox-brain is a point on which Tooby and Cosmides remain a bit vague. They suggest that it would have been somehow uneconomical for evolution to do so. In evolutionary psychology, the evolved context specific capabilities are commonly called "modules". One of the prime example for such a module of the adapted mind is that of language acquisition (Tooby and Cosmides, 1992, p. 70). If, as Tooby and Cosmides do, one follows Chomsky and assumes that there is a deep structure to language which underlies all world languages and which must for various reasons be connected to some inborn capability of language acquisition and language generation, then this inborn capability is indeed an excellent example for a highly specialized evolved module of the human brain.

(3) Research strategy and achievements

In connection with their so called "integrated causal model" Tooby and Cosmides propose a very concrete research design by which to prove the existence of a "module" of the mind. This design consists of five steps (Tooby and Cosmides, 1992, p. 73/74): a) Identification of an *adaptive target*, which is a certain challenge or problem in the life world of our ancestors to which the assumed module would pose a solution. b) Considering the *background conditions*, i.e. recurring structures of the ancestral world of hunter gatherer societies, under which the module has evolved. In relation to the ancestral world, evolutionary psychologists usually refer to the late Pleistocene. They speak of the human life conditions of this period as of the "environment of evolutionary adaptedness" (Tooby and Cosmides, 1992, p. 69) because they assume that major genetic adaptations cannot have occurred in the relatively short period of time after the invention of agriculture. c) Drawing up of a *design*: a description of the module itself under the assumption that it is designed to meet the requirements of the adaptive target. The last two steps would then be d) a *performance examination* and e) a *performance evaluation* of the design. Only if a design performs well (under ancestral conditions) can the researcher assume that he or she has identified an adaptation.

A great number of research projects in evolutionary psychology have made use of this research design scheme. One of the allegedly most impressive achievements in this respect is Leda Cosmides' research on psychological mechanisms for detecting cheaters (Laland and Brown, 2004, p. 168/169). Based on previous works of Peter Wason, she could show by a series of experiments that people have a highly developed ability for detecting violators of social rules, but easily fail to solve analogous tasks when these are presented in a different setting. The conclusion that the human brain is equipped with a special module for cheater detection rather than with the general capacity of solving logical puzzles that could then be directed to the task of cheater detection appears quite compelling in this case.

(4) Critical objections

However, in other areas such as mate choice, homicide and rape[7] the results evolutionary psychology has produced have been much more debated. But it would lead too far to enter into the details of these con-

---

[7]Evolutionary psychology seems to have inherited from sociobiology a certain liking for "sex and crime" themes (Dupré, 1996, p. 44ff.).

troversies here, which are well described in (Dupré, 2001, p. 48ff.) and (Laland and Brown, 2004, p. 170ff.). What is of interest here is how well genetic evolution can possibly account for altruism among humans. If the basic assumptions of Tooby and Cosmides (and the evolutionary psychologists following their approach) are correct, then altruism among humans would in some way or other have to be explained by an evolved altruism-module of the mind or by a reciprocity-module or by a morality-module which includes altruism. In order to examine the question whether an (evolutionary) explanation of human altruism should primarily be sought on a genetic basis, we will first ask how credible the evolutionary psychologist's approach by Tooby and Cosmides is in general when it comes to understanding human culture and then how the case is to be decided for the evolution of altruism in particular.

As far as the general case is concerned, Tooby and Cosmides have raised the bar for themselves quite high by the bold claim that any kind of human behavior could be explained in terms of the "integrated causal model". After all, they were aiming at a new unified approach to the science of human nature. But at the same time it is often very difficult to discern just when and to what degree a certain regular pattern of human behavior that we find in culture is due to an evolved module of the brain and when it is not. For example, we could think of a group of people that enjoys singing folk songs and dancing folk dances. Moreover, we know that dancing and singing are common patterns of human behavior found across all or at least most cultures. Now, are we to assume that there exists a module for folk dances or folk songs? Or, is there a module for singing and dancing? Or, is there maybe just a module for music and rhythm? If we decide for one of the latter two alternatives then this means that there remain interesting and important questions about singing and dancing that evolutionary psychology cannot explain on the basis of mental modules, namely the questions of how and why certain types of folk dances and folk songs evolved within a certain culture. But if in turn we are to decide in favor of the first alternative and assume that there exists a specialized module for folk dancing and folk songs then we are confronted with the problem that we would have to assume many more specialized modules of the mind in similar cases. We are then somehow left with the question where there is to be an end – if there ever is any – to postulating highly specialized modules of the mind.[8]

---

[8]For a more elaborate criticism of the use of "modules" in evolutionary psychology see (Dupré, 2001, p. 40ff). – As a historical side note it may be mentioned that a very similar discussion had many years earlier already arisen in another context in connection with the philosophical anthropology of the 20th century. Arnold Gehlen, when justifying his assumption that human nature is highly flexible and is shaped not

But it is not only the problem that there seems to be such a liberty of postulating modules that has caught the attention of critics of evolutionary psychology (Dupré, 2001, p. 40ff.). The research design proposed by Tooby and Cosmides is also flawed in another aspect, namely, regarding the identification of an *adaptive target* and the *background conditions*. If we are to believe the critics of this research design then the usual talk about the life conditions of our ancestors that appears in studies of evolutionary psychologists is often quite arbitrary and results in reiterating the same clichés and stereotypes about the life of hunter gatherer societies over and over again (Dupré, 2001, p. 23ff.). One of the common clichés about these societies is that they are highly egalitarian (Richerson et al., 2003, p. 372ff.). This may be empirically true, but at the same time we find in modern societies a psychology that is very well adjusted to the social hierarchies that pervade modern societies on almost all levels of professional and private life. Therefore, it is doubtful whether this assumption about the egalitarian character of ancestral societies is helpful when we want to understand the behavior of humans in today's societies. It is a feature not only of evolutionary psychology but also of other strata of Darwinian evolutionary theories of human culture that at some point or other they seem to revert to evolutionary just-so-story telling. In the case of evolutionary psychology this point seems to be reached when it comes to the question of the life conditions of our ancestors and the supposed consequences these have for how we handle modern life (Dupré, 2001, p. 21ff.).

If thus the "imperialist" claim of evolutionary psychology to provide a unified alternative to the "standard social science model" proves to be largely unfounded and leaves open the possibility to seek explanations for human behavior within other paradigms including that of a non-genetic theory of cultural evolution, the question still remains if the foundations of human altruism in particular are not, if only to some

---

by inborn instincts but by the institutions society provides had to argue against the then so common drive-theories in psychology, which in some respect resemble the "modules" of evolutionary psychology (Gehlen, 1983, p. 50ff.). Doing so he pointed to the simple fact that different authors postulated quite diverse numbers and kinds of drives, some authors needed more than 50 drives, others were content with only two or three. Gehlen concluded that other than for the organically represented drives (hunger and sex) there was no sure foundation for assuming the existence of drives and that therefore it was for pragmatic reasons advisable to circumvent the question of drives altogether and find some other key to the explanation of human behavior. Making this historical comment is not to say that the whole question would not have needed to be discussed in the context of evolutionary psychology if only the participants had known the history of philosophy a little better. Since the evolutionary psychologists had proposed a new research design, the question of innate capabilities (drives or modules) that direct human behavior certainly deserved reexamination, even if the result that the usefulness of the toolbox-metaphor of the human brain remains confined to only a limited array of questions touching human behavior has in the end turned out to be same as the one which philosophical anthropology had already arrived at half a century earlier.

degree, genetically determined. Generally, any trait that is constant across all human cultures is a good candidate for a genetically determined feature of human nature. In the case of altruistic behavior there are several indicators which render the assumption plausible: Moral behavior and understanding of basic moral categories is constant across different cultures. Even if the norms differ, one would expect to find some norms commanding altruistic behavior in any culture. Another pattern that is more or less universal is the markedly distinct behavior between in-group (family, tribe or other association) behavior and out-group behavior. Here again we could expect to find a kind altruistic behavior in in-group relations that probably also has a genetic basis. Finally, specific behavioral categories that can be found in any culture like that of reciprocity may be an indication for the existence of certain types of genetically programmed altruism.

The abstract models of altruism that will be discussed in chapter 4 can in principle be applied to both genetically and culturally evolved altruism. Since, as has just been argued, there is enough reason to assume that altruism among humans may also have a genetic foundation, the possibility of interpreting these models within a theoretical framework of genetic evolutionary theory of human behavior, i.e. evolutionary psychology, should not be dismissed altogether. On the other hand, there is no doubt that the scope, strength and specific form of most altruistic norms is shaped by culture. In the following we will therefore examine the theory of cultural evolution as an alternative (or supplementary) framework for understanding human altruism. A third possibility should at least be mentioned here: It is quite plausible to assume – as some researchers do (Laland and Brown, 2004, p. 241ff.) – that, for a certain period in the history of the human race, a co-evolution of genetic and cultural altruism in humans has taken place, where both forms of altruism evolved alongside each other mutually strengthening each other.

3.3.2 Cultural evolution as a Darwinian process

Once we reject the assumption that human behavior and, consequently, also the development of human culture is to the larger degree determined by the genes, a wide field of diverse theories that seek to explain the course of human history or the evolution of human cultures opens up. One of these theories, but – as has been stated earlier – by no means the only such theory, is the theory of cultural evolution that treats the evolution of human culture as a Darwinian process, where reproduction, variation and selection of cultural traits form the *agens* of human history. This theory comes in different flavors either as a theory or "science of cultural evolution" (Mesoudi et al., 2006) or as "memetics" (Blackmore, 2000), i.e. a theory of cultural traits called "memes", or as a "generalized theory of evolution" (Schurz, 2001). But I will in the following only speak of the theory of "cultural evolution" and occasionally point out the differences between its variants. Just as in the case of the genetic evolutionary explanations of human culture, I discuss (1) the intention and motivation of the theory of cultural evolution, (2) its basic assumptions, (3) its resarch strategies and achievements and (4) critical objections. Doing so, I rely mainly on the accounts given in (Mesoudi et al., 2006), (Schurz, 2001) and (Laland and Brown, 2004). I do not so much take into account the literature about "memetics" because the concept of a "meme" does not yet seem ripe for serious scientific application.[9] At the same time "memetics" is not at all indispensable for a theory of cultural evolution. For in any specific case of cultural evolution we can specify the entity the evolution of which is in question, say a social norm or a social institution, and study its evolution without assuming that this entity is an instance of or composed of some such things as "memes". The question whether memes exist or not is a question with respect to which one can remain completely neutral as long as only a specific instance of cultural development is to be explained on an evolutionary basis.

(1) Motivation and scientific intention

There exist several levels of motivation and justification for the Darwinian theory of cultural evolution, discerned by the ambition of the respective scientific program. On the lowest level, the Darwinian theory of cultural evolution tries to transfer the successful models and methods from evolutionary biology to the study of cultural development (Arnold, 2005b). It is assumed that there exist sufficient similarities between cultural development processes and evolution in nature to warrant such a transfer. On a more ambitious level, the theory of cultural evolution is motivated by the zeal to provide a unified coherent framework for the whole body of sciences dealing with human culture, just like the theory

---

[9]See my objections on page 43. – The concept of a "meme" was originally invented by the biologist Richard Dawkins (Dawkins, 1976, p. 304-322.). Later, however, Dawkins seems to have grown a bit suspicious of his own concept, for he writes "My own feeling is that its [the meme concept's, E.A.] value may lie not so much in helping us to understand human culture as in sharpening our perception of genetic natural selection." (Dawkins, 1982, p. 112). Dawkins preface to Susan Blackmore's manifesto "The Meme Machine" sounds equally sceptical (Blackmore, 2000, p. 7-21.). Even Laland and Brown have to admit that the idea of "memes" has mainly been popular among "computer geeks" but not among serious social scientists (Laland and Brown, 2004, p. 200).

of evolution provides the overarching conceptual framework in biology. At the same time it is assumed that applying the same methods that are successful in biology should allow the social sciences to yield much better results than has hitherto been achieved in the fragmented landscape of social science theories (Mesoudi et al., 2006, p. 329-332). This is very much the same "imperialist" story as it has been told by Tooby and Cosmides in their programmatic scripture on evolutionary psychology: The social sciences supposedly find themselves in a hopeless mess. In no way are they able to rival the success of the natural sciences. The reason for this annoying state of affairs is that they lack a unifying theoretical framework and proper exact methodologies. If only the social scientists were willing to learn from the exact sciences and adopt their methods and succumb to a unified theory then a great leap forward in the scientific advancement of the social sciences would be positively inescapable. (Or so the story goes...)

Yet another, though similar, motivation for the theory of cultural evolution is to fully exploit the potential of the Darwinian model of evolutionary processes and to give it as broad a scope as possible. This is the motivation behind the "generalized theory of evolution" (Schurz, 2001). The sort of generalization that is meant here, does not lie on the ontological level in the sense that one type of evolutionary process is meant to explain as many phenomena as possible, i.e. biological evolution as well as cultural evolution, as it is done in human sociobiology and in evolutionary psychology, both of which explain cultural developments largely by the same process of genetic evolution that does also account for the evolution of species. Rather, the generality is to be found on the level of theoretical abstraction. It is assumed that the same core principles of Darwinianism can explain evolutionary processes in different branches of science with different evolving entities. In biology they describe the evolution of genes. In social sciences they describe the evolution of diverse cultural traits or of "memes" (if we assume that such distinct entities as "memes" underlying all cultural traits do exist). Strictly speaking the generalized theory of evolution is not a single theory but encompasses a family of evolutionary theories. All of these have in common that they share the same three core principles of Darwinian evolution described above. But each member of the family is distinguished by additional specific principles or axioms which further describe the evolutionary process in its realm. Thus a theory of genetic evolution as one particular member of the family of evolutionary theories can be further narrowed down by adding the laws which describe genetic transmission and mutation. And a theory of cultural evolution, another member of the family, could contain principles that describe the transmission and change of cultural traits. In the following, however, we will not be concerned with the generalized theory of evolution in its broadest sense, but only with that part which concerns the evolution of culture.

(2) Basic assumptions

The central assumption of the evolutionary theory of culture is that some cultural developments – or, if we follow the more "imperialistic" programs, all cultural developments – can be explained as cases of Darwinian evolution by reproduction, variation and selection of certain cultural entities. What has to be clarified, when one wants to construct an evolutionary theory of culture in analogy to the theory of evolution in biology, is what the evolving entities are, and how reproduction, variation and selection of these entities takes place.

The entities of cultural evolution   A cultural entity that evolves can be about anything: It can be technology, it can be social norms and customs, it can be laws, it can be institutions, it could possibly also be economic or political systems and maybe, though this seems somewhat doubtful, it could be even arts. Generally speaking, an evolving entity in cultural evolution can be any discernible and identifiable cultural trait. As has been mentioned earlier, some authors apply the ubiquitous term "meme" for any of these entities. But there exist several drawbacks to the "meme"-terminology: 1) The above listed entities are of a very different kind and it must be expected that the conditions of reproduction, variation and selection also differ in each single case. But then it will not be of much use to try to generalize over all of these different instances of cultural evolution by inventing a "meme" theory. 2) Some authors hope that the just mentioned limitation can be overcome by a neuronal definition of the meme. A neuronal definition of the meme that defines the meme in terms of its neuronal representation in the human brain would have to be more atomic than the evolving cultural entities mentioned before. However, the research in this direction is not very far advanced to say the least. At present stage a neuronal definition of the meme is science fiction.[10] 3) In fact, there does not only exist no (generally accepted) neuronal definition of the meme, but there exists

---

[10]While the search for the neuronal basis of cultural traits may be an interesting research program of its own, theories about the neuronal representation of cultural traits will begin to be useful for the explanation of cultural developments (which, after all, is the primary purpose of the theory of cultural evolution) only by the time when the neuronal representation "can be clearly observed or measured" and at the same time unambiguously be linked to the cultural phenomena the explanation of which is in question. At present stage neuro-science seems to be far from fulfilling this requirement.

no precise definition of the "meme" at all. Usually what is offered is just examples and illustrations of a rather trivial kind. Instead of providing a workable definition of the meme, "memetics" is thus indulged in all kinds of dogmatic discussions concerning the nature and essence of a meme, like the question whether an evolving technology is itself to be considered a meme or the blueprints for this technology or just the mental representation of the blueprints in a person's mind.[11] But these dogmatic disputes are of little significance if one is primarily interested in explaining the evolution of some kind of technology or other cultural achievements.[12]

Fortunately, it is possible to circumvent the difficulties that surround the meme concept. For, when we want to explain the evolution of certain cultural traits like altruistic norms, we can simply study how these traits evolve in terms of reproduction, variation and selection without even bothering whether they are instances of some such thing as a meme or not.[13]

Reproduction, variation and selection in cultural evolution   In cultural evolution the three "Darwinian modules" reproduction, variation and selection take a form that is quite different from their counterparts in biology. More importantly, they can differ depending on the evolving entity that is under consideration. Here, only a very general overview can be given. *Reproduction* can take place either through teaching and learning or through imitation or through both. It seems obvious that some things can only be reproduced by teaching as, for the example, the knowledge how to read and write, while other things can easily be imitated. In contrast to the reproduction of genes in multicellular organisms in biology, knowledge and cultural techniques can be transmitted horizontally

---

[11]See (Salwiczek, 2001, p. 164ff.) for a number of such discussion points, most of which are peculiar to the meme concept.

[12]A very extreme example for this purely dogmatic (if not almost ideological) and thus very uninspiring mode of discussion about evolutionary theory in the social sciences is delivered by Alex Rosenberg (Rosenberg, 2005).

[13]One might object that any other concept in place of the "meme" would have to suffer the same drawbacks as the meme-concept. But this is not the case. Cavalli-Sforza and Feldman, for example, define the term "cultural trait" (which is roughly their equivalent for "meme") as "the result of any cultural action that can be clearly observed or measured on a discontinuous or continuous scale" (Cavalli-Sforza and M.Feldman, 1981, p. 73). The term "cultural trait" and the pertinent definition has several advantages over the "meme"-terminology: 1) Right from the beginning it is clear that cultural traits can be many different things and that it does not denote a single type of entities as the "meme"-terminology notoriously suggests. The largely meaningless question "What is a meme?" is thus evaded. 2) The requirement that the trait should be observable and measurable defies premature attempts at a neuronal definition of cultural traits (the other variant of the misleading attempt to find a fundamental, potentially hidden entity behind cultural evolutionary processes). 3) Finally, it is just a fact that memetics has spurred a good deal of poor quality literature on cultural evolution. It seems that despite Aristotle's saying that one should not argue about words, terminology does matter.

and not only vertically to descendants. Depending on the mode of reproduction and the entity reproduced a different rate of reproduction or imitation errors is to be expected. Such imitation errors already resemble one mode of *variation* in cultural evolution. Imitation errors occur unintentional, but variation in cultural evolution frequently occurs as the result of intended change. For example, many technologies we use are constantly being improved. The evolution of technology is therefore one where variation occurs to a high degree in the form of intentional change.

Selection is somewhat more difficult to specify for cultural evolution because when dealing with cultural evolution, there are two different kinds of selection that we can think of. First of all, there is the kind of selection that occurs when people choose to keep or adopt a cultural technique (in the broadest sense, encompassing technology as well as customs, norms, policies etc.) or not to do so. This kind of selection is the selection of cultural traits through the bearers of culture, that is, through humans.[14] A theoretical difficulty with this kind of selection is that there can be all kinds of reasons why people adopt cultural techniques and why not. They may do so because they believe that this will make their life better or allow them to compete more successfully with other people for power, wealth or prestige. But the reasons may also be of a wholly idiosyncratic nature. Therefore, the conditions of this kind of selection can be difficult to specify. The other kind of selection occurs when people that have adopted a certain cultural technology turn out to be very successful (or vice versa very unsuccessful) and simply drive out other people who have not adopted the respective techniques. This may be the case for intrasocietal competition as well as for intersocietal competition. Both kinds of selection are interrelated because, usually, if a certain cultural technique promotes success (in inter- or intrasocietal competition) then people will want to adopt it.

The basic assumptions of the theory of cultural evolution can thus be summed up: Cultural evolution in a Darwinian sense occurs when some cultural entity evolves through reproduction, variation and selection. The evolving entity can be of arbitrary kind with the only restriction that it must be a discernible and identifiable trait of culture. Similarly, the three "Darwinian modules" can take a somewhat different shape from case to case. Already at this point it may be remarked that lacking an equivalent for the sure foundation that the biological theory of evolution has in genetics, the theory of cultural evolution turns out to be much

---

[14]"Memeticists" also like to speak in this connection of "memes" competing for brainspace. If a cultural technique has been adopted then – described in "meme-speak" – its "memes" have successfully competed for human brainspace.

more vague and less concise. But this does not mean that it does not have its assets. Let us see what it can do:

(3) Research strategy and achievements

Given that it is reasonable to assume that at least some cultural development processes follow a Darwinian pattern, it appears only natural to try to apply some of the more specific methods used in evolutionary biology to problems of the social sciences where appropriate. This is what Mesoudi, Laland and Whiten suggest (Mesoudi et al., 2006) and they list a number of fields where this is already being done or can be done with some hope of success. In this respect they refer for example to linguistic studies of the development of languages that apply cladistic methods similar to those used in biology (Mesoudi et al., 2006, p. 333). The development of language seems particularly well suited for an evolutionary explanation because it is a gradual process and at the same time one that is largely unaffected by human intentions, which could distort the selection processes that assumedly promote the development of language. Another, even more striking instance of the transfer of methods from evolutionary biology to the social sciences is the use of evolutionary models borrowed from paleobiology by archaeologists in order to trace the lineages in the development of human artifacts such as coins or projectiles (Mesoudi et al., 2006, p. 334). Yet another field where similarities between biological and cultural evolution can be exploited is that of human behavioral ecology, which studies in how far patterns of human behavior or, likewise, other cultural traits result from an adaptation of human culture to the environment (Mesoudi et al., 2006, p. 335).

While the examples just given all more or less concern the evolution of cultures as wholes and are accordingly subsumed by Mesoudi, Laland and Whiten under the heading of macroevolution, Mesoudi, Laland and Whiten also find ample evidence for microevolution, that is, the evolution and selection of cultural traits within cultures or single societies. On a par with theoretical population genetics as a subdiscipline in biology they enumerate a number of mathematical and computer models of cultural evolution and gene-culture co-evolution as they have been put forward by Boyd and Richerson (Boyd and Richerson, 1985) and Cavalli-Sforza and Feldman (Cavalli-Sforza and M.Feldman, 1981) among others. So far this research has remained mostly theoretical and it therefore remains to be seen whether the reservations against it will eventually cease as they did in the corresponding case of the mathematical models of population genetics in biology (Mesoudi et al., 2006, p.

338). More empirically orientated research has been done on cultural transmission. Mesoudi, Laland and Whiten list several examples of experimental research. Many of these start with a group of people that has to solve certain tasks. Then, the members of the group are replaced one by one in order find out if and how traditions of solution strategies to the tasks evolve and are transmitted. There are indeed some similarities to research on the heritability of traits in biology. The respective field research on cultural transmission is criticized by Mesoudi, Laland and Whiten for its not identifying the putative selection pressure (Mesoudi et al., 2006, p. 340). But this criticism is somewhat question begging because the criticized deficiency could equally well be interpreted as reflecting the fact that the selectionist paradigm is simply not adequate for this type of research. Finally Mesoudi, Laland and Whiten mention some research on "memetics" as the cultural equivalent to genes in biology, but they admit that the concept of the "meme" is still very debated in many respects (Mesoudi et al., 2006, p. 342-344).

Summing it up, while it seems reasonable or at least worthwhile trying some of the methods of evolutionary biology in the social sciences, there obviously exist only few instances where this has already been done with success. But this also means that some instances do indeed exist. And further instances of the successful transfer of methods between evolutionary biology and the social sciences could certainly be added to what Mesoudi, Laland and Whiten mention. From its type of modeling and its kind of thinking, economics seems to be the branch of the social sciences which is the most akin to biology. As evolutionary game theory testifies, the transfer works in both directions[15] (which raises some further doubts about the "imperialist" claim of Mesoudi, Laland and Whiten). But it is only on certain occasions that the transfer works and many fields of the social sciences remain untouched by it. Therefore, one should conclude that rather than becoming the new overarching paradigm of the social sciences, the theory of cultural evolution marks a border region between the social sciences and biology where methods developed in biology can fruitfully be transferred to the social sciences (and vice versa).

(4) Critical objections

Surely, the weakest point of the theory of cultural evolution are the "imperialist" aspirations of some of its proponents. The naive expectation that everything in social science must fit into an evolutionary framework because this works so well in biology can of course hardly

---

[15]See (Arnold, 2005b) for further examples of the transfer of models between biology and economics.

be taken serious.[16] But then, the scientific value of the evolutionary theory of culture does not depend on the fulfillment of its far fetched "imperialistic" claims. If there exist but a few cases where it proves to be useful then this would suffice to justify the approach. But even as far as this goes the theory of cultural evolution has called forth severe criticism. The following critical discussion of the theory of cultural evolution is organized under the headings of three different questions each of which highlights a particular problem of the theory of cultural evolution. What will be discussed is 1) if the theory of cultural evolution is able to explain any phenomena that could not be explained otherwise at all and what these are ("What is the riddle?"), 2) where the theory of cultural evolution does not explain anything new, if it does at least offer better explanation ("Where are the advantages?") and 3) if there exist any monographic studies about cultural phenomena where the theory of cultural evolution has successfully been employed ("Where are the showcases?"). The discussion strongly relies on the criticism b Joseph Bryant (Bryant, 2004), which is a very acute criticism of the theory of cultural evolution. While there are certainly many scientists, especially in the humanities, who reject the attempt to apply Darwinian thinking to the evolution of culture, only few – like Joseph Bryant – have taken the pains to deliver a detailed criticism. Since in my oppinion such criticism is strongly needed and since on the other hand there are enough books and papers heavily advertising the Darwinian theory of cultural evolution (Mesoudi et al., 2006; Laland and Brown, 2004; Dennett, 2006, 1996), the following critical discussion is deliberately kept much more extensive than the previous description of this theory.

1. What is the riddle? A good scientific theory is one that gives us true answers to questions arising from the empirical world. That is, it tells us something we wanted to know or, to put it yet another way, it solves a riddle, right? Now, as has been mentioned earlier, the theory of evolution in biology is certainly a great theory because it solves some of the biggest riddles of our living world, among others, the riddle why all living beings are so extremely well designed to live in their respective habitats. But what is the riddle that the theory of cultural evolution could possibly solve? Design features of our cultural world provide certainly much less of a riddle than those in the natural world. Why is it, for example, that doors have handles? It does not take an evolutionary theory to answer this question because there exists a much simpler and

---

[16]Similarly, the expectation that the propagation of knowledge must be explainable with reference to self replicating entities called "memes", just because the metaphor of the "egoistic gene" worked so well in genetics must be regarded as quite naive.

straightforward answer: Doors have handles because it is very convenient to have a handle on a door and, therefore, people attach handles
to doors. Many functional adaptations in our cultural world can be explained by the fact that they were intentionally designed to be that way.
So, when the evolution or development of culture is concerned there exists right from the beginning much less of a riddle that a Darwinian
theory of evolution would be needed for to provide a solution.

There are two answers that can be given to this objection from the
standpoint of the evolutionary theory of culture. First of all, even
though many features of culture are intentionally designed and therefore
do not require an explanation by a selection process, many or even most
of the long term developments of culture can hardly be the result of con-
scious planning by humans. But also these long term developments do
often expose characteristics of functional adaptation either of the whole
culture or society to its living environment or of the mutual sectors of
the culture (religion, economics, law etc.) to each other. From the point
of view of the evolutionary theory of culture those features of cultural
development that result from intentional design merely represent single
steps in the long term evolutionary process. The fact that these single
steps are in many cases consciously designed (in contrast to the accidental mutations in genetic evolution) just means that the evolutionary
process will take place much faster (Schurz, 2001, p. 345) (Cavalli-Sforza
and M.Feldman, 1981, p. 66). Still, this means that the evolutionary
scheme will only be applicable in certain cases, while it will not be of
much use in many other cases: It will not help us along if the cultural
phenomena we want to explain represent just single steps in the evolutionary scheme. But it may be a good candidate for an explanation
if the cultural phenomena we want to explain are unplanned adaptive
long term developments of culture. But even then it may be a mistake
to assume that "directed mutations" (i.e. changes that are intentionally
brought about by humans with the aim of ameliorating some cultural
technology) merely speed up the processes of evolution. The existence
of directed mutations can lead to a totally different adaptation process
because adaptation can then occur as a sequence of directed mutations
on top of each other without any selection being involved.[17] Also, there
always remains the question whether it is really possible to spell out
such evolutionary explanations when it comes to explaining any such

---

[17]In this connection proponents of the evolutionary theory of culture sometimes casually refer to evolutionary "trial and error processes" just as if any trial and error process must by necessity be an evolutionary
one (in a selectionist sense). But this is of course not true. (If a counter example should seriously be
needed for proving this point: Backtracking algorithms rely on trial and error but are not evolutionary
nonetheless.)

long term developments of culture. This may be quite difficult to accomplish, as we will see when we look at some monographic studies which attempt to do so, later.

The other reply that could be given to the objection that there is not really a riddle for the theory of cultural evolution that needs to be solved is that even if this were true – which is only partly the case, as has just been argued – the theory of cultural evolution may still prove to be valuable in that it solves some of the problems of cultural developments that are already addressed by other theories better than these theories do. It is three advantages in particular that proponents of the theory of cultural evolution claim for their approach apart from potentially solving riddles about cultural developments yet unsolved: 1) *Generality.* The theory of cultural evolution allows for greater generalization. This would especially be the case if it is understood in the sense of the aforementioned generalized theory of evolution. 2) *Unity.* Closely linked with the claim of greater generality is the claim that it provides a unified scientific approach to the problems of the social sciences with all the supposed benefits that come with the unity of sciences. 3) *Greater scientific rigor.* Finally, it is often claimed that the evolutionary approach is more scientific than many other approaches in the social sciences. These three supposed advantages will be discussed in detail below.

So far, we can summarize that there exist at least some questions ("riddles") about cultural developments, namely about unplanned long term adjustments or adaptations within cultures, which it would be difficult to account for on the basis of historical of sociological theories which are centered around intentional action or intentional "responses" to "challenges" or the like and for which an evolutionary theory *might* provide answers. The theory of cultural evolution would then be worth while because it allows us to solve new scientific riddles that have not been solved or not even been taken notice of before. Other than that it is claimed that the theory of cultural evolution can give better answers to existing riddles. Whether this latter claim is warranted will be examined now.

2. Where are the advantages?   A new scientific approach or theory can be justified either because it opens up new fields of knowledge to us, formerly unknown or not paid attention to by science or because it gives us better insights into existing subject matters. As has been argued before, the theory of cultural evolution may be able to solve some riddles that have never properly been considered before and in this sense may allow us to gain new insights. But most of the time when proponents of the theory of cultural evolution give examples for instances of cultural evolution they refer to subject matter that is well known and covered by existing scientific theories already.[18] Where, then, are the great advantages of giving an evolutionary account instead of staying with conventional explanations? Supposedly, these advantages lie a) in the higher level of generality of the evolutionary approach, b) in the unification or linking of different fields of social sciences and even natural sciences (biology) and c) in its being more scientific than other approaches. Let's examine these claims one by one.

a) **Generalization.** Generalization could be a possible benefit of an evolutionary approach. However, regarding generalizations we have to distinguish between real scientific generalizations, where the relatively more specialized laws and concepts can be deduced from the more general laws and concepts, and a purely verbal generalization, where just the same kind of jargon is applied in many different cases. An example for the former, scientific type of generalization would be Newton's mechanics in relation to the laws of Kepler and other more specific laws like the law that states that the acceleration near the earth's surface is $9,81 m/s^2$. A good example for the latter kind is Hegel's dialectics in philosophy because Hegel believed that everything in this world follows the principles of dialectics and in his "Encyclopedia" he cast as much as he knew about any science or subject matter from physics to political philosophy and history into a dialectical jargon. But it is extremely doubtful whether in this way he achieved any informative kind of generalization beyond mere jargonization.[19] If Joseph Bryant's criticism of the theory of cultural evolution is right then the sort of

---

[18]This is particularly true for one topic that seems to be a favorite among evolutionary theorists of culture, namely, the history of religion. Examples of this brand are Wilson (Wilson, 2002) and Dennett (Dennett, 2006).

[19]The point I am making here against Hegel can most easily be explained using an example which Friedrich Engels, a most faithful adherent of Hegel's dialectics, has given (Engels, 1998, p. 248). The example which was supposed to demonstrate that everything in this world follows the dialectical scheme of thesis, antithesis and synthesis runs as follows: Take a grain of barley and plant it in the earth. The grain of barley is the thesis so to say. In the earth the germ buds and a new barley plant develops, which is the negation of the corn (antithesis). But then, as according to dialectics the negation is to be followed by a negation of the negation (or a synthesis) the barley plant itself produces many new barley grains. Unfortunately, far from demonstrating how general dialectics is, the example merely shows how useless it is. For, in order to know that what grows from a barley grain is a barley plant and not, say, potatoes we need to know – in addition to the dialectical principle – the laws of botanics. If, on the other hand, we already know the laws of botanics, we do not need to know dialectics any more to tell us what becomes of the barley grain. Because the same problem occurs in as good as every other application case of dialectics, dialectics is quite useless if considered as a scientific method or theory. A similar case can, as I believe, easily be made against most examples of memetics.

generalization this theory provides lies mainly on the verbal level of applying a vague and ubiquitous jargon to all kinds of already well known phenomena. Bryant speaks in this respect of a mere "schematic 'repackaging' " (Bryant, 2004, p. 471) and demonstrates in two examples of monographic evolutionary studies of cultural phenomena (Runciman's evolutionary interpretation of the replacement of "hoplite warrior culture" of Greek city states at the time of Alexander by larger kingdoms that relied on standing armies and mercenaries (Runciman, 1990) and the interpretation of the development of religion in evolutionary terms as it has been attempted among others by Wilson (Wilson, 2002)) that the evolutionary approach merely results in a much less concise if not distortive presentation of well known materials and at the same time falls short of the scientific level of conventional, non evolutionary accounts. Bryant's examples will be discussed in detail below.[20] In order to estimate in how far Bryant's criticism is not only confined to the two examples he discusses but resembles, as he believes, notorious weaknesses of the attempt to apply Darwinian figures of explanation in social sciences, it would of course be necessary to examine further examples of attempted evolutionary explanations of social or cultural phenomena, which goes beyond the scope of this book. Still, a few further considerations suggest that it may indeed prove difficult for the theory of cultural evolution to achieve a kind of generalization that is truly informative. As has been argued before, there exist different kinds of cultural entities and the way these entities reproduce, change and are selected is different according to the type of entity in question. (This is different in biological evolution, where reproduction and mutation occur in more or less the same way for most organisms.) But then the hint that all cultural entities, the evolution of which can be explained by a Darwinian theory of cultural evolution, evolve through the three Darwinian modules reproduction, variation and selection is just not very informative. In order to explain how and why a specific cultural entity, say, computer technology evolves, what we mainly need to know is the specific laws and circumstances that govern the evolution of this particular entity. But then we do not have much of a generalized theory any more. We will see that this particular limitation of the evolutionary approach will reappear when we examine the empirical applicability of simulation models from evolutionary game theory to the social sciences. Often when applying game theoretical models, the greatest part of the explanatory work is done not by the very abstract and general model but by the specific assumptions that enter into the determination of

---

[20]See page 56.

the input parameters with which the model is fed.[21] To be fair, it has to be said that it is always very difficult in the social sciences to find laws which are very general and at the same time highly informative. It seems that for the subject matter dealt with in the social sciences there usually is a payoff between generality and being informative and that the most useful laws and connections are to be found on an intermediate level of generality. If this is true, however, then it also shows how naive and misplaced some of the aspirations of the theory of cultural evolution are.

Another consideration that suggests that it is advisable to be suspicious of the generalizing claims of the theory of cultural evolution is the fact that it is all too easy to cast any conventional explanation of some cultural development into an evolutionary jargon. Just take an arbitrary explanation of any cultural development, relabel what would commonly be understood as "causes" into "conditions of selection" or some similar phrase from the evolutionary dictionary and, voilà, ready is your evolutionary explanation! It is in particular the branch of "memetics" that lends itself to this kind rephrasing. For example, assume social scientists had found out that more and more reports about terrorism in the news cause many people to live in fear of terrorism then here is the evolutionary explanation: Fear of terrorism spreads because the increasing number of reports about terrorism in the news exerts a positive selection pressure on the "be afraid of terrorists"-meme. Of course, nothing substantial is gained by this kind of rephrasing and certainly not a generalization of any valuable kind. The memetics-literature is full of examples of this very trivial kind of reframing common knowledge in an awkward evolutionary jargon.[22] Of course trying to understand so-

---

[21]See chapter 5.2.2 for an example where this problem occurs.

[22]The following excerpt from a manifesto on memetics may serve to illustrate this charge. It is typical for the way in which examples are constructed in memetics-literature: "A memetical example is the beginning of Christianity. Adherents of the new creed were prosecuted in order to conserve the previously dominant paganism and to destroy the upcoming religion. Kindreds of the faith in Jesus the Nazarean joined together, went into the underground and thus survived in the spiritual community. As the religious convictions, which one can also describe as memes, were adopted by those in power that is were copied, the memecomplex Christianity could prevail over the previous memepool (Constantinian turn!)." (Salwiczek, 2001, p. 129, my translation) This memetical account of a well known historical fact is distinguished from conventional descriptions by nothing but an awkward jargon. Technically speaking, the memetical account merely adds a few *irrelevant premises*, namely the laws of memetics. The qualification of religious groups as "memecomplexes" does not at all help us to explain why one of them (Christianity) won over the other (Paganism). For, since both are memecomplexes just the like, the explanation must lie within specific properties of each of them and cannot be due to their being memecomplexes. – More examples of this kind of trivial rephrasing of common knowledge in an evolutionary jargon can easily be found in Susan Blackmore's book "The meme machine" (Blackmore, 2000). Also quite notorious is the example of the chain letter, which is reiterated again and again in the memetical literature despite its utter triviality(Laland and Brown, 2004). One might object that examples such as the one just quoted were merely meant to explain what the meme concept means and not to prove its value. But then, the literature

cial developments in evolutionary terms is not necessarily bound to end up in trivial reframing of common knowledge. If done seriously it will be quite a demanding task, where one has to consider carefully whether and how the causes of the development in question can be interpreted either as conditions of selection or variation or reproduction. And one cannot be sure beforehand that the endeavor will be crowned by success. But there also exists the cheap way of doing it that bears a similar risk of intellectual self betrayel as Hegelian dialectics once did, which by ardent Hegelians was believed to capture a general pattern underlying any natural or historical process in this world whatsoever (Hegel, 1998; Engels, 1998).

b) **Unification.** Regarding the question whether the evolutionary theory of culture provides the right framework for a *unified science* of cultural evolution, it can only be repeated that at the present stage the Darwinian theory of cultural evolution is far cry from offering anything that could fulfill this claim. It may offer a few good models for a few special cases of cultural development, but it simply covers too little of the vast and varied field of the evolution (in a non Darwinian sense) of culture. At the same time it is by no means clear that the Darwinian scheme is in all cases better or at least as good as competing explanations for cultural development. Unified Science is a kind of pertinacious myth. Some scientists and philosophers seem to believe that whenever a science is being unified then this should give it a boost of scientific discoveries (Tooby and Cosmides, 1992, p. 19ff.) (Mesoudi et al., 2006, p. 329ff.). But in fact it is the other way round: Unification of sciences is the consequence rather than the prerequirement of dramatic scientific advances. It arises more or less by itself whenever different neighboring scientific fields have evolved far enough to merge. But it is not much use trying to impose a unification. Some philosophers of science even dispute that the sciences can be or should be unified at all (Dupré, 1996; Cartwright, 1999). Notwithstanding the question whether the skeptics of unified science are right or wrong, it seems fairly obvious that unity or, what amounts to the same, connectivity to other, specifically the natural sciences is a second rank criteria like generality, parsimony, simplicity and others. First of all it matters whether a scientific theory can explain anything and whether the explanation is true or false. And only if it is true, we can start worrying about whether it is parsimonious, general or how well it can be connected to other theories.

Besides, when talking about a unified science of culture, there is the

---

on memetics often does not advance beyond such trivial demonstrations.

question of why it must necessarily be a unified evolutionary theory of culture. One could equally well demand that it be a unified economic theory of culture based on the utility calculus and the laws of the market. Economics is, after all, no less rigorous than population genetics and it certainly is much closer to the other social sciences than biology. In the end it seems that the call for a unified science is just imperialist science badly disguised.

c) **Scientific rigor.** What about the evolutionary approach being *more scientific* than other approaches in the social sciences? When Mesoudi, Laland and Whiten complain that cultural or social anthropology has made so little progress in comparison with evolutionary biology (and similarly when Tooby and Cosmides complain that the social sciences in general have made very little progress lately) then what they imply is that this is due to a lack of proper methodology and scientific rigor. And they profess to offer a proper methodology by transferring methods and research designs from evolutionary biology to cultural anthropology. How successful this endeavor will be can ultimately be judged only by looking at the very results and concrete examples of this undertaking. But a few general considerations seem appropriate nonetheless: For example, it cannot generally be assumed that transferring certain concepts, methods or paradigms from one field of science where they have been employed with greatest success to another field will retain their success or even just their rigor.[23] Moreover, scientific rigor is not something that could be called in or that depends merely on the willingness of the scientists to apply rigorous methods. It also depends on the subject matter at hand. This is especially true for the application of formal or mathematical methods. Many branches of science simply do not lend themselves to mathematization. It would be laughable to complain that, say, classical philology has not made quite the same progress during the last two hundred years as astronomy or particle physics and to attribute this supposed defect to the lack of rigorous scientific methodology. On the other hand, it is of course always

---

[23]A comparison of genetics in biology and the parallel approach of "memetics" in cultural evolution is quite instructive in this respect. The usual bad excuse that "memetics" is only at its very beginnings won't do here. Apart from the fact that the "meme" concept is more than a quarter of a century old – which is ages on the time scale of modern science – and we still wait for great achievements, genetics in contrast was able to offer substantial new insights right from the beginning as is testified by the Mendelian laws. Daniel Dennet has a very simple explanation for the fact that memetics, despite its age and popularity, has hardly had any impact on cultural history. He believes that this omission is due to the wanton ignorance of " 'humanist' minds" (Dennett, 1996, p. 361). But surely, if the only explanation for the lack of secular success of memetics that an ardent proponent of this concept can find is a kind of conspiracy theory then it is much more plausible to conclude that the meme concept found no followers among the experts in the cultural sciences because memetics is simply a bad theory.

worthwhile trying. One just should not be overly optimistic about the theory of cultural evolution allowing for a more rigorous treatment of cultural developments than conventional theories of cultural developments. For the time being this seems to be a largely unfulfilled claim, but the future may still prove the opposite.

Summing it up, in those areas where the theory of cultural evolution does not solve any new riddles it does not have much to offer that would convince a scientist to give preference to this particular theory over other more conventional approaches. Its supposed generality seems to be accomplished mainly at the expense of a loss of substantial content. To effect a unification of cultural studies under its hood, it is just too sparsely applicable, and whether the acclaimed scientific rigour of its models really proves tenable remains to be seen. Of course, all of these considerations have remained somewhat abstract and tentative. In the end the decisive step to justify a scientific approach or paradigm is to employ it in scientific practice. If anybody were able to draw up a really convincing explanation of some cultural phenomenon based on the theory of cultural evolution then this would certainly do more to the justification of this paradigm (and to the abashment of its critics) than any abstract considerations. Therefore, let us now have a look at some case studies.

3. **Where are the showcases?** The best proof of the fertility of a general scientific theory is when it spawns many monographic studies where its laws and concepts find a useful and appropriate application to specific subject matters. How does the theory of cultural evolution fare in this respect? There certainly exist quite a few monographic studies dedicated to this paradigm. But are they good enough to convince us of the merits of this approach? For his criticism of the theory of cultural evolution, Joseph Bryant has examined two such studies (Bryant, 2004). Because the errors in reasoning he discovers seem to be quite typical for the evolutionary approach, it is worthwhile to take a closer look at his reasoning.

Bryant sets out with some general considerations about the question whether there really are any strong analogies between biological evolution and evolutionary processes in culture (Bryant, 2004, p. 459-469). His criticism suffers a bit from the fact that he assumes that the transfer of evolutionary constructs from biology to the social sciences would require that we find some kind of analogon to the laws of genetics in the cultural sphere, which is obviously very difficult to find(Bryant, 2004, p. 461ff.). But in fact the theory of cultural evolution does not at all rely

on such an analogy. Even those variants of the theory of cultural evolution that employ the concept of the "meme" as a parallel concept to that
of the "gene" in biology do not assume that the proliferation of "memes"
is guided by the same laws as govern the propagation of "genes" in biology. Still, Bryant hits upon an important point insofar as without any
analogon to genetics the theory of cultural evolution tends to be much
less concise than its biological counterpart. But more important than
Bryant's general criticism are his case studies of two attempts to employ
the theory of cultural evolution to the explanation of certain historical
developments. These attempts are: 1) Runciman's interpretation of the
displacement of the ancient Greek "hoplite" caste towards the end of
the classical period in ancient Greece (Bryant, 2004, p. 470-481) and 2)
Interpretations of the history of the Christian religion in Darwinian evolutionary terms, a typical example of which is D.S.Wilson's "Darwin's
Cathedral" (Wilson, 2002) (Bryant, 2004, p. 481-488). Both attempts
fall within scientific fields that are already well covered by a specialist
literature on the respective topics. It is therefore not new riddles that
Runciman and Wilson solve, but new solutions to old riddles they offer.
The question is: Are the evolutionary answers any better?

In Runciman's case, the vanishing of the "hoplite"-caste and its specific cultural codes in ancient Greece is interpreted as the result of evolutionary forces acting against it (Runciman, 1990). "Hoplites" in ancient
Greek were heavy armored soldiers that made up the core of the Greek
city state's armed forces. Because a full armour was expensive it was
the rich and nobles of the Greek cities that had the honor to fight in
the hoplite-phalanxes. An important aspect of the hoplite warrior culture was that the Greek city states did not entertain standing armies.
Those that fought for their city state in the army were citizens that
took part in seasonal warfares and pursued other obligations during
the rest of the year. According to Runciman the hoplite culture was
"doomed to extinction" towards the end of classical greek antiquity because it had evolved under different circumstances and could not adapt
quickly enough to a suddenly changed environment (Runciman, 1990,
p. 355f.). The hoplite armies with their part-time warriors and with
them the hoplite warrior and citizen culture became replaced by standing armies supplemented with paid mercenaries. The paradigmatic case
of these new and more successful formations is the Macedonian army
under Philipp and Alexander. This change in the military sector was
accompanied by changes in the social formation and political organization. Although they still remained important cultural centres for a long
time afterwards, the Greek city states were eventually replaced as major political players by the rising new empires like the Macedonian and,

later, the Roman empire. One of the main driving forces behind the erosion of the hoplite culture was the growing number of mercenaries as a result of continuous warfare and political unrest among and within the Greek *poleis*. People who became expelled from their home cities often did not have any other alternative than to let themselves be hired as soldiers, and in a time of constant unrest there were always those in need of their service. Runciman treats this process as an evolutionary selection process, wherein the social model of the hoplite culture, treated by him as a complex of interlocking social regulations on different sectors, military, economic, social and religious (Runciman, 1990, p. 351ff.), was ultimately replaced by more successful models of social organization.

Bryant finds fault with this evolutionary account of antique history for two reasons: The first objection is that Runciman's account is just another example of the mere rephrasing of terminology that, if we follow Bryant's criticism, is one of the main effects of the application of Darwinian evolutionary thinking to the social sciences. According to Bryant what Runciman tells us does not got beyond what we know from ordinary accounts of antique history. Nor is Runciman able to give a better explanation. He merely casts well known facts and connections into a peculiar evolutionary narrative (Bryant, 2004, p. 470). Without gaining any advantages by drawing on evolutionary concepts Runciman's account turns thus out to be just a less concise presentation of a well known subject matter. But Bryant finds an even greater flaw in Runciman's evolutionary presentation. By employing evolutionary concepts which just do not fit very well to the subject matter in question, Runciman slips into the error of *retrospective determinism* (Bryant, 2004, p. 478).[24] Because evolutionary accounts of cultural processes typically downplay the role of human intention, they underestimate the degree to which the outcome of historical processes is liable to human action and planning. According to Bryant the social and cultural transitions that took place at the end of the Hellenic age can be much better understood with the figure of *challenge and response* than in evolutionary terms.[25] The Greek city states faced a challenge in form of growing num-

---

[24]Next to the fault of *retrospective determinism* Bryant identifies four other pitfalls that Runciman's evolutionary approach has fallen into: 1) Misidentification and misrepresentation of causal processes, 2) supplanting and effacing of the intentionality of real flesh-and-blood actors by ambiguous and implausible biological hypostazations such as memes, mutants and environmental pressures, 3) obfuscatory superimposition of internally most differentiated social processes and arrangements by screening abridgments such as fitness, adaptation and extinction, 4) Underplaying or bypassing of the "ideational or symbolically constructed dimensions and characteristics of social life … in a strained effort to reconfigure the field of action along the lines of an organism-environment duality" (Bryant, 2004, p. 481).

[25]To people unacquainted with the way explanations in social sciences usually work, the figure of "challenge and response" might as such appear much more vague, ambiguous and less concise than the

bers of soldier armies and the visible military advantages that could be gained with professional combatants instead of part time combatants. But in no way they were thereby "doomed to extinction" as Runciman believed. Rather, the question was if they were able to find an adequate response to this challenge. And indeed they did respond to the challenge by employing professional militias themselves and by forming alliances (Bryant, 2004, p. 480). In the end they were not successful, which may partly also be due to contingent factors such as the loss of a small number of decisive battles. Had the response been successful, the "hoplite culture" could have been retained with only minor adjustments.

Of course one could ask at this point whether the fault really lies with the theory of cultural evolution. Maybe Runciman just did not make a very clever use of the evolutionary concepts. After all, there is no strict necessity by which an evolutionary account of some process in cultural history must slip into the mistake of retrospective determinism or any of the several other defects that Bryant diagnoses (Bryant, 2004, p. 481). Maybe, such mistakes could be avoided, while still employing evolutionary concepts. But then, specific theoretical approaches are often in a certain way suggestive. And it seems that the evolutionary approach is just not very appropriate to explain the kind of short term cultural transition processes that Runciman submits to an evolutionary analysis. Further below, however, we will see that even for long term cultural development processes it can be very difficult to draw up a precise evolutionary description.

Taking Bryant's criticism a step further and linking it with some of our previous reflections about suitable application scenarios or application limits of a Darwinian evolutionary theory of culture, we can conjecture[26] that Runciman's basic mistake was to apply the evolutionary scheme to a process that took place on a time scale which is short enough to fall into the time horizon of human planning. Now, while the theory of cultural evolution does take account of intentional or planned human action by treating it as "directed mutations" (kinds of mutations for which there exists no analogon in biological evolution, where mutations are always random mutations) it does not explain the single directed mutations itself. Therefore, the theory of cultural evolution will not yield an appropriate explanation of cultural development processes that consist, technically speaking, only of one or a few single

---

concept of a Darwinian evolutionary process. But as spelled out by Bryant in the case of the "hoplite culture" it is in fact no less concise but at the same time much more appropriate to the subject matter than Runciman's evolutionary account (Bryant, 2004, p. 470ff.).

[26]To actually demonstrate this conjecture a more detailed analysis of Runciman's evolutionary concepts would be necessary.

"mutations".

The other one of Bryant's two case studies of the failure of the evolutionary theory of culture concerns the possibility of interpreting the genesis of the Christian religion on the basis of Darwinian cultural evolution. An ambitious study that follows this approach is David Sloan Wilson's "Darwin's Cathedral" (Wilson, 2002). Wilson, who is otherwise known for his collaborate work with Elliott Sober "Unto Others", where they make a case for group selection (Sober and Wilson, 1998), sets out to describe the mechanism of group selection and to explain why he sees human groups as adaptive units that are subject to group selection mechanisms. This part, where Wilson is completely on his own terrain is still the best part of his book (Wilson, 2002, p. 5ff.). But then his reasoning becomes rather naive. Because group selection is a mechanism that renders functionalistic explanations[27] plausible (under certain conditions) he hopes to revive a kind of sociological structural functionalism, just as he and Sober were able to revive group selection which had formerly fallen into disgrace among biologists due to its seemingly functionalistic nature (Sober and Wilson, 1998, p. 55ff.). But then he never really shows just how the evolution of religious movements that demand a high degree of dedication and, in extreme cases, even self sacrifice from their members was due to group selection mechanisms or to Darwinian evolutionary mechanisms in general. In this respect his treatment unfortunately remains very vague. Also, as Bryant contends, Wilson's Sketch of early Christianity almost entirely rests on the works of the rational choice school of the sociology of religion like those by Rodney Stark as one of its most prominent representatives (Bryant, 2004, p. 482). Wilson has hardly any insights to offer that go beyond what rational choice sociologists like Rodney Stark have already said about the Christian Religion (Wilson, 2002, p. 147ff.).[28] Therefore, Wilson's "Darwin's Cathedral" is again an example where the evolutionary theory of culture offers just old wine in new bottles.

In the two examples discussed by Bryant the Darwinian evolutionary theory of culture was thus not able to provide any new insights. On the contrary, it led in the case of Runciman even to a somewhat distorted interpretation of the analyzed historical process. But are these two examples really symptomatic for the weaknesses of the evolutionary theory

---

[27] A *functionalistic explanation* is an explanation where a phenomenon is not explained by its causes (*causal explanation*) but by its function, e.g. "ants are collaborative animals because this contributes to the survival of the anthill (or of the ant species etc.)". Functionalistic explanations are never proper explanations because serving a certain function is not a sufficient reason for the existence of a certain trait.

[28] This is also true of Wilson's other examples, the presentation of which to a large extent consist of lengthy quotations of what other author's have said on the topic.

of culture, as Bryant holds, or are they just examples where the evolutionary theory of culture has been badly applied? A complete answer to this question would require carrying out a systematic survey, which goes beyond the scope of this book. However, there is a provisional short cut which can help us to get around this difficulty: Instead of looking at further examples of evolutionary theory in order to find out how well they deal with cultural history, we can also look at some examples of cultural history in order to find out in how far they are evolutionary. There is one very prolific recent author whose latest works seem particularly well suited for such an attempt. This author is Jarred Diamond who has presented in his books "Guns, Germs and Steel" (Diamond, 1998) and "Collapse" (Diamond, 2005) a fascinating and fresh approach to the study of cultural history based on geological and archeological data. Diamond is an evolutionary biologist who only lately turned to cultural history. He therefore knows the Darwinian theory of evolution very well. If we can expect anyone to transfer Darwinian evolutionary concepts from biology to the study of human culture then we can expect this the most likely from a biologist turned historian of culture.[29] The first of the two mentioned books "Guns, Germs and Steel" covers roughly the last 13 000 years of human history and tries to answer the question as to why some civilizations were more successful than others and why ultimately the Europeans won over most of the other civilizations and not the other way round. The book thus covers processes within a very large time horizon, large enough so that the problem of the short time horizon which rendered Runciman's evolutionary account of a phase in ancient Greek history implausible will not interfere. The second book is about past and present environmental catastrophes. The subtitle "how societies chose to fail or succeed" suggests that societies differ in whether they manage to solve the environmental problems or whether they fail to do so. Is there maybe a process of selection going on here?

Let us look at "Guns, Germs and Steel" first. Diamond examines the question why some civilizations develop technologies that make them stronger than others, why some are faster doing so than others and why some societies carry germs with them that are lethal to others but not the other way round. Why, for example, did the Indians die from the diseases the European invaders brought to them, while the European invaders did not die from any Indian diseases? The answer that Diamond gives, and which is strikingly well supported by the empirical evidence Diamond relates to, is that this depends primarily on the habitat a society lives in and the environmental conditions it faces. Why do some

---

[29]In fact, Diamond's "Guns, Germs and Steel" is a favorite reference of adherents of a Darwinian evolutionary theory of culture. See, for example, (Dennett, 2006, p. 104f.).

societies have agriculture and others do not? Because plants that are suitable for agriculture (and there exists only a small number of plant species for which this is the case) grow naturally only in some specific areas of the world (Diamond, 1998, p. 131ff.). Why do some societies raise livestock and others don't? Again, only very specific animal species can be kept as livestock. And these are not spread all over the globe (Diamond, 1998, p. 157ff.). Why did the technology of agriculture spread much faster in Eurasia than in America after it had been discovered? It did so because the Eurasian continent stretches along an east-west line with roughly similar climate and environmental conditions, which means that the cultivation of the same crops can spread easily and without many adjustments along the east-west line (Diamond, 1998, p. 176ff.). Why are the Australian aborigines not organized in large hierarchical kingdoms? Because, for the reasons mentioned above, they did not even get as far as inventing agriculture. How could they possibly have taken the further steps of civilizational development that are based on agriculture (Diamond, 1998, p. 295ff.)? So, the explanation that Diamond offers for the civilizational development of societies consists in describing the natural environmental conditions they live in and in how far the invention and use of certain cultural techniques requires certain environmental conditions to be fulfilled. It should be observed that Diamond only talks about what is required for certain cultural developments to take place. Very little is said about how these processes take place and it is completely left open if they follow a Darwinian evolutionary scheme or not. The case that gets the closest to an evolutionary description of the process of the development of a cultural technique is Diamond's account of the invention of agriculture. Agriculture comprises several interlocking work phases (sowing, harvesting, threshing, grinding and baking), the suitability of which for the purpose of food production can impossibly have been known to humans before they had agriculture. Therefore, agriculture cannot simply have been invented but must have been introduced stepwise in a gradual process. The question is then, what the intermediate steps between hunting and gathering and fully fledged agriculture are. Diamond suggests a slow replacement of hunting and gathering as means of food production starting with "accidental" grain fields on rubbish dumps, continuing with garden keeping by hunter-gatherers and, finally, resulting in cultivation (Diamond, 1998, p. 104ff.). Is this then an evolutionary process that Diamond describes? It could be, but neither Diamond's description nor the empirical data that it is based on could really sufficiently support this claim. The processes could also be one of a linear sequence of inventions building on top of each other with no selection taking place other than a simple choice of preferred technology.

Only where Diamond discusses the role that germs played in the world-conquest of the Europeans, he employs evolutionary theory. But here it is solely biological evolution that he refers to. The most lethal germs originated from livestock. Since Europeans (or Eurasians, for that matter) had been raising livestock for many centuries before they made contact with the cultures on other continents, the European population had had time enough to evolve resistance against the associated diseases, but not vice versa (Diamond, 1998, ch. 11).

The conclusion to be drawn about Diamond's "Guns, Germs and Steel" is that it provides little evidence for the benefits of an evolutionary theory of culture. There is no denying that it would surely be possible to rephrase the whole book in an evolutionary jargon. But what would be the point of doing so? And to base an empirically well founded evolutionary explanation on Diamond's book would require gathering much more empirical data on the civilizational development processes taking place than is presented by Diamond.[30]

In Diamond's other book that touches on human cultural history the non-evolutionary character of Diamonds explanations is even more obvious. Just as if he had read and taken to heart Bryant's criticism of the evolutionary theory of culture, he avoids the evolutionary jargon but employs instead non-evolutionary explanatory figures such as that of "challenge and response". Why did the Norse culture in Greenland cease to exist after a few hundred years while the Inuit continued to live in the same hostile environment? According to Diamond, who traces back the downfall of the Greenland Norse in great detail, the Norse and the Inuit faced the same environmental challenges but the Norse failed to develop an adequate cultural response to this challenge (Diamond, 2005, p. 248ff.). In his presentation of this processes Diamond does not make any use of evolutionary assumptions.[31] In order to explain the failure or success of societies in general, Diamond develops a five tier model that comprises environmental as well as political factors (Diamond, 2005, p.

---

[30]The data that would be needed for such an endeavor may not even be available at all. The elegance of Diamond's approach is among other things due to the fact that he makes good use of his data, but, at the same time, does not overinterpret it. He does not try to answer questions that cannot be answered with the help of the accessible geographical, biological and archaeological data, and neither does he indulge in theoretical disputes that could not be decided by the same empirical data.

[31]An adherent of evolutionary explanations might be inclined to interpret the prevailing of the Inuit over the Norse as an instance of selection in the evolutionary sense. But then only the terminology but not the concept of selection from evolutionary theory would be applied because in biology natural selection is the very factor that shapes all features of an organism. In analogy, one would have to explain how the many particular features of the Inuit and the Norse culture (technology, diet, social order etc.) have been shaped by processes of selection. This would be a much more ambitious project and it would most probably also require to gather much more data about these cultures than Diamond had available.

10-15), rangeing form climate conditions and and environmental damage to hostile or friendly neighbours and ultimately the sociatal responses to these hazards. There is nothing particularly evolutionary about his model. Also, in his whole book, Diamond strongly emphasizes the role and importance of human decisions. For him it is primarily a matter of choice whether human societies fail or succeed. This emphasize is partly due to Diamond's political legacy, which is to warn his readers about the dangers of environmental catastrophes. Therefore, it is understandable that he presents the cultural processes that lead to the destruction of the environment not as anonymous evolutionary processes beyond human design and intervention. Still, his presentation is very convincing as it stands.

In neither of his two books on human culture has Diamond had much use for a Darwinian concept of cultural evolution. Obviously, if a biologist turns to the study of human culture and is not absolutely bent on applying evolutionary concepts to human culture, he will quite naturally end up with the same kind of explanations (like, for example, explanations in terms of "challenge and response") that are used by historians, archaeologists, social scientists etc. What distinguishes Diamond from the typical historian or social scientist is the great importance he attributes to the natural environment in shaping human culture. Beyond that, there is little in his books that betrays the biologist. The little use Diamond makes of evolutionary concepts underlines the impression that Bryant's criticism is not merely an outcome of the usual prejudices of a group of scientists (in this case social scientists) against fresh approaches developed by outsiders but that the use of Darwinian evolutionary concepts for understanding the development of human societies and cultures is indeed strongly limited. At any rate, Diamond's books provide excellent examples for *non-evolutionary* explanations of cultural developments.

Despite all this criticism it should not be forgotten that the theory of cultural evolution certainly also does have its assets (see section 3.3.2). Therefore, summing the discussion of the evolutionary theory of culture up, it can be concluded that there is good reason to assume that there are some evolutionary processes in human history and cultural development that can be understood as Darwinian evolutionary processes. However, this also means that it is *only* some of the many and varied types of development processes occurring in human societies that can reasonably be described in Darwinian evolutionary terms. It is therefore not to be expected that a Darwinian evolutionary theory of culture will ever attain the rank of the one great frame paradigm for social sciences as the theory of evolution does in biology. To call for a unified theory of cultural evolution, as Mesoudi, Laland and Whiten do, can thus only be regarded as a mistake. The imminent danger of a unified theory of cultural evolution is that it induces us to disregard other and possibly better alternative explanations for cultural development processes. At any rate, we must neither assume that all cultural phenomena can be explained on an evolutionary basis, nor can we assume without further reason that if we have an evolutionary explanation for a certain cultural phenomenon that it will be the only possible explanation or that it really tells us everything there is to know about it. This has important consequences for the way we have to look at the evolutionary models of altruism discussed in the following chapter. While when applied to biology these models encompass all possibilities how altruism can evolve that have hitherto been conceived of, we cannot assume that these models cover all or even just the most important possibilities of how altruism evolves in culture. At most, it can be maintained that the evolutionary models describe mechanisms of the evolution of altruism that – under the reserve of its empirical verification[32] – may be at work in human culture side by side with other non-Darwinian mechanisms that produce altruism. For example, one of the major factors that promote altruistic or cooperative behavior (in a broad sense) in human societies are the institutions of law and law enforcement. This factor is nowhere adequately captured in any of the common models of the evolution of altruism.[33] Of course a Darwinian theory of the evolution of law and the institutions of law enforcement does not seem completely inconceivable. But so far no such theory has been produced. Therefore, the existing evolutionary explanations for altruism cannot claim to offer a comprehensive answer to the question how altruism evolves in human societies.

3.4 Theory and models

In the preceding subsections different strata of the Darwinian theory of evolution have been presented and discussed in some detail. What remains to be clarified is the place that the models of the evolution of altruism discussed in the following chapter take within this theoretical framework.

As has been shown, there are basically three types of Darwinian evolutionary theories. There is the – well known – theory of evolution in bi-

---

[32]See chapter 5.
[33]One would have to look in other places such as institutional economics to find models that come closest to this.

ology which can be characterized in contradistinction to the other types as a theory of genetic evolution of living organisms including humans. Then there is evolutionary psychology (the successor of sociobiology) which is a theory of genetic evolution of human nature and behavior in particular. Because evolutionary psychology relies solely on genetic evolution, it could be regarded as a branch of the common biological theory of evolution. But because its claim to explain human behavior and psychology as a part of the genetically evolved human nature is highly controversial – much more controversial than the biological theory of evolution is nowadays among scientists – it is advisable to treat it as a different stratum of evolutionary theory. Finally, there is the theory of cultural evolution which applies Darwinian evolutionary thinking and evolutionary models to the development of human culture but does not assume that human culture is determined by the genes.

The models that will be examined in the following chapter are game theoretic models of evolving strategies. No claim is made about how these strategies are implemented, e.g. whether they are coded by the genes of an organism or whether they represent some kind of learned wisdom of human individuals. Therefore these models should be understood as models within the theoretical framework of a generalized theory of evolution. In principle, they can be applied to both genetic and cultural evolution. The "Darwinian modules" enter into these models mainly through the replicator dynamics that is used in these models. Variation or mutation is (except for a very trivial form) not present in the models presented in the following. Still, they suffice to model typical selection processes as they occur once a certain "meaningful" mutation has appeared on the scene and challenges the existing types.

The models themselves remain abstract that is, they do not specify how reproduction, variation and selection takes place. When applying the models to a biological context, this does not pose a problem because what is meant is always reproduction of genes, mutation of genes (variation) and selection of organisms (and thereby indirectly of genes, too). But when applying evolutionary models to the social sciences, these must be specified empirically. Such a specification or explanation of what reproduction, variation and selection means will to some degree be context specific as there are different kinds of reproduction, variation and selection in cultural evolution. An abstract evolutionary model can – in principle – be applied to social sciences if there exists at least one context for which the mechanisms of variation, reproduction and selection can be specified empirically. Whether the application of the model in this context is meaningful in the sense of providing new insights and empirically testable hypotheses is yet another question. In the next chapter different models for the three basic types of evolutionary altruism will be presented and supplemented by considerations concerning their interpretation in a cultural context. The question of their empirical impact will not be considered until the subsequent chapter.

Chapter 4

Modeling the evolution of altruism

In the previous chapter different variants of Darwinian evolutionary theories were introduced. While the general approach of each of these theories was sketched and discussed in some detail, nothing has so far been said about how the evolution of altruism in particular is to be explained. In this chapter the different evolutionary explanations for altruism will be set out. These explanations will be described with the help of simulation models. Simulation models are an easy way to examine 1) if a certain explanation works in principle, i.e. if it is conclusive and does not rest on self contradictory assumptions and 2) how the explanation works. It sometimes appears that scientists also believe that by studying computer simulations of the evolution of altruism, one could learn something about how and why altruism evolves (Axelrod, 1984). But this belief is mistaken. By studying computer simulations alone, one cannot learn anything about how altruism evolves, unless the simulations have been empirically validated. And this has been achieved for almost none of the many computer simulations of the evolution of altruism so far. The choice of computer simulations rather than mathematical models is motivated by the fact that computer simulations are often more intuitive and can very easily be extended. Purely mathematical models in contrast set much stronger limits to the complexity of what can be modeled. Also, it seems that computer simulations have been much more popular than purely mathematical models for modeling the evolution of altruism.

Within the evolutionary paradigm there are basically three different explanations for the existence of altruism. These explanations are 1) the theory of reciprocal altruism, 2) the theory of kin selection and, finally, 3) group selection theory. The theory of reciprocal altruism explains altruism by the assumption that altruism may serve the benefactor himself (or herself) if there is some way of ensuring that the benefits are returned. The theory of kin selection explains altruism by the genetic relatedness of the partners of altruistic exchange. A special twist has been given to this theory by Richard Dawkins who concludes that what appears as altruism is just the egoism of the genes which related individuals share (Dawkins, 1976, p. 278ff.). In contrast to this, the theory of group selection can even explain the existence of genuine altruism. According to the theory of group selection, altruism may evolve in populations that are divided into relatively isolated subpopulations (called "demes") because it enhances the fitness of a subpopulation.

In the following three sections these explanations for the evolution of altruism will be described one by one. The explanation of reciprocal altruism will be examined in greatest detail. Because the main goal of this book is to examine how explanations of altruism work (and not so much to explain altruism itself, which is more of a task for specialist scientists than for philosophers) the simulation models will be developed stepwise. At every step it will be examined how this type of modeling works, i.e. what basic modeling choices are taken, what the model can demonstrate and what it cannot demonstrate and how the model can be refined to possibly increase its demonstrative power. This procedure will be followed in all detail for the models of reciprocal altruism. As the epistemic conditions for modeling are exactly the same in the case of kin selection and group selection, these will be discussed only briefly. The presentation and discussion of the models will in this chapter remain largely immanent. No empirical considerations enter into the discussion at this point. These will be reserved for the following chapter. However, since it is not altogether obvious how the models can be used outside a genetic contest, some brief indication will be given for each model concerning how it can possibly be applied to a cultural context.

4.1 Reciprocal altruism

The theory of reciprocal altruism was first proposed by the biologist R. Trivers (Trivers, 1971). According to Trivers "altruistic" cooperation among animals that are not close relatives could be explained by reciprocity. Examples of reciprocal cooperation in biology are grooming among primates but also mutualisms like that of hermit crabs and sea anemones,[1] where the partners of cooperation are not even of the same species. The core of the reciprocity argument runs as follows: Altru-

---

[1]In the case of hermit crabs and sea anemones, however, it is – without precise empirical information – hard to tell whether it is an instance or reciprocal altruism, which requires that the partners have the option to cheat, or byproduct mutualism, where no such option exists, or even simply parasitism by the sea anemone if the benefits for the hermit crab do not outweigh the disadvantage of carrying sea anemones around.

ism subsists, because it is conditioned on the return of the investment by the partner of cooperation. If this condition is fullfilled cooperation can result in a fitness benefit for both partners of cooperation. This turns cooperation into an evolutionary advantage, which explains why reciprocal altruism appears in nature.

The greater part of the modeling on reciprocal altruism centers around the repeated two person Prisoner's Dilemma. The paradigm example of modeling reciprocal altruism is the computer tournament Robert Axelrod has conducted in order to explain the evolution of cooperation (Axelrod, 1984). But there are of course great differences with regard to the setting and parameters under which simulations of this type have been carried through. Interestingly, many of these later models suggest quite different conclusions from those Axelrod drew from his simulations (Binmore, 1998, p. 313ff.). Generally, scientists are nowadays much more careful about drawing sweeping conclusions from their models than Axelrod was. Some variants of these models will be discussed further below (see section 4.1.5).

When casting the concept of reciprocal altruism into a model or formal description two types of such models can be distinguished: (1) Formal descriptions of the concept of reciprocal altruism as such. These are typically sparse and do not go beyond rendering the very concept of reciprocal altruism in formal terms. (2) Rich and detailed models of diverse situations, in which reciprocal altruism can occur. As appears naturally, the formal descriptions of the first type have been developed first. Trivers, in his famous article (Trivers, 1971), uses the following equation to describe the conditions for the evolution of reciprocal altruism:

$$\frac{1}{p^2}(\sum b_k - \sum c_j) > \frac{1}{q^2}\sum b_m \qquad (4.1)$$

p frequency of the altruistic allele
q frequency of the non altruistic allele
b_k an altruistic benefit an altruist receives
b_m an altruistic benefit a non altruist receives
c_j costs that an altruists takes upon itself
      for bestowing an altruistic act
      (on either an altruist or a non-altruist)

(Trivers, 1971, p. 37)

The left hand side of the inequation tells us the fitness of an average altruist, which is calculated by determining the overall benefit of altruism on the the altruists ($\sum b_k$ is the overall benefit that only *the altruists* receive from altruism and $\sum c_j$ is the overall cost the altruists have to pay) and dividing it by the frequency of the altruist. (Trivers considers only those types as altruists both of whose alleles are altruistic.) Thus the fewer altruists are present, the higher is the share each gets from the overall net benefits on altruists. (This should not let us overlook the fact that the overall net benefit typically increases with the number of altruists.) The right hand side of the inequation in turn delivers the fitness of an average non-altruist.

Now, what the equation tells us is simply that we should expect altruism to spread in a population if the fitness of the altruists is higher than that of the non-altruists and that this in turn depends on the respective fitness benefits and costs. More simply put, altruism will evolve if $\sum b_m$ is kept relatively small. If it is assumed that this will be the case when the altruists stop being altruistic in case their altruistic acts are not being reciprocated (that is, if they find out that they have met a non-altruist) (Trivers, 1971, p. 37) then it becomes understandable how the inequation describes the evolution of reciprocal altruism. Strictly speaking, the inequation as such does not say anything about *reciprocal* altruism in particular. It could therefore also be interpreted as a general inequation of altruism.

Apart from Trivers' inequation also other basic general models of altruism or "cooperation" have been suggested. Dugatkin, for example, outlines a "cooperation game" that consists basically of a game matrix filled in with variables, which if for the variables parameter values within a certain range are chosen yields the one or the other of the typical dilemma games like the Prisoner's Dilemma, the stag hunt game or the chicken game (see page 74 for an explanation of these game types) (Dugatkin, 1997, p. 34ff.). Further alternatives can be found in Boorman and Levitt's treatment of the genetics of altruism (Boorman and Levitt, 1980). However, all of these models do hardly more than render the basic concept of altruism in a formal notion. In order to turn a general model of altruism such as Trivers' inequation into a specific model of the evolution of reciprocal altruism, or, even more specifically, the evolution of altruism in a certain empirically given or imagined situation, it would at least be necessary to give an interpretation of how the single terms of the equation such as $\sum c_j$ or $\sum b_m$ are to be determined. This may of course depend on specific conditions and assumptions.

Therefore, it should not surprise us that when we turn from the sparse and very basic models of altruism of the first kind to the rich and detailed models of the second kind, we find a baroque variety of different models and approaches that in one way or other claim to describe the "evolution of altruism". It is not in the least the multitude and diversity of models of the "evolution of altruism" that has called forth criticism. Especially when computer simulations come into play, it seems that nothing is easier than setting up a model of reciprocal altruism. But exactly because it is so simple to produce models, and because there are so many different models which lead to different – and often even contradictory – conclusions (Binmore, 1994, p. 198ff.) (Dugatkin, 1998, p. 42-44), and because hardly any of these models has been supplemented by empirical research, the impression is hard to avoid that most of the models of reciprocal altruism are mere "toy models" (Hammerstein, 2003b, p. 92) that provide more of an obstacle than an inspiration to the research on altruism. We will come back to this important criticism later, but first we will try to see how the modeling of reciprocal altruism with the help of computer simulations works, and in how far the imminent danger of arbitrary modeling can possibly be kept in check when constructing such models.

In order to get a grip on reciprocal altruism, the first step will be the construction of a very simple model of reciprocal altruism which does at best serve as a sort of "in principle" explanation. The purpose is to discuss the general features and premises that enter into the explanation of reciprocal altruism on an evolutionary basis. The second step will be a fully-fledged computer simulation of reciprocal altruism that would also allow studying the influence of different parameters (correlation, degeneration, noise etc.) on the evolution of altruism in the model. However, as the model is not based on any empirical data, it would be futile to try to draw far reaching conclusions from the model. Its purpose is mainly to demonstrate how unstable such models of reciprocal altruism typically are, which forshadows a central difficulty of the modeling approach that will be discussed later in this chapter (see sections 4.1.4 and 4.1.6).

4.1.1   A simple model of reciprocal altruism

There are many different ways to model reciprocal altruism. The most popular models of reciprocal altruism are game theoretic models. Usually the game theoretic models are based on the *Prisoner's Dilemma* game. Although other alternatives are sometimes discussed like the so called "stag hunt"-game (Skyrms, 2004), the Prisoner's Dilemma does in a certain sense depict the most crucial cooperation dilemma. In the most simple case of the symmetric two person Prisoner's Dilemma there are two players, each of which can choose either to *cooperate* or to *defect*. ("Defect" is the terminus technicus for "do not cooperate".) Depending on the choices of both players each player gains a certain payoff. There

		Player 1	
		cooperate	defect
Player 2	cooperate	3 / 3	0 / 5
	defect	5 / 0	1 / 1

Figure 4.1: The Prisoner's Dilemma

exist four possible combinations of actions by the two players. In the Prisoner's Dilemma a player gets the highest payoff if she or he chooses to defect while the other player cooperates. This payoff is commonly denoted by the letter T for "temptation to cheat". If both players cooperate, each of them gets the "reward" R for cooperating. If neither player cooperates, both get a payoff of P for "punishment". In the Prisoner's Dilemma P is smaller than R, but R is yet smaller than T so that the players have an incentive to cheat even at the risk of being punished. This holds all the more, because the worst alternative for each player in the Prisoner's Dilemma is to cooperate when the other player does not cooperate (that is, when the other player "defects"). In this case the cooperating player is left with a "sucker's payoff" of S, which, in the Prisoner's Dilemma game, is even smaller than P.

More schematically the Prisoner's Dilemma is depicted in table 4.1. For the purpose of illustration the letters T, R, P, S have been replaced by the numbers $5, 3, 1, 0$. Of course, any other quadruple of numbers could have been chosen as long as the condition $T > R > P > S$ holds, which defines the Prisoner's dilemma in the two person case. If the chosen parameters do not fullfil this condition, then it is not a Prisoner's Dilemma any more, but a different kind of game. For example, if $R > T$ instead of $T > R$, the game defined is a *stag hunt game*. As has already been said, the stag hunt game is also sometimes used to model cooperation problems. But in fact the stag hunt game does at best describe a coordination problem, because in the stag hunt game any rational player should choose to cooperate as long as he or she has reason to assume that the other player also cooperates. Thus, cooperation in the stag hunt game is just a matter of coordination. Yet another alternative for a cooperation dilemma would be the *chicken game*. The chicken game is very similar to the Prisoner's Dilemma with the only difference that the worst alternative is that of mutual defection ($S > P$). In the chicken game it would thus be better to be cheated alone than to cheat mutually.

This is different in the Prisoner's Dilemma. In the Prisoner's Dilemma a rational player will never cooperate, even if the other player were willing to cooperate. This is easy to see if we look at figure 4.1:

Assume that the other player does cooperate, then it is best not to cooperate, because this increases one's own payoff from 3 to 5. And if the other player does not cooperate? Then again, it is best not to cooperate oneself, because by defecting one still gains a payoff of 1 instead of being left with 0. Therefore, whatever the other player does, it is always best not to cooperate in the Prisoner's Dilemma. This result is of course not very satisfactory, because both players end up with less than they could. With the numbers from above, both get a payoff of 1, although they could both get 3 if only they were able to cooperate. In the more technical language of game theory this state of affairs can be described as a consequence of the Prisoner's Dilemma having only one Nash equilibrium (a state of affairs where no single player can increase his or her own payoff by choosing a different course of action) which is not Pareto-efficient. Pareto efficiency means that no one could be better off without anybody else getting less. In the Prisoner's Dilemma all players would be better off if they did cooperate. Therefore, the non-cooperation equilibrium is not Pareto-efficient.

There is no way of getting around this unpleasant state of affairs, which means that without a change of boundary conditions the Prisoner's Dilemma would be a very boring model for the evolution of reciprocal altruism as altruism simply cannot evolve in the "one shot"[2] Prisoner's Dilemma. This changes when moving from the one shot Prisoner's Dilemma to the reiterated Prisoner's Dilemma. In the reiterated Prisoner's Dilemma several rounds of the Prisoner's Dilemma are played repeatedly by the same players. The reiterated Prisoner's Dilemma thus opens up a whole set of strategic opportunities, because the players can choose their actions with regard to what the other players did in the previous rounds. A player could for example choose to cooperate when the other player has cooperated in the previous round and not to cooperate otherwise. This strategy will in the following be called *Tit for Tat*. It is now easy to see that in the reiterated Prisoner's Dilemma playing uncooperatively is not always the best choice. A notoriously uncooperative player (whose strategy will be named *Hawk* in the following) that meets *Tit for Tat* will receive a payoff of T (or 5 points in our example) in the first round and a payoff of P (or 1 point) in all subsequent rounds. If the Prisoner's Dilemma is repeated often enough, the average payoff of the uncooperative player will be close to P (1 point). The player would have fared much better by playing cooperatively, in which case the average payoff would have been R (3 points), which by the definition of the Prisoner's Dilemma is higher than P.[3] Thus, unlike

---

[2] The "one shot Prisoner's Dilemma" is called thus to emphasize that it is not repeated.

[3] It should be kept in mind that the goal of the players is to receive as high a payoff as possible and

the one shot Prisoner's Dilemma, unconditional non-cooperation is not always the best strategy in the repeated Prisoner's Dilemma. This said, the question naturally arises what is the best strategy in the repeated Prisoner's Dilemma. The answer is that there is no single best strategy in the repeated Prisoner's Dilemma. The reason for this is simple: Assume a strategy named *Grim* that cooperates as long as the other player cooperates but ceases to cooperate for the rest of the game if the other player fails to reciprocate cooperation even in one single instance. Obviously, against *Grim* it is (except for the very last round of the game) best to cooperate. More specifically, against *Grim* it would be a very bad idea to fail to cooperate in the first round. Now, assume a strategy that is a best reply[4] to *Grim*. This strategy cooperates in the first round. But if this strategy is run against *Hawk*, it is obviously not a best reply, because any best reply against *Hawk* should never cooperate, not even in the first round. Thus, any strategy that is a best reply to *Grim* is not a best reply to *Hawk*. Therefore, in the reiterated Prisoner's Dilemma, there exists no strategy that is a best reply to all other possible strategies, which means that in the reiterated Prisoner's Dilemma there is no best strategy.

How then should a rational player act to maximize the payoff in the repeated Prisoner's Dilemma? There is a certain argument, the importance of which is sometimes overrated, to the effect that also in the repeated Prisoner's Dilemma rational players will never cooperate. This is the argument from backwards induction. It runs as follows: Whatever strategy a player chooses in the repeated Prisoner's Dilemma if the player cooperates in the last round the strategy can still be ameliorated by defecting in the last round. (The last round is a single one-shot Prisoner's Dilemma where non-cooperation is always the best strategy.) The same line of reasoning applies to the opponent so that both players, if they are rational, will defect in the last round. But if both players defect in the last round anyway then neither player has an incentive to cooperate in the last but one round. The same logic then applies to the round before the last but one round and so on, until the first round is reached. In the end both players play *Hawk* all the time. There is nothing to be said against the logic of this argument, only that it rests on a very strong assumption that can hardly be called realistic. The assumption is that both players behave strictly rational and also know

---

not primarily to win the match, i.e. to receive a higher payoff than the opponent. If it was only about winning the match then *Hawk* would be the best strategy, because *Hawk* either wins or the game ends in a tie.

[4]A "best reply" is a strategy that gets as much payoff in a game against some given strategy as is possible.

that they both do. If there is only a slight chance that the strategy of one of the players deviates but a little bit from strict rationality, it might not pay for the other any more to play *Hawk*. Moreover computer simulations show that in an evolutionary scenario it takes millions and millions of generations, until a population of *Tit for Tat* players is finally replaced by *Hawk* through a process of gradual degeneration in the manner of a backward inductive process (see Appendix 8.6, where this is spelled out). Finally, the argument of backward induction fails if the number of rounds in the reiterated Prisoner's Dilemma is unknown. Therefore, if the number of rounds is unknown or if there is any reason to assume that players are not always strictly rational, it remains impossible to single out one strategy as the best or the only reasonable strategy in the reiterated Prisoner's Dilemma.

In the repeated Prisoner's Dilemma, there is therefore room for cooperation. But how much room is there for cooperation? Is it better to be hesitant when cooperating with other players, or should one be generous and cooperate even if the other player does not always reciprocate? Mathematical game theory does not have much to say about these sorts of questions, except that – according to the folk theorem – there exist innumerous equilibria. Any combination of payoffs of a repeated game in the cooperative payoff region that assigns each player at least the player's minimax value is arbitrarily close to the outcome of some Nash equilibrium (Binmore, 1998, p. 293). Without entering into the mathematical details of the folk theorem, its validity in the case of the repeated two person Prisoner's Dilemma can easily be demonstrated by a few simple considerations: Assume a sequence of moves of the two players that generates a payoff of at least P for each player and that is repeated throughout the game. For example, we may assume that player one plays a sequence of three cooperative moves and one defection in the fourth move while player two plays a sequence of four cooperative moves without defecting. If we stick to the payoff values from figure 4.1 above, player one gets an average payoff of 3.5, while player two gets 2.25. Now let us further assume that any deviation from this repeated sequence of moves by one of the players is punished by the other player by switching to *Grim* instantly, that is, by playing non cooperatively for the rest of the game. In the long run the other player would then only get a payoff close to P. This will keep the player from deviating from the equilibrium path. And this is the case, even if the equilibrium path leads to an inefficient or unjust outcome as in our example. Although player two gets much less than player one, player two would even be worse off if he (or she) was trying to change the situation by deviating from the equilibrium path.

There could be an objection that if one player chooses to deviate from the equilibrium path, the other player does not have an incentive any more to enforce the equilibrium by punishing the deviating player. (In the technical language of game theory one would say that the equilibrium is not "subgame perfect".) If, in the above example, player two chooses not to accept the defection of player one every fourth round, but to counter by playing *Tit for Tat*, player two does not really have an incentive to punish player one, because by doing so player two would earn a much lower payoff (close to 1) than by cooperating (close to 3). However, this argument is only compelling if we think of two players playing the repeated Prisoner's Dilemma. In an evolutionary scenario the two players of the example represent strategy types rather than individual players. Each of the strategy types is chosen by a large share of a population. If a few individual players single-handedly deviate from the equilibrium path this does not have any noticeable impact on the equilibrium. Therefore, the conclusion remains valid that the folk theorem leaves us with a large number of equilibria and no hint which strategy is generally to be considered a good strategy and which is not.

If there is no single best strategy in the reiterated Prisoner's Dilemma and if there exist many equilibria, how are we to find out what kind of strategy will be evolutionarily successful? The approach pioneered by Axelrod (Axelrod, 1984) was to simulate the games in the computer and then just see which strategies are successful and which strategies aren't. In the most simple case one picks a number of arbitrarily chosen strategies and lets each strategy play a match against each other strategy. A match is a repeated Prisoner's Dilemma of a fixed number of rounds. How many is unknown to the players so that any end game effect can be avoided. (Alternatively, one could also let the match stop with a certain probability after each round.) When the match is finished the average score each player has earned in a single round is calculated. After every player (or strategy, respectively) has played a match against every other player, the overall average score of each strategy is determined and the different strategies are ranked according to their score. The whole procedure somewhat resembles a tournament in sports, with the important difference that it is the average score that matters and not how many other players a player beats in the matches. (If it were the object to beat as many opponents as possible then the strategy *Hawk* would always be a sure bet, because *Hawk* cannot be beaten by any other strategy.) The result of such a tournament is depicted in figure 4.2. For the tournament a reiterated Prisoner's Dilemma of 200 rounds

Ranking	Strategy	Score
1.	Tester	2.2524
2.	TitForTat	2.2067
3.	Pavlov	2.1544
4.	Grim	2.1377
5.	Random	2.0137
6.	Hawk	1.9024
7.	Tranquilizer	1.8625
8.	Dove	1.8288
9.	Joss	1.6319

Figure 4.2: A tournament of the reiterated Prisoner's Dilemma

with the parameters $T = 5, P = 3, R = 1, S = 0$ was carried through.[5] Except that a much smaller number of strategies was used for the purpose of illustration the tournament resembles exactly the one described by Axelrod (Axelrod, 1984).

The winner of the tournament (figure 4.2) is a strategy called *Tester*.[6] The strategy *Tester* starts off with two defections. If the opponent does not answer these defections by defecting, *Tester* classifies the opponent as an exploitable strategy and defects every second round during the remainder of the match. Otherwise *Tester* switches to the fairly reliable strategy *Tit for Tat* after two rounds of unconditional cooperation in order to appease the opponent. The strategic advantages *Tester* gains over *Tit for Tat* can easily be traced in the match logs. If *Tester* meets an exploitable strategy like *Dove* the beginning of the match log looks like this:

```
Dove : Tester                1.485 : 4.010

1 0   1 0   1 0   1 1   1 0   1 1   1 0   1 1   1 0   1 1
. . .
```

The log is to be read as follows: The top line tells which strategies have played the match and what their respective average score was for

---

[5]The strategies that take part in this tournament are described in detail in Appendix 8.1.1. The simulation software for this and the following simulations can be downloaded from www.eckhartarnold.de/apppages/coopsim.html. The version of the software on this website is most probably different from the version used for the simulations in this book. Readers who want to take a closer look on the software version that was used for this book may want to write to eckhart_arnold@hotmail.com. I promise to send you a DVD that contains the complete browsable simulation results as well as the software used to produce these results. See Appendix 8.7 for a brief description of the contents of the DVD.

[6]This strategy was designed by David Gladstein for Axelrod's computer tournament (Axelrod, 1984, p. 39).

this match. In the line below, each pair of numbers resembles the moves of both strategies in one round of the reiterated Prisoner's Dilemma. "1" means that the player has cooperated, "0" means that the player has defected. The first of the two numbers in the pair tells the move of the strategy that appears first in the top line (in this case *Dove*), the second number stands for the move of the other strategy (here it is *Tester*). As can be seen, *Dove* cooperates indefatigably, while *Tester*– after having noticed the exploitability of *Dove* after the second round – rips off a benefit of 5 points every second round by defecting. (*Tester* could do even better against *Dove* by betraying every single round instead of every second round, but it must be remembered that all strategies must try to be as universal as possible, and while *Tester* would indeed be better off betraying every round against *Dove* the damage might also be the greater in cases where the strategy of betrayal employed by *Tester* fails.) In comparison the match log of the match *Dove* against *Tit for Tat* looks as follows:

```
Dove : TitForTat          3.000 : 3.000

1 1   1 1   1 1   1 1   1 1   1 1   1 1   1 1   1 1   1 1
...
```

Both strategies cooperate throughout the game. The score *Tit for Tat* gains is reasonably good (compared to an average score of the winner of the tournament of only 2.2617), but it is certainly lower than the 4.1 points, *Tester* was able to achieve. For a final comparison, let us look at the log of the match *Tester* vs. *Tit for Tat*:

```
Tester : TitForTat          2.985 : 2.985

0 1   0 0   1 0   1 1   1 1   1 1   1 1   1 1   1 1   1 1
...
```

Tester starts with two defections again, but because *Tit for Tat* reciprocates these defections, it decides for the better and plays cooperatively for the rest of the game, thereby still achieving almost the maximum possible score against *Tit for Tat*. Thus, *Tester* is smart enough not to mess with revengeful strategies, but flexible enough to exploit weaknesses. It is only against absolutely unforgiving strategies such as *Grim* that *Tester* does not do so well. The success of *Tester* can to some degree be understood by looking at the tournament chart and by interpreting the match logs. It must, however, be admitted that there is a great deal of contingency involved in the success of *Tester*. For, *Tester's* success crucially depends on the set of strategies that take part in the tournament, on the choice of payoff parameters and on the absence of disturbing factors such as noise etc. How to deal with these contingencies will be discussed shortly. Before that there is yet another step to take in order to find out something about the possible *evolutionary* success of a strategy like *Tester*.

To determine the evolutionary success of a strategy like *Tester* the simulation can be extended in such a way that a sequence of tournaments is played. The average payoff every strategy receives in a tournament is interpreted as a fitness value which serves as input for the next tournament in the sequence. In contrast to the original tournament it is not silently assumed any more that there is exactly one player for each strategy, but that there exists a very large population of players which is divided among the strategies. Successful strategies receive a larger share of the player population in the next round than less successful strategies. (We could imagine that if a strategy proves to be very successful in the tournament a certain percentage of the players that have previously played less succesful strategies will adopt the more sucessful strategy in the next round. For a biological setting the interpretation would even be easier as the average payoff could be interpreted as a fitness value that directly transforms into the relative reproduction rate.) The partitioning of the player population does have an impact on the outcome of the tournament, because the outcome of a match between strategies with large population shares does have a greater weight on the the average payoff of the respective strategies than when the population shares are small. For example, assume that both the strategies *Dove* and *Hawk* are present in the tournament, and assume further that the population share of *Dove* is extremely small (because *Dove* is typically a low performer, especially when exploitative strategies like *Hawk* are present), then even though *Hawk* performs extremely well against Dove (5 points average) this will hardly affect the overall performance of *Hawk*. This has just been a rough and sketchy description of the population dynamical process that is assumed in the evolutionary extension of the simulation. For the mathematical details and technical realization of the population dynamical process in the simulation see Appendix 8.2.

The results of the population dynamics of the repeated Prisoner's Dilemma with the parameters and strategy set above are shown in figure 4.3. While the original tournament was clearly won by *Tester*, the population dynamic leads to quite a different result after only 50 generations. As can be seen on the table below, this time *Tit for Tat* clearly leads the way. Also, between the other strategies the ranking has shifted

82

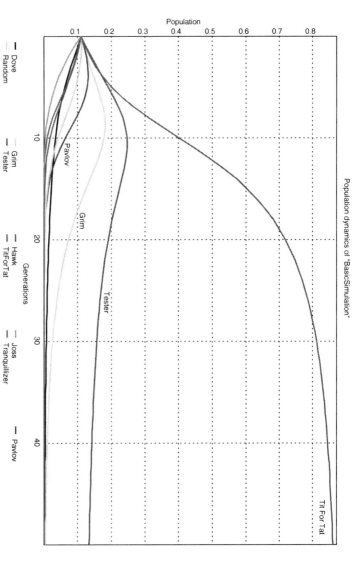

Figure 4.3: An evolutionary simulation of the reiterated Prisoner's Dilemma.

Ranking	Strategy	Population share
1.	TitForTat	0.8606
2.	Tester	0.1342
3.	Grim	0.0037
4.	Dove	0.0015
5.	Random	0.0000
6.	Pavlov	0.0000
7.	Tranquilizer	0.0000
8.	Joss	0.0000
9.	Hawk	0.0000

Figure 4.4: Ranking in an evolutionary simulation of the reiterated Prisoner's Dilemma after 50 generations

significantly. (Note that in this table the population share is rounded after 4 digits, so that what appears as zero can still be a small population share greater than zero.) The phenomenon is easily explained: *Tester's* success in the tournament depends largely on the presence of exploitable strategies like *Dove*. As the population share of *Dove* is reduced over time, so is the success of *Tester*. Interestingly, the strategy that fares worst is that of unanimous non-cooperation (*Hawk*). Another interesting phenomenon is that *Dove* catches up over time and ends up on place 4 (of 9) after 50 generations.

4.1.2 Discussion of the simulation

What conclusions can be drawn from the simulation? The model certainly demonstrates that a strategy that relies on (reciprocal) altruism (as *Tit for Tat* does) can be very successful in situations such as the repeated Prisoner's Dilemma. This, however, is hardly more than a trivial consequence of the folk theorem mentioned earlier: *Tit for Tat* is just one of the many equilibria in the repeated Prisoner's dilemma and obviously the dynamical system of the simulation was located somewhere in the basin of attraction of *Tit for Tat*. But the simulation also exposes other phenomena that the mathematical description of the dynamical system would hardly have drawn our attention to. The poor performance of *Hawk* and the comparative success of *Dove* after just a couple of generations suggest the conclusions that on the one hand, even in face of the danger of being exploited, strict egoism[7] is not at all a safe

---

[7]By *strict egoism* I mean the attitude of not bestowing any benefit unto another unless at least an equal return is guaranteed. Other than rational egoism, which is supposed to be free from envy and simply aims at the maximization of profit no matter how good or bad the others fare, strict egoism is not compatible with altruism as defined in chapter 2.2

84

strategy to play and that on the other hand in a millieu of reciprocal altruists (e.g. *Tit for Tat*) even genuine altruism (e.g. *Dove*) can strive. It would be tempting to continue in this fashion by drawing further generalizing conclusions from the simulation, and in fact this has historically been the naive approach to the employment of computer simulations in the social sciences as well as biology.[8] But this modus operandi is liable to serious objections. First of all, any general conclusion that is drawn from the simulation has been demonstrated only under the very special conditions of the simulation. There is no guarantee that, if we change the values of the parameters or the setup of the simulation but a little bit, any of the conclusions will still be valid. Secondly, we cannot know whether the results that are obtained under the highly artificial conditions of a computer simulation have any empirical impact. Even if the simulation resembles more or less certain empirical situations – as does the repeated Prisoner's Dilemma that can be taken to resemble repeated interactions of trade partners or political actors – it is by no means assured that any results of the simulation can be transferred to the empirical situation in question. The weak relation of more or less resemblance may not preserve the results of our simulation study, so to speak. Addressing the former of these problems may lessen the latter problem, because an increase in generality is also likely to increase the scope of possible empirical applications, although it certainly cannot solve it alone. The crucial question of empirical applicability will be discussed in chapter 6 in greater detail. It is a question to which so far no fully satisfactory answer has been given. Still, even computer simulations as simple as this one can have some (if only slight) scientific value. They can help to demonstrate or to create an awareness of interesting and unexpected phenomena (such as the possible evolutionary success of reciprocal altruists among a mixed population of altruists and egoists). And even with extremely simple computer simulations *theoretical possibilities* can be proven (Schüßler, 1990, p. 91). This is very helpful to find out whether a certain concept or a set of hypotheses is sound or suffers from internal contradictions. If it is possible to design a computer simulation in which a certain phenomenon occurs, this suffices to prove that the occurrence of the phenomenon is *theoretically possible*.[9]

But before we can even dare to draw any further conclusions from our computer simulation regarding the nature of reciprocal altruism as an empirical phenomenon, we do at least need to take care that the results

---

[8]This is mostly true for Axelrod (1984), but some scientists still proceed in this fashion today like Skyrms (1996, 2004), which is of course legitimate for purely illustrative purposes, but insufficient if explanations for empirical phenomena are being sought.

[9]See also chapter 6.1.1 where different possible purposes of computer simulations are discussed.

of the computer simulation are not merely a contingent artifact of the choice of certain parameter values. For this purpose a more refined computer simulation that addresses the problem of generalizability will be introduced shortly hereafter (see chapter 4.1.4). Before, it will briefly be considered how the concept of reciprocal altruism can possibly be applied to cultural evolution.

4.1.3 Reciprocal altruism in cultural evolution

The concept of reciprocal altruism originally stems from biology. Cast into a game theoretical simulation model it mixes concepts that were originally developed in a social science, namely economics (game theory), and in biology (replicator dynamics). When arguing that an abstract theoretical model is transferable to a certain scientific subject area, one has to indicate what the empirical correspondents to the modeled processes and parameters could possibly be. In this case the involved parameters and processes are primarily the payoff parameters of the Prisoner's Dilemma game and the replicator dynamical process. If applied to a biological setting the replicator dynamics do not pose a problem as it resembles just the simplemost form of modeling genetic replication. The payoff parameters need a little more consideration. What is important with regard to the payoff parameters is that because the input of the replicator dynamics is derived from the payoff parameters they must resemble the *fitness-relevant payoff* that results from a certain kind of behavior. If we take grooming as one of the popular standard examples of reciprocal altruism in the animal kingdom then the payoff we assign to grooming or being groomed must in some way resemble the increase (when being groomed) or decrease (when grooming) of fitness, i.e. the average number of offspring, that an animal derives from grooming. As we shall see later (chapter 5.1, page 152) this poses no small challenge for the respective empirical research in biology.

When trying to transfer the insights such models provide to the social sciences, a reasonable interpretation must be given to the payoff parameters and the replication process. The game theoretical payoff parameters are usually understood in terms of some sort of utility that individuals derive from the interaction in the game. Regarding utility, economists distinguish between different utility concepts. The two basic types are ordinal utility and cardinal utility. Ordinal utility means that the utility values (i.e. payoff values) are understood as representing only the order of preference between different alternatives and that the numeral utility values have no further empirical meaning beyond indicating that order. Therefore, if the payoff parameters are understood as expressing merely an ordinal utility the Prisoner's Dilemma with the payoff parameters $T = 5, R = 3, P = 1, S = 0$ represents exactly the same game as the Prisoner's Dilemma with the payoff parameters $T = 10, R = 9, P = 2, S = 1$. This is different when cardinal utility is assumed. Here the concrete numerical values matter. In the most literal interpretation of "cardinal utility", the utility values express just that: A numeric value for the utility an alternative has for an individual.[10] The concept of cardinal utility is much harder to justify than the concept of ordinal utility. When one wants to rely merely on ordinal utility one has to be careful to use only models which are not sensitive to a change of the numerical payoff values as long as the order of the values is the same. Vice versa, if models are used that react sensitively to a change of the numerical values of the payoff parameters then these models rest on an implicit commitment to the concept of cardinal utility. The simulation model of reciprocal altruism presented above does indeed react sensitively to a change in payoff parameters (within the bounds of the repeated Prisoner's Dilemma),[11] which means that the model implies cardinal utility. Or, to put it in another way: Conclusions from the model can only be drawn in contexts where the concept of cardinal utility is justifiable.

How can the replicator dynamics the model uses be understood when the model is meant to describe a process in cultural evolution? As has been hinted at earlier (page 44) there exist many diverse replication and selection processes in cultural evolution. One of the most simple assumptions that can be made in this context is that norms (represented by strategies in the reiterated Prisoner's Dilemma) are replicated and selected, because people tend to imitate the behavior of successful people. If it is assumed that this is a stochastic process where the fraction of people that change from a bad strategy to a good strategy depends on the differential success of these strategies then we come very close to the replicator dynamics used in the model. Thus, it is in principle possible to offer an interpretation of the population dynamical process that seems plausible in a social science context. However, just as in the case of the payoff values, there is a silent commitment that goes along

---

[10]More common, however, are somewhat lesser conceptions of cardinal utility like the Neumann-Morgenstern utility function (which is commonly used when it becomes necessary to include some kind of probability or risk assessment into the utility valuation). According to this concept of cardinal utility, two utility functions are not only equivalent when they assign exactly the same numerical values to the same alternatives, but already when the functions can be transformed into each other by some positive affine transformation. Still, cardinal utility if understood in this way rests on much stronger assumptions about the empirical content of the assignment of utility values than the concept of ordinal utility.

[11]To verify this, it suffices to run the evolutionary simulation with the strategies *Dove, Grim, Hawk, Joss, Random, Tat for Tit, Tit for Tat, Tranquilizer* and then change the payoff parameter R from 3 to 3.5 . In the first case (R=3) *Tit for Tat* wins, in the latter case *Dove* plays best.

with the assumption that norms (or types of behavior) "reproduce" in proportion to the success of their adherents. For, this furthermore requires that people can compare their success among each other. It is thus silently assumed that intersubjective cardinal utility comparisons can be made. This may not be so problematic in empirical situations where the payoff is a monetary payoff. But outside strictly economic contexts the assumption of intersubjective cardinal utility can become hard to justify.

Summing it up, it is in principle possible to give the parameters and processes of population dynamical simulation models of the repeated Prisoner's Dilemma an interpretation that gives some credence to the attempt to transfer theoretical insights from the model to empirical phenomena that are studied in the social sciences. However, this attempt implies certain strong theoretical commitments which, if taken seriously, limit the probative force of conclusions drawn from the model. On the other hand, one might reason that the strong assumption of intersubjective cardinal utility may be acceptable if we confine ourselves to drawing conclusions that remain valid over a wide range of different parameter settings. Such an attempt will be made with the following extension of the simulation model to a series of simulations.

4.1.4 A more refined model of reciprocal altruism

A Simulation series instead of single simulations

There are two different kinds of conditions that limit the generalizability of the results of computer simulations such as the one presented before: 1) conditions that define the simulation setup and 2) the values of the parameters used. In our simulation the values of the parameters are the payoff parameters of the Prisoner's Dilemma ($T = 5, R = 3, P = 1, S = 0$) and the number of repetitions of the Prisoner's Dilemma (which is 200). The presuppositions that enter into the simulation setup include that the basic game is a two person Prisoner's Dilemma, that the payoff parameters are symmetric and remain the same in every round, that all strategies start with the same population share in the evolutionary simulation, that the average payoff in the tournament and not the number of won matches is taken to determine a strategy's fitness. One of the most important prerequisites that enter into the simulation setup is the set of strategies that play the tournament. The set of strategies strongly influences the outcome of the simulation, because whatever strategy is winning the tournament, it can only be one of the strategies from the set of strategies that takes part in the tournament. And it is well possible that the potentially most successful strategies will never be found out, because they were not among the player's strategies in the first place. Also, the success of a strategy depends highly on the other strategies that are present: A strategy that is very successful among one set of opponent strategies may not fare so well if it has to deal with other opponents. And there are many more, mostly silent assumptions that enter into the simulation setup. It is in fact impossible to enumerate all these assumptions, because they also include negative assumptions like the fact that noise or distortions are absent in the simulation or that no new strategies ever enter the evolutionary process and so on. One can easily think of further silent assumptions that underlie the simulation setup.

How then, are we to deal with these contingencies? To reduce the contingencies introduced by the arbitrary choice of parameter values, the obvious solution would be to let the simulation run several times, changing the values of the parameters in a controlled way with every run. But it soon becomes apparent that there are limits to this approach. If, for example, we were to choose three different values for the above mentioned five parameters then already 243 ($= 3^5$) simulation runs would be needed. This can still be handled, but with more different parameter values to test and with every new parameter that is introduced to increase the generalizability of the simulation, this figure increases very rapidly and the simulation soon becomes unmanageable. A remedy is to pick only the extreme values from the parameter ranges and apart from that to pick random parameter values for a fixed number of simulation runs ("*Monte Carlo simulation*"). This allows to keep the number of necessary simulation runs manageable, while at the same time catching possible exceptional cases which are primarily to be expected for extreme parameter values.

It is a more difficult matter to reduce the contingencies that concern the simulation setup. Of course it is impossible to eliminate all such contingencies. As the simulation is to simulate something, the setup must necessarily be to some degree contingent. When applying simulations empirically the setup could be chosen to closely model the empirical situation (which still leaves the problem of which idealizations and abstractions from the situation are to be considered acceptable). But as this simulation is not designed with any *particular* empirical situation in mind, the choice of the basic simulation setup is solely a matter of convenience and plausibility, which unavoidably entails a certain degree of arbitrariness. As has been hinted at earlier, it is just a matter of imagination to find further conditions that define the simulation setup and which could – with plausible reasons – be changed to produce another simulation. Just as in the case of the choice of parameter values it is necessary for pragmatic reasons to limit the variability of the simulation setup.

The setup of the simulation series

But how can a variable setup be integrated into the simulation, anyway? It would be quite laborious to write a separate program for every new simulation setup. A much easier way is to parametrize the conditions of the simulation setup. The setup of the simulation series described in the following is defined by six parameters, each of which can take one from two up to four different values. These parameters describe (1) the *strategy set*, (2) the *correlation* between players with the same strategy, (3) the *in game noise* which switches an intended move of a player into its opposite with a certain probability, (4) the *evolutionary background noise* that is modeled as a random distortion on the fitness values, (5) the *set of payoff parameters* of the Prisoner's Dilemma and (6) a *mutation rate* by which a certain percentage of strategies degenerates into one of several simpler types. In detail these parameters work in the following way:

1. *Strategy Set* (varied in the simulation series between either "Automata" or "TFTs") : There are two strategy sets in the race, the set of all *Two State Automata* (i.e. a strategy representation by deterministic automata that can remember exactly one move) and a set of variants of *Tit for Tat*, which are called *Parametrized Tit for Tats*.

   The set of strategies that can be represented by Two State Automata is described in detail in Appendix 8.1.3. The motivation behind using the set of Two State Automata as one of the base sets of the simulation series is that this strategy set does – in a sense – represent all strategies of a certain complexity.[12] It contains all deterministic strategies that can remember exactly one move. Of course there is still some arbitrariness involved, because there is no reason why one should choose memory constraints as criterion for complexity limits instead of, say, calculation time. Also, it should be noted that the set of all Two State Automata contains some rather "unrealistic" strategies, like for example the strategy "DHDHD" (see Appendix 8.1.3 for an explanation of the string encoding of the automata strategies) that punishes cooperation and

---

[12]The idea of using the set of Two State Automata as the base set in the reiterated Prisoner's Dilemma goes back to Linster (Binmore, 1998, p. 315).

rewards defection. In the evolutionary race one would expect such strategies to die out quickly, but even then they can give other strategies that exploit such characteristics a head start which under "normal" circumstances would seem "unrealistic".[13]

The second strategy set is gained by adding the two parameters *good rate* and *evil rate* to modify the behavior of *Tit for Tat*. The *good rate* is a probability with which the *Parametrized Tit for Tat* makes a cooperative move when the ordinary *Tit for Tat* would not. And, conversely, the *evil rate* defines a probability with which the parametrized strategy defects when normally *Tit for Tat* would cooperate. If both the *good rate* and the *evil rate* are zero then the parametrized strategy is the same as the ordinary *Tit for Tat*. For this simulation series, strategies with all combinations of good and evil rates from 0% to 100% in steps of 20% are included in the base strategy set. This strategy set is highly symmetric and, differently from the case of the Two State Automata, there is a random element in most of these strategies.

2. *Correlation* (values selected from: 0%, 10% and 20%): The correlation factor describes the probability by which players are more likely to meet opponents with the same strategy than opponents with a different strategy. A correlation of 0% means that the players are randomly matched, while with a correlation of 100% players do exclusively play against players of the same strategy. Typically, cooperative strategies profit from correlation.[14]

3. *Game Noise* (values selected from: 0%, 5%, 10%): In order to model some such thing as possible misunderstandings between players, the intended move of a player is randomly turned into its opposite with the probability of the game noise parameter. If game noise is 5% then there is a five percent chance that a player who cooperates in one certain round will really defect in the same round instead. Typically, when game noise is present, strategies that have some kind of error detection mechanism (like, for example, *Generous Tit for Tat*) will do better than strategies that don't (like the ordinary *Tit for Tat*).

4. *Evolutionary Noise* (values selected from: 0%, 5%, 10%, 15%): A random distortion of the given percentage will decrease or increase

---

[13]Of course none of the simulations of this type is ever realistic. At best they rely on plausible assumptions. As will be argued in greater detail in chapter 6 this restriction imposes strong limitations on the potential scientific value of such simulations.

[14]This very simple way of modeling correlation is taken from Brian Skyrms (Skyrms, 1996).

the fitness value of each strategy in the population dynamics. It should be noted that the impact of the evolutionary background noise modeled in this way is relative to the population share of the strategies. A strategy that has almost died out can hardly get back on track just because of the random shocks caused by evolutionary background noise.

5. *Payoff Parameters* (values selected from the (T,R,P,S)-tuples: (5,3,1,0), (3.5,3,1,0), (5.5,3,1,0), (5,3,2,0)): The payoff parameters define the Prisoner's Dilemma. In the simulation series discussed below they are not selected individually, but as a tuple. All tuples fulfill the two conditions for the reiterated Prisoner's Dilemma: $T > R > P > S$ and $2R > T + S$.

6. *Mutation Rate* (values selected from: 0%, 1%, 5%): During each generation of the population dynamical process the given percentage of the population of each strategy mutates to a simpler strategy. In the case of the Two State Automata, an automaton mutates to *Dove* if its string representation contains the character "D" three or more times (that is if the strategy already has a tendency to be friendly). Otherwise, it degenerates to *Hawk*.

In the case of the *Parametrized Tit for Tat* strategies, degeneration is modeled by rounding the "good rate" (gr) and the "evil rate" (er) to 1 or 0. Consequently there are four different "degenerated" strategies: *Dove* (gr=1,er=0), *Hawk* (gr=0,er=1), *Tit for Tat* (gr=0,er=0), *Inverted* (gr=1,er=1), where *Inverted* is the "inversion" of *Tit for Tat* (it rewards defections and punishes cooperation).

The choice of the degenerated strategies is, of course, arbitrary. It is motivated merely by the assumption that degeneration should somehow result in a simplified version of the original strategy. One could certainly think of other degeneration schemes or introduce more varied and more complex types of mutation. The latter however would most certainly require the introduction of further parameters which in turn would drastically increase the number of possible parameter combinations for the simulation series.

Two simulation series (named "big simulation series" and "Monte Carlo series" respectively) have been run, the results of which will be discussed in detail in the following. In the "big simulation series" all of the above described parameters have been varied systematically. As there are 864 possible combinations of parameters, it contains 864 single simulations. In the "Monte Carlo series" the parameters are not varied systematically, but chosen randomly within the upper and lower bounds for simple scalar parameters (*correlation, evolutionary noise, game noise, mutation rate*) or randomly from the different values mentioned in the list above (*strategy set, payoff parameters*). The "Monte Carlo series" also contains 864 simulations, although in this case the number represents the arbitrary choice to let the "Monte Carlo series" be as big as the "big simulation series". Since the "Monte Carlo series" is not restricted to a given number of combinations it could of course also be made arbitrarily long. Comparing the results of the "big simulation series" with that of "Monte Carlo series" will help us to detect artifacts or contingencies which are due to the choice of the parameter values.

The variety of evolution - A quick look at some of the results of the simulations of reciprocal altruism

Before analyzing the results of the simulation series systematically, a quick look at some of the individual simulations of the series may help to give an impression of what to expect. What should not come as a surprise at all is that both the outcome of the evolutionary processes and the courses that the evolutionary processes take are highly diverse. A typical result is shown on figure 4.5 (simulation no. 580 of the "big series"), where the system converges after only about 50 generations to a stable mixed equilibrium with *Tit for Tat* as the winning strategy. In the "slip stream" of *Tit for Tat* several even more cooperative strategies (good rate > 0% and evil rate = 0%) survive, including even *Dove*, which still occupies a noticeable share of the population. In this case the parameters are very favorable to cooperation, the payoff for successful cheating $T = 3.5$ is only slightly higher than the reward for mutual cooperation $R = 3.0$. Furthermore a correlation of 10% encourages cooperation for this particular strategy set.[15]

That the success of cooperative strategies in repeated games is by no means a necessity, is demonstrated by the example in figure 4.6 (simulation no. 106 of the "big series"). Here, the completely non cooperative strategy *Hawk* finally dominates the whole population. In this case the payoff parameter P was set to 2 instead of 1 and there is a relatively high game noise of 10%. That *Hawk* turns out to be a pure equilibrium strategy is not just due to the fact that it is an evolutionary stable strategy (that is, a strategy that cannot be invaded by any mutant). For,

---

[15]That it is not generally true that correlation strengthens cooperation is demonstrated by the strategy *Signaling Cheater*, a strategy that plays a predefined sequence of cooperative and non-cooperative moves in the beginning as a signal and only cooperates in the following rounds if the opponent has played the same sequence of signaling moves. *Signaling Cheater*, although generally a non cooperative strategy, profits from correlation just like any cooperative strategy.

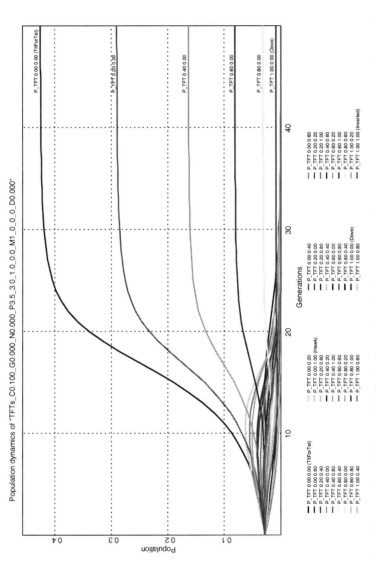

Figure 4.5: A stable mixed equilibrium with *Tit for Tat* as the winning strategy and even more cooperative strategies surviving in the "slip stream" of *Tit for Tat*. The simulation (no. 580 of the "big series") uses the payoff parameters T=3.5, R= 3, P=1 and S=0 and a correlation value of 10%.

Hawk sets out with the same small population share at the beginning as all the other strategies. *Hawk* wins simply because it is strong under the given conditions.

Both examples show what happens when the system converges, either to a mixed equilibrium (figure 4.5) or to a pure strategy equilibrium (figure 4.6). But the simulations of the series do not only differ with respect to their possible results. Also, the evolutionary process itself can differ in various respects. It is not a necessity that the evolutionary system converges at all. Figure 4.7 (simulation no. 55 of the "big series") depicts a situation where the evolutionary system evolves through expanding cycles. Eventually, it may arrive at a point where one of the cycling strategies drops out and cannot recover any more.[16] As can be seen, the pattern of these cycles can become quite complex. There are primarily six strategies involved in the cycles: The automata: DDHDD (*Tweedledee*), DDHDH (*Tit for Tat*), DHHDD, DHHHD, HHHDD, HHHHD. The parameters used were a payoff parameter T of 5.5 and an in game noise of 5%, all other parameters were left at the standard values. Since with a game noise unequal to zero there is a random element involved in the simulation, the same parameters may produce a different outcome if the simulation is run again. In this case several passes of the simulation show that diminishing cycles can occur as well, in which case the system finally converges on a mixed equilibrium. This in turn suggests that in the surrounding of these parameter values the simulation becomes unstable. (See chapter 6.1.2 for a discussion of the implications of limited model stability.)

The evolutionary process can develop even more intricate patterns. Figure 4.8 is taken from the "Monte Carlo series" (simulation no. 634). Here the game noise is 2.56%, there is a correlation of 7.93% and a steady flow of degenerating mutations in the above described manner of 1.19% and finally there is an evolutionary noise of 10%. As can be seen on the graph, the evolutionary process interchanges between four clearly marked phases of different and mostly cyclical processes. In *phase one* the strategies HHHHH (*Hawk*) (dark blue line), DDHDH (*Tit for Tat*) (medium blue line) and DDDDD (*Dove*) (pink line) follow each other in close cycles with an amplitude of roughly 0.6 (population share) and a length of roughly 30 generations. (This more detailed information can be read off the simulation log in addition to the graph.) Phase one is followed by *phase two*, during which the population is almost completely held by the five strategies DDHDH (*Tit for Tat*), DHHDH, HHHDH,

---

[16]As described in Appendix 8.2 the theoretical model underlying the simulation does not allow the extinction of a population. At worst a population becomes infinitely small. But in the computer simulation the population share of a strategy can still become zero due to the limits of arithmetic precision.

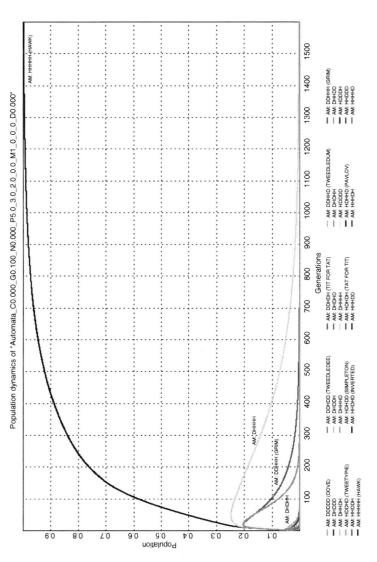

Figure 4.6: Example of a pure strategy equilibrium. In this case the non-cooperative strategy *Hawk* takes over the whole population. In the simulation (no. 106 of the "big series") a strong game noise of 10% was present. The payoff parameters were set to T=5, R=3, P=2, S=0.

96

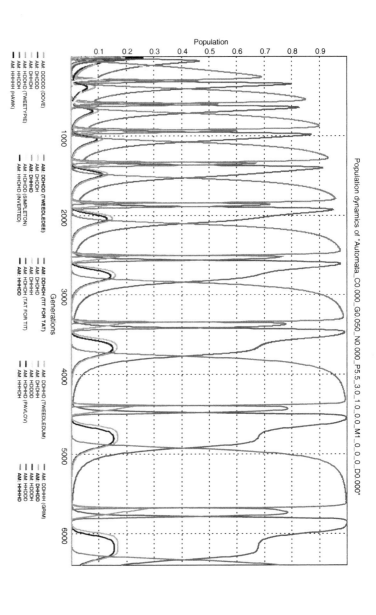

Figure 4.7: Example of strategies dominating the population in interchanging cycles. The result occured in simulation no. 55 of the "big series" under a game noise of 5% and the payoff parameters T=5.5, R=3, P=1, S=0.

DDDDD (*Dove*) and HHHHH (*Hawk*). Although it cannot clearly be discerned, the strategies do not seem to cycle in this phase. The relative changes in frequency are then mainly due to the 10% artificial evolutionary background noise in this simulation. Sometimes, though not always, phase two is followed by the somewhat irregular intermediate *phase three*, where HHHHH (*Hawk*) gets stronger, the amplitudes rise and strategy DDHDD (*Tweedledee*) comes into play. When phase three does not occur, phase two is followed immediately by *phase four*. Otherwise, phase three is followed by phase four, which consists of a short cycle where the population is dominated by the strategy DDHHD (*Tweedledum*) directly followed by a longer cycle of HHHHH (*Hawk*) with "maximum" amplitude. In contrast to the other phases which consist of an irregular number of cycles, phase four always consists of these two cycles of DDHHD (*Tweedledum*) and HHHHH (*Hawk*) after which it is "resolved" into phase one. This suggests the conclusion that the transition from phase four to phase one occurs inevitably while the other transitions are due to random shocks caused by the evolutionary background noise.

Altogether these examples give an idea of the great variety of evolutionary developments that are possible starting from the same setting within a not too wide range of initial conditions. This should be kept in mind when we now turn to the analysis of the systematic results. For, the systematic analysis described in the following paragraph relies heavily on aggregated data and is thus apt to level the qualitative differences between the evolutionary processes of the individual simulations.

A more systematic analysis of the simulation results

With a figure of 864 simulations in the "big series" it would be quite impractical to analyze each simulation individually. It is therefore unavoidable to analyze the simulation results in some automated way. For this purpose the simulation results are aggregated according to the following scheme: All results are recorded separately for both strategy sets (the set of *Two State Automata* and the set of *Parametrized TFTs*). Both the tournament results and the results of the evolutionary simulation of each strategy are recorded. From these a tournament ranking and an evolutionary ranking is computed for each strategy set. The *tournament ranking* is in lexical order, which means that if a certain strategy has won the tournament more often than some other strategy during the series then it gets a higher tournament ranking, no matter how often it gained a second place. The choice of the lexical ordering is arbitrary. Other ways of ordering the tournament results would also

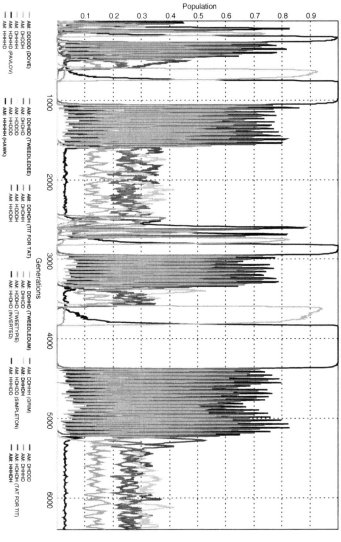

Figure 4.8: Example of strategies dominating the population in interchanging cycles. The simulation was taken from the "Monte Carlo series" (simulation Nr. 634). It uses the standard payoff parameters of T=5, R=3, P=1, S=0 with a correlation factor of 0.079301, a game noise of 0.025585, 0.09998, an evolutionary noise of 0.99980 and degenerative mutations that occur with a proability of 0.0191.

have been possible. To determine the *evolutionary ranking* of a strategy its average final population over the whole simulation series is used. In cases where the simulation does not reach an equilibrium state the simulation is stopped after 25,600 generations and the last population distribution in the 25,600th generation is taken as the final population. This procedure is somewhat arbitrary, especially in cases of a cyclical evolutionary processes, but detecting and treating these special cases separately would not have been feasible due to the complexity of the required algorithms and the additional computing time. Since breaking off the simulation after a certain generation and taking the population share of this generation as reference is like taking a random sample, the error incurred should diminish if a similar situation (i.e. the same strategies entering into a cyclical process) appears more often in the series. And if it does not, the error does affect the aggregated results only slightly.

Because the primary interest of making this simulation lies in the two questions 1) whether altruism is apt to evolve under the conditions of the simulation and 2) what kind of altruism (reciprocal altruism or genuine altruism) can evolve, the strategies are visualized in the graphical representation of the simulation results with different colors which indicate their "degree" of altruism. For the sake of simplicity only three different colors are used: Red, green and blue. The color red is used for non altruistic or exploitative strategies. Green is the color for altruists that are more than merely reciprocal altruists. And the color blue is used for all other strategies, reciprocal altruists as well as other strategies which cannot easily be classified.[17] In the case of the *Parametrized TFT* strategies, the green color (for genuine altruism) is assigned to all strategies for which the "good rate" exceeds the "evil rate" by at least 0.5, which means that the forgivingness of the strategy is 50% higher than its tendency to unnecessary defection. The color red is assigned to those strategies that have a "good rate" that is smaller than their "evil rate". The color blue is assigned to all remaining strategies.

In the case of the *Two State Automata* a strategy is considered genuinely altruistic and thus marked with the color green if the five character string encoding of the automaton (see appendix 8.1.3 for an explanation) contains at least four Ds (the character "D" (Dove) being the marker for cooperative moves). If the automaton contains one or zero Ds it always gets the color red. When there are three Ds in the

---

[17]Experimenting with different color schemes for visualization, I found this to be the most useful one. One could also mark the "absurd" strategies with a separate color in order to distinguish them from the reciprocal altruists, but this is not really necessary since these strategies do not play a dominant role anyway.

program string of the automaton, it is assigned the color blue if the second and the fourth character are Ds, which means that the strategy answers cooperation with cooperation. If this is not the case, three out of five Ds do not suffice to classify the strategy as "indifferent" and it therefore gets the color red for being non cooperative. If there are exactly two Ds in the program string then the strategy gets the color blue only if it is the strategy DDHHH (*Grim*) and red otherwise. The color scheme may appear unnecessarily complicated, but it roughly matches (my) intuition about which strategy can be considered (genuinely) altruistic and which cannot. At any rate the color scheme is only meant to simplify the reading of the charts. It helps immensely if the results of the different simulation series can be grasped at one glance, but no conclusions are based on the color of the charts alone.

The overall picture   Figure 4.9 shows a graphical representation of the aggregated results of the "big simulation series" for the set of *Parametrized TFTs*. The column on the left hand side shows the aggregated tournament rankings over the whole simulation series. The strategies appear very nicely ordered with the non cooperative strategies on top, *Hawk* being the most frequent winner. (As a look at the detailed charts 4.9 confirms *Hawk* has in fact won every tournament of the series!) This should not come as a surprise, because, as has been mentioned earlier, the strategy set of *Parametrized Tit for Tat* strategies is highly symmetric. The middle column shows the evolutionary ranking. The picture here is much more diversified with strategies of all three types spread over the whole ranking. Interestingly, even some genuinely altruistic strategies like *Dove* were able to gain a good ranking. The overall highest final population share was attained by *Tit for Tat*. Just how much of the average final population share *Tit for Tat* was able to gain can be seen on the third column, where the strategies are drawn in boxes of sizes proportional to their population share. Over the whole series *Tit for Tat* ended up with an average population share of 39%, followed by *Hawk* with 28%. The strategy *Dove* takes the fourth place with an average population share of 8%. This is a surprising result. In order to explain it we need to examine some of the individual simulations, which will be done later. But before, we will continue with the analysis of the aggregated results and cast a look at the results of the simulation series for the set of *Two State Automata*.

Since the set of *Two State Automata* is a strategy set with quite different characteristics from the set of *Parametrized TFTs* different results should be expected. And indeed the tournament ranking is not as neatly

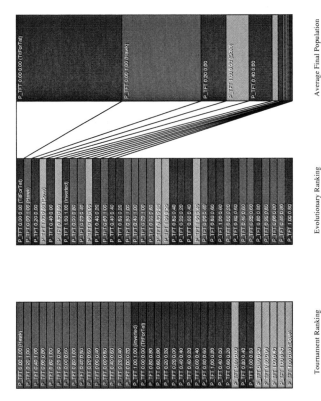

Results for strategy set: "TFTs"

Figure 4.9: The aggregated results of the 432 simulations from the "big simulation series" using the set of *Parametrized TFT* strategies.

ordered any more as is the tournament chart of the *Parametrized TFTs* (see figure 4.10). While the genuine altruists stay at the bottom just as well,[18] the reciprocal or indifferent strategies are spread out over the whole ranking. The evolutionary ranking shows a greater similarity to that of the *Parametrized TFTs*. Both the reciprocal and the the genuine altruists have moved up in the ranking as compared to the tournament results. As on the previous figure (figure 4.9), genuine altruists are still able to obtain a respectable average population share in the evolutionary simulations. The strongest of these is the strategy DDDDD (*Dove*) that placed 5th with an average population share of 9%. The winner of the evolutionary simulation is the strategy *Hawk* with an average population share of 35%. So, even in this very different milieu *Hawk* appears to be an extremely strong contender.

Having described the results of both strategy sets individually, what should concern us now is the features they have in common, because these are potentially features that can be generalized and at the same time it is these aspects that require explanation. The following characteristics are remarkable and raise specific questions about the nature of the evolution of altruism:

1. In both cases altruists gain from the evolutionary setting as compared to the tournament setting. Is this a general trend? How can it be explained?

2. Within both strategy sets the strategy *Hawk* is extraordinarily strong in the evolutionary simulation. Given the assumption that *Hawk* can fairly easily be invaded[19] by reciprocal strategies, what are the reasons for the success of Hawk?

3. The most surprising aspect is the considerable success of the strategy *Dove*. It is sometimes assumed that the only chance to account for "true" or "genuine" altruism in an evolutionary framework is by relying on group selection (see chapter 4.3). But group selectionist mechanisms were not present in this simulation. Some of the simulations of the series had mutations included, where *Dove* would be one of the targets of mutation. But the mutation rates were

---

[18]The strategy DDHDD (*Tweedledee*) is an exception here that cannot be given too much weight, because it is the least altruistic from the strategies classified as genuine altruists. It is best understood as a kind of *Lesser Tit for Tat* that never punishes two times in sequence.

[19]A small group of *Tit for Tat* players can easily invade a population of *Hawks*, because *Tit for Tat* plays much better against itself than *Hawk* and can at the same time not be exploited by *Hawk* (i.e. it plays almost as well against *Hawk* as *Hawk* plays against itself). On the other hand, because *Hawk* plays badly against itself, even a big group of *Hawks* will hardly be able to spread in a population of *Tit for Tat* players.

Results for strategy set: "Automata"

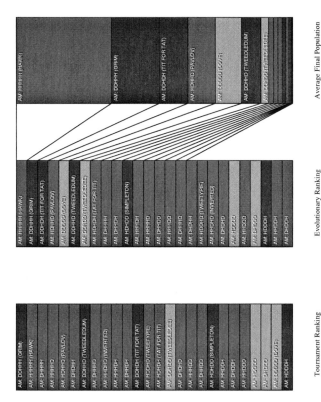

Figure 4.10: The aggregated results of the 432 simulations from the "big simulation series" using the set of *Two State Automata* (see appendix 8.1.3) strategies.

typically low (1% and 5%) and genuinely altruistic strategies still retained some measure of evolutionary success in those simulations of the series where no mutations occurred. If it was not for this reason, how could *Dove* then survive?

The first question is fairly easy to answer. Exploitive strategies require the presence of other strategies that can be exploited to be really successful. But then the exploited strategies quickly die out in the evolutionary process so that the exploiters are left without the comparative advantage they have over the reciprocal strategies in the tournament. (The question remains, however, how this explanation can be reconciled with the fact that the (exploitable) genuine altruists do not always die out as has been shown by the simulation charts in figure 4.9 and 4.10). To answer the latter two of these questions a more detailed analysis of the simulation results is required, which will be given in the following.

Reasons for the success of the strategy *Hawk* In order to explain the success of the strategy *Hawk* we first need to find out what are the determinants of this success. One method to find this out is to keep each parameter fixed at one of its possible values at a time and to vary only the other parameters. This yields the aggregated results for the subset of the simulation series corresponding to this particular parameter value. If the phenomenon in question (in this case: the success of *Hawk*) depends on a single parameter only then this should become apparent on the charts for the subseries of this parameter.[20] And indeed the charts testify that there exists a strong correlation between the existence of *game noise* and the success of strategy *Hawk*. Figures 4.11 and 4.12 depict the situation when the game noise parameter is set to 0%.

The enormous difference that the absence of game noise makes becomes immediately apparent from the colored charts. In the case of the *Two State Automata* it is the strategy DDHHH (*Grim*) that leads the race this time with 38% of the average final population. It is followed by the strategy DDDDD (*Dove*) which occupies 23%, a very much larger share than in the overall statistics. The third and fourth rank are taken by DDHDH (*Tit for Tat*) (16%) and HHHHH (*Hawk*). The latter still takes a considerable average final population share of 7.5%. The picture is even clearer for the strategy set of *parametrized TFTs*: Here *Tit for Tat* takes over almost the whole average final population (82%), leaving only little space for other strategies such as a slightly more friendly version of *Tit for Tat* ("good rate" = 20%) and *Dove*, both of which take an

---

[20]The comprehensive results for each single parameter are listed in appendix 8.3. Here only those results are picked out for discussion that help to answer the questions raised above (page 102).

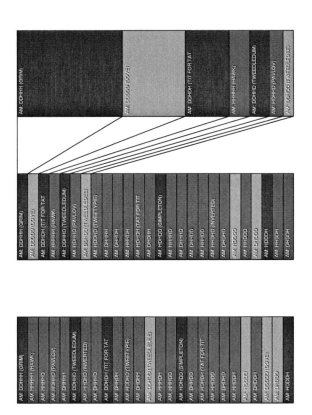

Results for strategy set: "Automata"

Figure 4.11: Absence of *game noise* strongly increases the success of reciprocal and altruistic strategies. (See figure 4.10 in comparison.)

average final population share of roughly 7%. The suspicion that it is the game noise parameter which is responsible for the success of *Hawk* in the overall picture, is strengthened even more when we look at the charts for the subseries with game noise = 5% and game noise = 10%.

Table 4.13 shows a comparison of the average final populations of the best strategies with and without game noise. With increasing game noise the success of the most uncooperative strategy *Hawk* increases sharply in both cases, from 7.4% (no game noise) over 36.4% (game noise = 0.05) up to 60% (game noise = 0.1) for the automata strategies and from 0% (no game noise) over 27.4% (game noise = 0.05) up to 58.1% (game noise = 0.1) in the case of the *Parameterized Tit for Tat* strategies. Conversely, the success of reciprocal strategies decreases with rising game noise. In the case of the two state automata the most dominant reciprocal strategy is *Grim*. *Grim's* average final population share amounts to 38.2% when game noise is absent, but is reduced from 10.4% to 3.2% as game noise rises from 5% to 10%. Within the strategy set of *Parameterized TFTs* the strategy *Tit for Tat* features as the most dominant of the reciprocal strategies. Its performance falls sharply from 82.4% to 19% when the game noise is set to 0.05 and again a little softer to 14.2% when the game noise is increased to 0.1. Interestingly the strategy PTFT 0.2, 0 (which is very close to *Tit for Tat* in so far as it usually plays Tit for Tat, but forgoes punishment with a probability of 20%) shows the opposite tendency as its average final population share slightly increases from 6.8% (no game noise) over 8.6% (game noise = 0.05) to 11.5% (game noise = 0.1).

It seems as if some of the population share that *Tit for Tat* occupies is shifted towards a somewhat lesser variant of itself as the game noise increases. This would not be suprising, because *Tit for Tat* is characterized by a specific weakness in face of game noise: When playing against itself and being disturbed by noise it may enter into cycles of interchanging cooperation-defection, defection-cooperation moves or – in rare cases, when two disturbances follow each other and do not cancel each other out – even into cycles of continued mutual defection. These cycles can only be broken if another disturbance happens that cancels the effect of the previous disturbance. An excerpt from the match log of a noisy *tit for tat* vs. *Tit for Tat* match demonstrates this phenomenon:

```
TitForTat : TitForTat   2.349 : 2.309

1 1   1 1   1 1   1 1   0 1   1 0   0 1   1 0   0 1   1 0
0 1   1 0   0 0   1 0   0 1   0 0   0 0   0 0   1 0   0 1
1 1   0 1   1 0   0 1   1 0   0 1   0 0   0 0   0 0   0 0
```

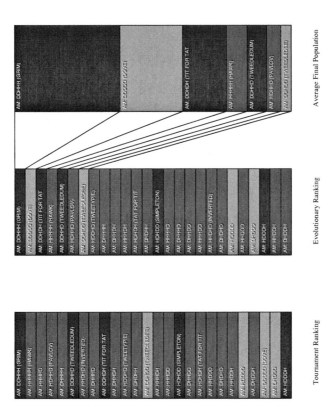

Results for strategy set: "Automata"

| Tournament Ranking | Evolutionary Ranking | Average Final Population |

Figure 4.12: The absence of *game noise* has the same positive effect on the evolution of cooperation for the strategy set consisting of the *parametrized TFT* strategies. (See figure 4.9 in comparison.)

108

Strategy	Average Final Population Share			
	overall	no game noise	5% noise	10% noise
Automata				
Hawk	34.6%	7.4%	36.4%	60.0%
Grim	17.3%	38.2%	10.4%	3.2%
TitForTat	10.2%	15.8%	7.8%	7.1%
Pavlov	10.0%	5.0%	16.5%	8.5%
Dove	9.3%	22.6%	3.7%	1.6%
...	...	...	...	...
Parametrized TitForTats				
TitForTat	38.5%	82.4%	19.0%	14.2%
PTFT 0.2,0	9.0%	6.8%	8.6%	11.5%
Dove	8.3%	6.5%	11.8%	6.6%
Hawk	28.5%	0.0%	27.4%	58.1%
...	...	...	...	...

Figure 4.13: The influence of game noise on selected altruistic and non altruistic strategies.

...

In the fifth round of the match a disturbance pushes the players into a cooperation-defection, defection-cooperation cycle. In the 13th round another disturbance pushes them into mutual defection but is luckily canceled by a new disturbance in the following round. The same happens again in the 16th round, only that this time mutual defections last for three rounds. The same pattern continues throughout the match with the players eventually being pushed back to cooperation from non cooperation or to non cooperation from cooperation. The overall result of 2.349 : 2.309 is far below the cooperative equilibrium (without noise) of 3:3. In contrast, a lesser variant of *Tit for Tat* that forgoes punishment once in a while can get the cooperative exchange back on track all on its own. For comparison: *Generous Tit for Tat* gained a score of 2.632 : 2.620 under the same conditions.

But even if we consider the combined performance of *Tit for Tat* and PTFT 0.2,0 the pattern that the reciprocal strategies decrease with increasing game noise remains the same. Given that non-altruistic strategies profit from game noise and that reciprocal strategies lose, one should expect that genuine altruists are on the losing side as well. This is true for the automata strategy set, where the average final population share of *Dove* falls from 22.6% if no game noise is present to 3.7% and finally 1.6%. Interestingly, the picture is not so clear cut for the set of *Parametrized TFTs*. Here *Dove* gains 6.5% when game noise is absent. Strangely, the share of *Dove* rises to 11.8% when game noise is 0.05 and it goes back to 6.6% for a game noise of 0.1. This phenomenon looks like an anomaly and it is not quite clear what the reason for it is.

Now that we have seen that the extraordinary success of *Hawk* is mostly due to the effect of game noise and that we have described in some detail just what this effect consists in, the question remains still open, why it is the strategy *Hawk* that profits from game noise and not *Dove* or some lesser *Tit for Tat* variant like PTFT 0.2,0 or DDHDD (*Tweedledee*)? A possible answer can be found by looking at how *Hawk* plays against the strategy *Random*. Most strategies have some trouble playing against *Random*, but *Hawk* does extremely well. On average it gains a score of $(T + P)/2$ (which is 3.0 for the standard parameters) against *Random*, because random cooperates roughly in 50% of all moves, which gives *Hawk* a payoff of T $(= 5.0)$, while for the other 50% of the moves it still receives the punishment P $(= 1.0)$. Compare this to the performance of *Tit for Tat* against *Random*: Since *Random* defects for an average 50% of all moves, half of *Tit for Tat's* moves are punishments (defections) and the other half are rewards (cooperative moves). Now, since *Random* neither cares what moves the other player makes nor what the semantics of the other player's moves are, it answers – on average or in the long run – half of the punishments by *Tit for Tat* with defection and half of them with cooperation. The same holds for the rewards of the *Tit for Tat* player. Consequently, *Tit for Tat* gets an average score of $(T + P + R + S)/4$ $(= 2.25$ for the standard payoff parameters), which is considerably less than what *Hawk* gains. That *Dove* fares even worse hardly needs to be explained. Taking the reasoning one step further it can even be shown that *Hawk* is in fact the single best reply to *Random*. For, since *Random* does not at all take into account the other player's moves and therefore *Random's* future moves cannot be influenced by them, the reiterated Prisoner's Dilemma dissolves into a number of one shot Prisoner's Dilemma's. But for the one shot Prisoner's Dilemma there exists a single best reply no matter what the other player does and that is non cooperation. Therefore, against *Random* it is best to play *Hawk* and the more randomness there is in the game, the more it pays to play *Hawk*. This is the likely explanation for the growing success of *Hawk* with the increase of game noise.

The evolution of genuine altruism in the slip stream of reciprocal altruism
The second question concerns the considerable success of genuinely altruistic strategies like *Dove*, DDHDD (*Tweedledee*) and PTFT 0.8,0 (which is 80% Dove and 20% Tit for Tat). The following table lists the average final population of these strategies over the whole simula-

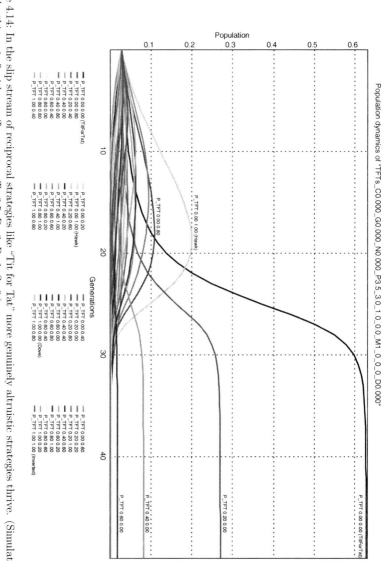

Figure 4.14: In the slip stream of reciprocal strategies like "Tit for Tat" more genuinely altruistic strategies thrive. (Simulation no. 436 from the "big series" with payoff paramters T=3.5, R=3, P=1, S=0.)

tion series and over the subseries without degenerative mutations (as described on page 91):

Strategy	whole series	no mutations
DDDDD (*Dove*)	9.3%	1.7%
DDHDD (*Tweedledee*)	2.9%	6.8%
PTFT 1,0 (*Dove*)	8.3%	1.5%
PTFT 0.8,0	2.2%	6.5%

Obviously, the success of *Dove* is to a high degree due to the mutations by which some of the strategies are continuously converted to *Dove*. But this factor does not suffice to account for the success of genuinely altruistic strategies. For, even without mutations *Dove* still ends up with a noticeable average final population share of 1.7% and 1.5% respectively. Also, *Dove* may be in a certain sense the most altruistic of all strategies but it is not the only genuinely altruistic strategy. For the sake of classification, all strategies that are considerably more friendly than *Tit for Tat* have been classified as genuinely altruistic. By this standard DDHDD (*Tweedledee*) and PTFT 0.8,0 are both genuinely altruistic strategies, because DDHDD (*Tweedledee*) punishes at most every second time and PTFT 0.8, 0 answers only 20% of the opponent's defections with punishment. Both these strategies, which are not generated by the sort of mutations that are included in some simulations of the series, obtain a non-marginal average final population share. How can the success of these strategies be explained?

One proximate explanation is that genuine altruism can develop in the "slip stream" of reciprocal altruism. The reciprocal strategies clear the way and when the exploiting strategies are practically extinct then genuine altruists thrive in the slip stream of the reciprocal altruists. This situation can well be observed in figure 4.14. In the beginning *Hawk* emerges as the dominant strategy followed by other only slightly more cooperative strategies like PTFT 0,0.8. It takes almost 30 generations until *Hawk* and its spouse are subdued by the reciprocal strategies. The equilibrium that emerges shows *Tit for Tat* at the top, followed by a sequence of continuously more altruistic strategies with PTFT 0.2,0 as the second, then PTFT 0.4,0, PTFT 0.6,0, PTFT 0.8, 0 and *Dove* on the 6th rank. The parameters of this simulation are admittedly quite favorable to cooperation with a "temptation" payoff T=3.5 (instead of T=5). Still, the tournament winner is *Hawk* while *Dove* takes the last place. It is only through the evolutionary process that reciprocal strategies win over the population and that genuine altruists survive in the slipstream of the reciprocal altruists.

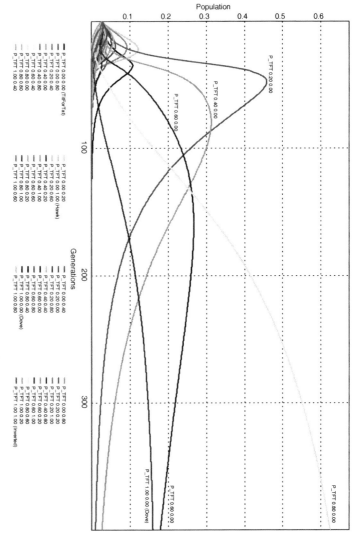

Figure 4.15: Another example of how genuine altruism may evolve in the "slip stream" of reciprocal altruism: After the reciprocal strategies have cleared the way the genuine altruists take over the population. (Simulation no. 628 from the "big series" with a correlation factor of 10%, a game noise of 5% and payoff parameters T=3.5, R=3, P=1, S=0.)

The metaphor of "slip stream altruism" seems even more appropriate to describe the results of the simulation depicted in figure 4.15. The simulation depicted in this figure deviates from the standard parameters by a correlation of 10%, a game noise of 5% and – like the simulation in figure 4.14 – a payoff for one sided defection of $T = 3.5$. Both the correlation and the relatively low reward for cheating, encourage cooperation, while a certain game noise may strengthen a generous type of reciprocity over strict reciprocity. The result is that the genuinely altruistic strategies become even more successful than the reciprocal strategies. After 400 generations, PTFT 0.8,0 leads the race with a population share of 62.5% while PTFT 0.6,0 and PTFT 1,0 (*Dove*) follow with 17.9% and 16% respectively. But they succeed only in the "slip stream" of the more reciprocal strategies PTFT 0.2,0 (dark green line) and PTFT 0.4,0 (orange line) that have cleared the field from initially successful exploitative strategies like PTFT 0,1 (*Hawk*) (pink line).

The latter result according to which genuinely altruistic strategies may – under favorable circumstances – even turn out to be more success-ful than reciprocating strategies in a dilemma setting that is designed to bring out reciprocal altruism seems so surprising that one might doubt whether the calculations are correct. In order to understand why this is indeed possible we can try to isolate the effect in a simpler simula-tion which is designed to produce only this effect. Figure 4.16 depicts a simulation that contains only the strategies *Dove*, *Hawk*, *Tit for Tat* and *Tat for Tit*. The parameter R (payoff for mutual cooperation) has been changed from 3 to 4 to demonstrate the effect. (Such parameter tweaking is admissible, because we only want to demonstrate the pos-sibility of a certain phenomenon with no claim to its being widespread or even typical.) Under these circumstances, *Dove* wins the tournament and thus enjoys an evolutionary head start right from the beginning. The following table shows the payoff score with which *Dove* gains the tournament as well as the population share and weighted score after 50 generations.

Ranking			After 50 generations	
Rank	Strategy	Score	Population Share	Score
1.	Dove	2.9950	0.5718	4.0000
2.	TitForTat	2.8738	0.4282	3.9999
3.	TatForTit	2.1262	0.0000	3.3604
4.	Hawk	2.0050	0.0000	3.2959

How come that *Dove* wins the tournament and gets even more points than *Tit for Tat*. Shouldn't *Tit for Tat* be at least as good as *Dove*?

After all, it cooperates whenever the opponent does. The answer to this question becomes obvious when looking at the outcomes of the matches between the contenders:

Match	Result
Dove : TatForTit	3.980 : 4.005
Dove : TitForTat	4.000 : 4.000
TatForTit : TatForTit	1.000 : 1.000
TatForTit : TitForTat	2.500 : 2.500
TitForTat : TitForTat	4.000 : 4.000

As can be seen, *Dove* plays very well against both *Tat for Tit* and *Tit for Tat*. But *Tit for Tat* and *Tat far Tit* do not do so well against each other. The reason is that *Tat for Tit* plays the same strategy as *Tit for Tat*, only that it starts with a defection. This leads to a sequence of alternating defection-cooperation, cooperation-defection moves, which results in a comparatively poor average score of 2.5 for the two reciprocal strategies when playing against each other, even though they both play well with *Dove* and, being reciprocators, they are both successful in suppressing *Hawk*. It should be noted, however, that *Tat for Tit* does not play too well against itself either, because it contains no kind of mechanism to detect its own kind. To describe the phenomenon one could say that *Tit for Tat* and *Tat for Tit* are *conflicting reciprocators*. They are both reciprocal altruists, but they are not attuned to each other. Therefore, they come into conflict. As *Dove* is not concerned by this conflict, the presence of conflicting reciprocators allows the genuine altruist *Dove* to become the evolutionarily most successful strategy. It should be observed that because of the presence of (conflicting) reciprocators *Dove* is still protected against an invasion of *Hawks*. In this sense the "slip stream" metaphor still captures the situation, although it does not seem as appropriate a depiction any more as in the previous cases of successful genuine altruists.

Summing up our considerations, we can now give a plausible answer to the question as to why genuine altruists gain a noticeable average population share in the simulation series by referring to the phenomenon of "slip stream altruism". Actually, there are (at least) two types of "slip stream altruism": One type where genuine altruists play the role of a minor contender in a mixed equilibrium of reciprocal altruists and genuine altruists, and another type where genuine altruists even dominate the population after reciprocal altruists have successfully extinguished all exploitative strategies. Under certain conditions (presence of conflicting reciprocal strategies) genuine altruists may even enjoy a head

115

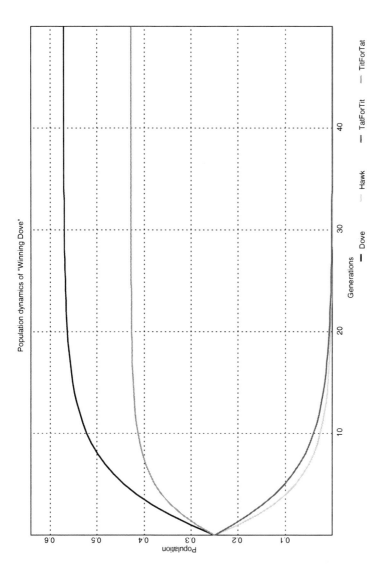

Figure 4.16: If the reciprocal strategies in the simulation are of conflicting types (like *Tit for Tat* and *Tat for Tit*) then "naive" or genuine altruists like *Dove* can become the "laughing third" and win the evolutionary race. (This simulation uses the payoff paramters T=5, R=4, P=1, S=0.)

start right from the beginning. For this last case, however, the "slip stream" metaphor may appear a bit overstretched.

Conclusions

The simulation series produced certain "interesting" results regarding the success of altruistic strategies in the repeated Prisoner's Dilemma. We have found that under the conditions of the simulation (a clause that should never be omitted when discussing the results of computer simulations) the main contributor to the breakdown of altruism is the presence of what has been called "in game noise", which is the sort of noise that disturbs the matches between individual players (in contrast to evolutionary noise that distorts the population dynamical process). Another interesting result is that even though the simulation was constructed as a simulation of reciprocal altruism, there exists – under the conditions of the simulation! – a certain albeit limited opportunity for genuinely altruistic strategies to survive in the "slip stream" of reciprocal altruists.

Of course it would be possible to carry on with the analysis of the generated simulation data and to check for interactions between the different variables etc. (See appendix 8.3 for an overview of the aggregated results for each single variable.) But then, what would be the point of performing an extensive analysis of merely computer generated data? When applying the tool of computer simulations in science or philosophy, there is always the question "Do the simulations prove anything?" or "What do they prove?". Computer simulations as such can of course prove nothing more than the theoretical possibility of the phenomena they produce. Thus, the simulation described before proves that such a phenomenon as "slip stream altruism" is theoretically possible. This, however, says nothing about its empirical impact. We do not know whether "slip stream altruism" is a widespread phenomenon in reality. We do not even know whether it exists in reality at all. And finally, one could even go so far as to doubt whether "slip stream altruism" is possible in reality (as opposed to merely "theoretically possible") at all, for it could still be the case that there exist laws of nature that contradict one or more of the basic assumptions on which the simulation rests. The latter, however, seems very unlikely, because – save for the rather artificial setting of the simulation – no unduly implausible assumptions have been made.

Moreover, since the setting of the simulation is highly artificial and in no way realistic (just think of the two hundred times repeated Prisoner's Dilemma with always exactly the same symmetric payoff), it is virtually impossible that this particular model will ever be applied to any empirical situation in a strict sense. The best that can be hoped for is that for the phenomena the model produces an analogon can be found somewhere in empirical reality. In view of this possibility the model offers at least some idea of some phenomena the empirical researchers might look for. But such purely theoretical models can at worst also distract the attention of researchers from the processes and mechanisms of the evolution of altruism that are relevant in an empirical sense (Hammerstein, 2003a) (Dugatkin, 1997, p. 167).

The same restrictions apply to almost all computer simulations of reciprocal altruism and also to many of the mathematical models that have been constructed in the aftermath of Axelrod's book on the "Evolution of Cooperation" (Axelrod, 1984). This becomes very obvious when looking into these simulations and their results. Since their scientific relevance is extremely doubtful, only a brief overview will be given about some of these simulations in the following.

4.1.5 A quick look at other models and simulations of the same class

It would hardly be possible to list all the models and computer simulations on the evolution of reciprocal altruism that have been published over the last twenty or more years.[21] And, what is more important, it would hardly be worth the trouble, because almost none of these models has ever been applied empirically.[22] Moreover, it is not to be expected that many of these models will ever be applied, because they typically represent highly artificial settings just as the computer simulation presented before. It seems that the empirical research on reciprocal altruism is quite detached from this sort of modeling and that when it develops its own models they are at best remotely inspired by the theoretical modeling and simulating that went on during the last twenty years. We will elaborate this topic a little more later (see chapter 6) and then try to explain the reasons for the apparent empirical failure of models of this type. At any rate, the conclusion to be drawn is that such models do at best represent some kind of theoretical speculation

---

[21] An overview on the literature on Axelrod is given by Robert Hoffmann (Hoffmann, 2000). A compact overview over the most important of these models is found in (Dugatkin, 1997). A broad overview with some discussion on agent-based simulations in the social sciences in general is offered by Gotts, Pohlhill and Law (N.M.Gotts et al., 2003).

[22] Hoffmann maintains of Axelrod's framework that " This general framework is applicable to a host of realistic scenarios both in the social and natural worlds (e.g. Milinski 1987)."(Hoffmann, 2000, section 4.3) However, the only example he mentions (Milinski) turned ultimately out to be a failure of Axelrod's simple model. See chapter 5.1.3.

about the evolution of altruism.

As far as this speculation goes, Dugatkin (Dugatkin, 1997, p. 24ff.) gives an overview of the most prominent of these speculative models, which will briefly be reviewed in the following, highlighting some of the more important points and adding some further sources. According to Dugatkin a wide range of topics have been covered by theoretical models. Theoretical research has been carried out on N-person games, one result among others being that "increasing group size hinders the evolution of cooperation" (Dugatkin, 1997, p. 25). This is at least true if the only form of punishment is defection in the next round, for, in an N-person game there is only the chance to either punish none or all other players, which will in turn induce the "unjustly" punished players to punish the punisher in the following round. As Boyd and Richerson demonstrate (Boyd and Richerson, 1992), cooperation can evolve in an N-person game if punishment is allowed in the form of "retribution", that is, specific acts of punishment that do not form a part of the usual cooperative or non cooperative interactions. However, here the problem emerges how punishers can avoid being invaded by non punishing cooperators if – as would only be "realistic" to assume – punishment is costly.[23]

Other model research concerns the question how the environment and population structure influence the evolution of cooperation. There are results according to which a spatial environment allows for the coexistence of *Tit for Tat* and *Hawk* and others according to which very generous cooperative strategies can evolve in spatial Prisoner's Dilemmas (Dugatkin, 1997, p. 24). Yet another model shows that spatial mobility may allow *Tit for Tat* to invade a population of *Hawk* players much easier than without mobility (Ferriere and Michod, 1996). However, it can also be shown – under the conditions of a certain model – that spatial effects alone do not suffice to maintain cooperation (Frean and Abraham, 2001). Kirchkamp (Kirchkamp, 2000) examines a spatial model which, among other things, shows that cooperation can be sustained even with asynchronous timing, thereby refuting a contradicting result that Huberman and Glance (Huberman and Glance, 1993) had obtained under different model assumptions.

Quite a few models center around the stability conditions of *Tit for Tat* and related strategies (Dugatkin, 1997). Dugatkin and Wilson (Dugatkin and Wilson, 1991, p. 24) examine a spatial scenario where a population of *Tit for Tat* players can be invaded by "roving" defec-

---

[23]Empirical research indicates that people do in fact "altruistically" punish, even if punishment is costly for themselves. But this still does not answer the question, why they do so. See chapter 5.2.1, where an example of the respective empirical research is discussed.

tors. Depending, as usual, on the choice of certain parameter values, the population either stays clear of *Rovers* (as Dugatkin and Wilson call the roving defectors) or moves to a mixed equilibrium or *Rover* "sweeps to fixation" (Dugatkin and Wilson, 1991, p. 694ff.). An important necessary precondition for the success of *Rover* and at the same time a feature that distinguishes Dugatkin's and Wilson's model from almost all other models of the "evolution of cooperation" is that *Rover* is allowed to break off interaction with its partner. One of the few other models that also allowed the players to break off cooperation is Schüßler's simulation of cooperation on anonymous markets (Schüßler, 1990, p. 61ff.). Here each player is allowed to break off the sequences of iterations whenever he or she wants. One should expect that this encourages a kind of "hit and run" tactic, but interestingly – under certain model conditions and within a certain parameter range – even here reciprocal altruism can evolve. Since the continued interaction between players is in no way enforced in Schüssler's simulation, this seems to contradict one of the few general conclusions which otherwise remains true for almost all of the simulations of reciprocal altruism, namely the conclusion that the evolution of reciprocal altruism depends on the "shadow of the future", i.e. the continuation of interaction as necessary precondition of reciprocation. But in a certain sense the "shadow of the future" also plays a role in Schüßler's simulation: Those strategies that use a "hit and run" tactic and break off cooperation have to pick their partner from a pool of free strategies. But, typically, the pool of free strategies consists largely of cheaters as the non cheaters tend to stay engaged in successful cooperative relations. In this model the "shadow of the future" does not mean that a cheater must fear being punished by a reciprocator in the future, but that non-cheaters will be rewarded by keeping up a prosperous relationship. (See appendix 8.5 for a simplified version of Schüßler's simulation that demonstrates this point.)

Another modification that has grave consequences with regard to the evolutionary stability of *Tit for Tat* is the introduction of noise into the models of the repeated Prisoner's Dilemma. In the simulation presented above we found that noise was one of the major sources of the breakdown of cooperation. But as always, this connection depends on the specific model. In a very different model, Nowak examines "Stochastic Strategies in the Prisoner's Dilemma" (Nowak, 1990) with the result that in an "error prone" world *Tit for Tat* is not a very good strategy, but rather a more generous version of *Tit For Tat* is appropriate. The same author, together with Sigmund also examined the case when interactions between players in the repeated Prisoner's Dilemma are alternated instead of taking place simultaneously (Nowak and Sigmund,

1994). They arrive at the result that the alternating interaction in contrast to simultaneous interaction does make a decisive difference. In the cases which they examine the strategy "win stay, lose shift" (termed *Pavlov* in my simulations) is best suited to simultaneous interaction, while in a situation of alternating interactions a generous version of *Tit For Tat* proved to be most appropriate.

Where does this all lead us to? The overview just given of simulations and – in some cases – mathematical models of the reiterated Prisoner's Dilemma did, of course, only present a small selection of the models and simulations that have been published on that topic. But this selection of models should suffice to demonstrate that there are innumerable plausible ways to model reciprocal altruism. And this fact alone raises questions concerning whether these models can tell us anything about how reciprocal altruism evolves. It has been mentioned before that it is very dangerous to draw generalizing conclusions from single simulations with arbitrarily chosen parameters (see chapter 4.1.2), because the results may be very different for different parameter values. "Massive simulations", where one runs a series of simulations over a range of parameter values, can to some degree provide a remedy to this problem. They allow us to draw conclusions with some level of generality (see sections 4.1.4 and 4.1.4). But still, this generality is confined to the setting of the particular simulation series. Relying on models alone, it is practically impossible to draw any general conclusions regarding the evolution of reciprocal altruism beyond this level. As it seems that for any candidate for such a general law or principle governing the evolution of reciprocal altruism a simulation can be found (or easily be constructed if it did not exist already) where this law is not valid any more. For example, if we believe that it would be a general truth about reciprocal altruism that continued interaction is a necessary requirement for its evolution then Schüßler's simulation (see Appendix 8.5) convinces us that this is not the case. Or, if we were inclined to follow Nowak's plausible conclusion (Nowak, 1990) that in a noisy world *Generous Tit for Tat* is a very suitable strategy then our simulation series above demonstrates that this is not generally the case (see chapter 4.1.4).

There are two possible reasons to account for the fact that hardly any general conclusions can be drawn from purely theoretical simulations[24] of reciprocal altruism: First of all, it is well possible that no such general laws exist. There is no *a priori* reason why the evolution of reciprocal altruism should be governed by the same set of general laws in every

---

[24]Under a "purely theoretical" simulation I understand a simulation that is not connected to any particular empirical process it simulates and by comparison with which its empirical validity could be tested, but one that does at best rest on plausible assumptions about processes of a certain kind.

instance of reciprocal altruism that exists. It is possible to characterize the bare concept of reciprocal altruism in a broad and general way by Trivers' equation or similar formalisms. And, of course, we can always presuppose the validity of the laws of evolution and, in the animal kingdom, of genetics as well. But these alone do not suffice to provide an explanation for specific occurrences of reciprocal altruism. Such a specific occurrence of reciprocal altruism would be, for example, the sort of altruism that shoal fish supposedly adhere to when inspecting a predator (see chapter 5.1.3). Now, in order to explain this alleged case of reciprocal altruism, it would be very helpful if we had some laws on an intermediary level of abstraction (that is, laws that are less abstract then the laws of evolution or genetics but still general enough to apply not just to the specific case in question) like a law that says: In situations of prolonged or repeated interaction (where mutual cooperation would be beneficial to all partners) those individuals that regularly punish cheaters but skip punishment once in a while usually gain the highest average fitness payoff. But it may also be the case that no such laws of reciprocal altruism on the intermediary level exist and that in order to construct explanations for specific occurrences we will have to rely on the laws of evolution and on laws which are specific to the case in question. The fact that there are hardly[25] any general laws on this intermediary level which are valid across different simulations of reciprocal altruism strongly suggests that this is indeed the epistemological situation that we find ourselves in.

But it may also be otherwise, and this is the second possible reason for why the model research on reciprocal altruism did not yield any intermediary laws or any one specific model which could be understood as *the* role model of reciprocal altruism: We may not have been able to find any laws of reciprocal altruism with the help mathematical modeling or computer simulations just because there are so many possible ways of modeling it. One could conceive of arbitrarily many different settings for simulations of reciprocal altruism and certainly each single one of them could be justified by plausible reasons as long as the scientist proves eloquent enough. But this does not necessarily imply that no such intermediary laws of reciprocal altruism exist, because the range of possible theoretical models of reciprocal altruism of course by far exceeds the range of models appropriate for empirical application. And it may still be possible that all of the empirical occurrences of reciprocal

---

[25]I say hardly, because there exist boundary cases of almost trivial laws for which the statement that no intermediary laws of reciprocal altruism have been confirmed by model research may be disputed. An example would be that "the shadow of the future matters". In a very broad sense this might be true despite the simulations of Schüßler, which challenge this assumption (see Appendix 8.5).

altruism follow a certain pattern or do at least fall under a manageable number of different types which can be described by laws on an intermediary level of abstraction. But then, the way to find these laws or patterns will not be by research of purely theoretical models alone but only by investigating models that are closely connected to empirical research.

4.1.6 Summary and conclusions about modeling reciprocal altruism

Summing it up, what can be said about the results of theoretical simulation models of reciprocal altruism is that they provide us with certain insights about how reciprocal altruism works and why it can be evolutionarily successful. Most of these insights come close to truisms and as such they hardly justify the technical effort put into the manifold simulations of cooperation and reciprocal altruism. Still, they are not totally devoid of content. And they might be considered to be of some philosophical importance regarding the question if and how altruism has a realistic chance of survival in this world. The most important insight in this respect is that configurations are conceivable under which reciprocal altruism can evolve and survive in dilemma situations. (We have to say that such configurations are conceivable and cannot yet say that they exist, because we have not touched upon any empirical matters by now.) What is more, not only the sort of strict reciprocal altruism that is embodied in reiterated Prisoner's Dilemma strategies like *Tit for Tat* has a chance to thrive in a world that is governed by the principle of the "survival of the fittest". Under some configurations among the many conceivable simulation setups also strategies that are more generous than *Tit for Tat* and even genuinely altruistic strategies may thrive, if only in the slip stream of strictly reciprocal altruists. If *Tit for Tat* marks the borderline between egoism and altruism then this means that there is some chance for real altruism to appear in evolution.

These "results" are admittedly somewhat trivial. But being so they can teach us an import lesson about the deficiency of pure model research. Of course many more and more detailed conclusions could be drawn from the individual models, but the range of validity of any of these conclusions is confined to the respective model, because usually it is possible to find another model where the same conclusions are not valid any more. Therefore, the study of models of reciprocal altruism can hardly teach us anything about how and why altruism evolves. In order to learn something about the evolution of altruism or cooperation it would first be necessary to check the empirical validity of these models or of the conclusions these models suggest. As we shall see subsequently, this goal has hardly been achieved so far, mostly because the majority of the models and simulations presently at hand are so artificial that they do not easily lend themselves to empirical testing.

The epistemological requirements for "explanatory" models will be discussed in detail in chapter 6. For the time being the following analogy might help us to understand the epistemic status of models and computer simulations of reciprocal altruism and why we cannot expect to gain much knowledge about the evolution of cooperation from simulations alone. Computer simulations as well as specific mathematical models of the evolution of altruism relate to the mathematical background theories they are based on (such as game theory or the theory of dynamical systems) as curve sketching relates to calculus. While calculus is as such of a certain mathematical and therefore scientific interest, curve sketching is more of an exercise. It gains scientific interest only when the curves sketched represent functions that are laws of nature in some scientific context. For example, it might be a nice exercise to determine the derivative, the extreme values, the zero points etc of some arbitrarily chosen function like $f(x) = (x^2 - 2)/(2x^3 - 5x)$. But it would not be of any great scientific interest. Only, if we did the curve sketching of some such function like $F(d) = Gm_1m_2/d^2$ this might indeed be of scientific interest, because (if we interpret G as the gravitational constant, m_1 and m_2 as masses of two solid bodies and d as the distance between those bodies) $F(d)$ determines the gravitational force between two bodies as a function of its distance. It could be used, for example, to determine the acceleration of an asteroid approaching earth. Now, while the second function is about as trivial as the first one, it is – differently from the first one – of scientific interest, because it relates to something that happens in nature and it is science's business to understand what happens in nature.

With the computer simulations and models of the evolution of cooperation this is quite similar. As long as these models do not relate to any processes in nature, they are nothing more than mere exercises in computer programming (or mathematical modeling), data visualization and data analysis. Now, of course, most of the authors publishing such models and simulations are careful not to do so without adding some story which seemingly relates them to real world events. For example, they might tell us that we find Prisoner's Dilemma situations all around us all the time and that upon closer inspection many of these Prisoner's Dilemma situations turn out to be really repeated Prisoner's Dilemmas. Therefore, a model of the repeated Prisoner's Dilemma will tell us a lot about what happens around us. But this amounts to nothing more than story telling. Only when the models are so closely related to empirical processes or events that we are able to check which models (from the many plausible or imaginable models) are appropriate,[26] do these models start to become scientifically relevant. Without that they remain mere exercises in computer programming, just like curve sketching is an exercise in calculating.

4.2 Kin selection

From the three fundamental explanations for the evolution of altruism kin selection is probably the only mechanism that has always been completely undisputed. And this is quite understandable: Kin selection basically states that individuals will behave altruistically towards other individuals depending on how closely related they are. This view fits in nicely with the received understanding of evolution as a process where evolutionary success of an organism depends on the successful propagation of the organism's genes. By supporting a related individual an animal may further the propagation of its own genes, because up to some proportion the other individual carries the same genes. Furthermore, the degree of genetic relatedness and thereby the average amount of shared genes between two individuals can easily be determined with great exactitude as it depends on the kinship relation (i.e. the relation of being brother or sister or niece or nephew etc.) and on the type of inheritance of the respective species, that is, whether the species has a diploid set of chromosomes as all mammals do or a haplodiploid set of chromosomes as some insects.

In the following, the concept of kin selection will be rendered more precise by putting it into simple mathematical terms. Also, it will be described how the concept can be understood in biological settings (about which a few hints have just been given) and whether analogous processes of kin selection in the realm of cultural evolution are conceivable.

4.2.1 The fundamental inequation of kin selection

The concept of kin selection was originally described by the biologist William D. Hamilton (Hamilton, 1964). It is also known under the title "*inclusive fitness* theory", because it describes the "all inclusive" reproduction rate of an organism's genes. The condition under which

---

[26]See chapter 6.1.2 for a detailed account of the criteria which allow to check whether a model is "appropriate".

altruism can evolve through kin selection, can be stated in the form of a very simple inequation.

$$C \leq rB \tag{4.2}$$

C the cost (in terms of reproduction rate or number of offspring) for the donator

B the benefit (in terms of reproduction rate) for the recipient

r the degree of genetic relatedness

If the cost for the donator is smaller than the benefit of the recipient discounted by the degree of genetic relatedness then altruism towards the relative will increase the overall ("inclusive") fitness of the donator that is, the donator's genes will spread at a higher rate than they would if the donator was not altruistic. For example, in diploid species[27] brothers and sisters are on average related by 50%. Theoretically, it would therefore pay for an individual to sacrifice itself for the survival of at least two siblings. An often used example to illustrate the power of kin selection to generate altruism is that of eusocial insects. Since, due to the genetics of eusocial insects, sisters are closer related to each other (75%) than they would be to their offspring (50%) it is, as the story goes, more advantageous for them to partake in the raising of sisters than in rearing their own offspring. Although, this would nicely illustrate how kin selection works, there are two counter arguments to this kind of reasoning: First of all, not in all eusocial animals are the circumstances of genetic relatedness as just circumscribed. Some eusocial insects live in "states" with several queens, which leads to kinship relations between sisters and offspring quite different from those described above. Secondly, it is not important how closely sisters are related to each other if none of the sisters ever reproduces itself. If, say, a worker ant or a worker bee is to maximize its inclusive fitness it does not at all pay if it invests in the rearing of genetically strongly related individuals (its sisters) if these do not reproduce. Therefore the coefficients of relatedness that should be compared are those of the relatedness of a worker to its potential offspring and the relatedness to those siblings that will become queens or males. Since the queen sister of a worker is not more closely related to her offspring than a worker would be to her own, the worker would in principle be better off rearing its own offspring, unless for some further reason inequation 4.2 holds. The case of eusocial animals is quite a complicated one and will be discussed in connection with the empirical findings in chapter 5.1.1. Here, the example shall

---

[27] *Diploid* species are species that have two sets of chromosones. All mammals are diploid species.

only serve to illustrate how the concept of kin selection as described by equation 4.2 works in principle.

4.2.2 Transferring the concept of kin selection to cultural evolution

So far, kin selection has been described as a mechanism of genetic evolution. In a genetic context genes for altruism towards relatives spread, because if altruistic benefits are bestowed on a relative then there is a certain chance (depending on the degree of genetic relatedness) that the relative carries the same genes for altruism and will transmit them to its descendants.

It is not implausible to assume that genetic kin selection for altruism has also been at work in the evolutionary history of humans. For example, it is common practice and also sanctioned by common moral opinion in virtually all cultures to assume that one has more and higher obligations towards one's own family members than to other people. But already when it comes to friendship which incurs similar duties and obligations, or when considering the fact that obligations due to family relations also exist towards non-consanguine relatives, it becomes clear that the genetically determined kinship altruism is strongly formed by culture. The latter does of course not necessarily mean that it is formed by a cultural analogue to *kin selection* if such an analogue should exist. Whether such an analogue exists, is the question which shall be considered now. The question is somewhat more problematic than in the case of reciprocal altruism, because as far as reciprocal altruism is concerned, there exists an understanding of reciprocity in many areas of social life which is very akin to the concept of reciprocal altruism as it is applied in biology.[28] For all three kinds of evolutionary altruism there exists the problem of giving a sufficiently precise quantitative empirical interpretation for the parameters that appear in the respective equations or computer models. But in the case of kin selection even a merely qualitative interpretation poses an additional difficulty, because it is not quite clear how to interpret relatedness in the cultural context. Other than in genetic evolution, cultural traits are not necessarily transmitted as whole packages but can be broken up and recombined almost arbitrarily. So, who is to be considered a relative of an altruist? Is it any other altruist, or is it only other altruists that share the same (religious, ethnic, national or other group) affiliation, or is it other people with the

---

[28]It may even be the case that the concept of reciprocal altruism is more appropriate in a cultural than in a biological context, because there exist very few clear cut empirical examples of reciprocal altruism in biology (see chapter 5.1).

same affiliation regardless whether they are altruists or not? Probably any of these possibilities could be considered with some credibility.

Let us first assume that relatedness is to be understood in the sense that an altruist considers other altruists as kin with no further requirements concerning group affiliations. Then an altruist will condition his or her altruism on the recipient being altruistic as well. The difference to reciprocal altruism is that the recipient is expected to act altruistically towards other individuals but not necessarily to return the favor to the altruistic benefactor. Can altruism spread under this assumption? If we assume as replication and selection mechanism that people copy the behavior of successful individuals then it can spread. For, since egoists will not be recipients of favors, altruists will be more successful. Just as in the case of reciprocal altruism this does of course also depend on the narrower circumstances such as the possibility or impossibility of cheating and cheater detection etc. Because of the similarity to reciprocal altruism, the mechanism just sketched is usually discussed under the title of "indirect reciprocity" or "image scoring", because altruistic acts are not directly reciprocated and individuals are treated according to their image (of being altruists or non-altruists).

Regarding the other case when altruism is conditioned on the group affiliation of the recipient rather than on the the image of the recipient, two subcases must be distinguished, one where the group consists entirely of altruists and one where altruism is not necessarily a group trait. The latter case is better understood in terms of group selection, which will be discussed in section 4.3. As to the former case, if altruism is tied to group affiliation and is at the same time a group trait it can spread for just the same reasons as have been described above, only that it furthermore helps to promote other group traits. It should be noted that if we conceive of "cultural kin selection" in this way, the concept of a group is a very peculiar one, where group membership depends entirely on adopting a certain behavior. For most social groups this is not sufficient. Usually group membership depends on other factors as well such as being appointed a member for example. In this context it may not be superfluous to indicate that the concept just sketched of a mechanism of "cultural kin selection" should not be confused with what is commonly discussed as "in-group" and "out-group" behavior of social groups, which is something quite different. The analogy to kin selection in biology remains somewhat coarse, anyway, because it is difficult to give a precise interpretation to the term "degree of relatedness" in a context of cultural evolution. This again should warn us that – contrary to the expectations of advocates of the application of an evolutionary approach to the social sciences (see chapter 3.3) – precise scientific concepts often lose their rigor and precision when they are transferred to a different scientific subject area.

Still, an interpretion for the mechanism of kin selection in the realm of cultural evolution does not seem completely inconceivable. Whether it has a strong empirical impact (i.e. is applicable to many and important empirical phenomena of social life and at the same time better suited to deal with these phenomena than alternative concepts) is a question that is up to empirical science to decide.

4.3 Group selection

The probably most astonishing mechanism by which the evolution of altruism can be explained is that of group selection. The concept of group selection explains the evolution of altruism by the usefulness that altruistic traits of individuals within a group have for the group as a whole. On a naive level this explanation appears seductively simple: Cooperation and altruism even to the point of self-sacrificial behavior exist, because they serve the most useful purpose of contributing to the preservation and well-being of the group or species that the individual belongs to. Nothing seems simpler than that: Some species have developed altruistic behavioral traits, because these are necessary for the preservation of the species. If the species hadn't got this trait, it would simply die out or, *vice versa*, since this species has not died out, the existence of altruistic behavioral traits must be explained as a consequence of its self preservation.

But there is a problem with this kind of naive reasoning. The mere fact that a certain trait serves a useful purpose for the group or species does not tell us what the causes were that made this trait come into existence or even whether there are sufficient causes for its existence at all. A functional explanation that relates certain means to a certain end does not explain by which causes these means have been brought about. A sufficient explanation of any natural phenomenon can thus only be a causal explanation. The standard causal explanation in evolutionary theory is the explanation by fitness dependent selection. Unfortunately, it is just this mechanism that renders group functionalism seemingly impossible. For, suppose there was a certain altruistic trait in a species that enhances group fitness. And suppose that this altruistic trait reduces individual fitness in comparison to other "egoistic" individuals within the group (otherwise the trait would not be truly altruistic, would it?). Then, even though the group profits from the existence of the trait, this very trait will be selected against within the group so that after a couple of generations it will most probably have died out. Moreover, since the altruistic trait is constantly being selected against, it would not even have the chance to ever invade a population, thus rendering altruism improbable even as a transitory phenomenon if it was only by group selection that altruism could be brought about.

It is for this reason that group selection has long been regarded among biologists with a similar suspicion as Larmarckian inheritance. But just as for Lamarckian inheritance there exists a special case, called the Baldwin effect, where under certain circumstances an acquired property can become a genetically inherited property,[29] it can be shown that group selection, i.e. the selection of traits because they are beneficial to groups even though they may be impedimental to the reproductive success of the individuals that carry these traits within the group, is indeed possible. This possibility has recently been described very elegantly by Elliott Sober and D.S.Wilson (Sober and Wilson, 1998). In the following, however, I do not intend to reiterate the description of group selection that Sober and Wilson have given, but I present a computer model of the evolution of altruism through group selection. Group selection is the kind of mechanism where the method of computer simulations really shines. While the mechanism of kin selection is very straightforward and while the evolution of altruism on the basis of reciprocity is also fairly intuitive, group selection seems *prima facie* almost impossible. What could be said against the line of reasoning above? Doesn't it clearly show that group selection is quite impossible? Yet, if we succeed in constructing a numerical model where group selection produces results that differ even in the long term significantly from the results in a non group selection scenario, this suffices to prove that group selection is a possibility that we have to take into account. In other words, in the case of group selection, already its theoretical possibility constitutes an important problem. But this theoretical possibility can be demonstrated by a computer simulation.

4.3.1 A toy model of group selection

The ingredients needed for our group selection model of the evolution of altruism are a population that is divided into relatively isolated subpopulations, which are commonly called "demes". There must be two

---

[29]The reasoning behind the Baldwin effect is this: Learned behaviour creates a "cultural environment" that favors genetic adaptations that are adjusted to this "cultural environment" (Depew, 2003, p. 6ff.). One can reason that as a special case acquired properties that increase the fitness of its bearer in the cultural environment may eventually be replaced by genetic adaptations that "hard code" these properties if acquiring the property by leraning is costly so that having it inborn increases the relative fitness. The existence of the Baldwin effect is a much disputed issue, however.

different selection processes, one between the individuals inside a deme and one that takes place between the demes themselves. It is also possible to imagine more than two levels of selection.[30] But as our model is only to demonstrate the principle of group selection, it is advisable to keep things as simple as possible. The important point is that the sub-populations (demes) are only *relatively* isolated, i.e. there will be a certain amount of exchange of individuals between the demes. As the fitness of the deme depends on its composition of individual types, the exchange of individuals between demes will ensure that there is always a fitness difference between the demes.[31]

If this sounds a bit too abstract, we can imagine an area in the Savannah that is inhabited by a population of monkeys. The monkeys live in small packs, each of which occupies a certain territory. We assume that the monkeys within a pack (or group) compete for the food they reap from the group's territory and that this competition has the structure of a one shot Prisoner's Dilemma, i.e. the average fitness of all monkeys within the group will be highest if they share the food without engaging in fights over the food among each other. However, a monkey that engages into fights with his more peaceful minded group fellows will be able to obtain more food than it would when sharing food. But as every fight costs a lot of energy, the average fitness of the whole group will be less than in the case of mutual cooperation. This means that within the group the competitive monkeys will probably produce more offspring than the cooperative monkeys, but at the same time the offspring that a group produces as a whole will be greater if there are fewer competitive members in the group. For the sake of simplicity, we will assume that the size of the territory that a group occupies is always proportional to the number of its members, that is the ratio of food resources per group member is the same for all groups. Finally, we assume that from time to time some monkeys leave their group and join other groups. Now the question is: Will the group beneficial cooperative type survive?

It should be observed that in this example the cooperative type corresponds to the naive strategy *Dove* in the repeated Prisoner's Dilemma model while the competitive type corresponds to the strategy *Hawk*. With only these two strategies, the situation in the repeated Prisoner's Dilemma is exactly the same as in the one shot Prisoner's Dilemma.

---

[30]See (Sober and Wilson, 1998) for a discussion of multilevel selection as well as for an alternative way to model group selection not by a computer simulation but by mathematical equations.

[31]This is, of course, true only *ceteris paribus*. If we imagine a non random exchange process that operates in such a ways as to level the differences in composition between the demes then this will not be the case. For a random exchange process this could also happen as an extremely unlikely exception. Finally, the selection process within the demes could be such that it leads to a leveling of the differences in the inner composition of the demes which the exchange cannot compensate.

But we will stick to the repeated Prisoner's Dilemma, because it later allows us to introduce further strategies. The payoff parameters of the Prisoner's Dilemma are the same as in the simulation of reciprocal altruism before, that is, $T = 5, P = 3, R = 1, S = 0$. In order to model group selection, we assume that the population of *Doves* and *Hawks* is divided into 25 demes, each of which contains both strategies, albeit in different ratios. The selection process within the demes follows the same replicator dynamics as in our simulation of reciprocal altruism, taking the average payoff for each strategy as fitness value. (See appendix 8.2 for the details.) For the selection process between the demes the average payoff of all strategies within the deme is taken as fitness value. Just as in the simulations of reciprocal altruism, the population size is represented by fractions of one, which are to be understood as the share of an arbitrarily sized whole population that is occupied by the deme. Similarly, the populations within the demes are represented by the fractions of the population that use the one or the other of the two strategies. To determine the respective population shares of *Hawk*'s and *Dove*'s in the overall population, it is only necessary to add up the population shares of a strategy within each deme weighted (multiplied) by the population share of the deme. The graphs presented in the following always display the aggregated population shares of each strategy.

The exchange process between the populations of the demes is modeled as a kind of reshaping of the deme composition. Every ten rounds all demes are dissolved and the whole population is redistributed randomly to 25 new equally sized demes. For a detailed description of the reshaping algorithm and its implementation see appendix 8.4.

Group selection and genuine altruism

Does group selection make a difference and, if it does, is the group selection effect only transitory, as the critics of group selection claim? The results of the computer simulation show that group selection can have a lasting impact on the evolution of altruism. Figure 4.17 depicts what happens to a population of *Dove*'s and *Hawk*'s under group selection.

In the group selection setting the strategy *Dove* emerges as the clear winner with roughly between 80% and 90% of the population playing *Dove*. How can it be explained that *Dove* earns a lasting success even though – as we know – the population share of *Dove* within every deme is constantly decreasing? The reason why the population share of *Dove* increases in the overall population is that those demes that contain many *Dove* players have a strong fitness advantage over demes where the fraction of *Hawk* players is high. Therefore the demes that contain a

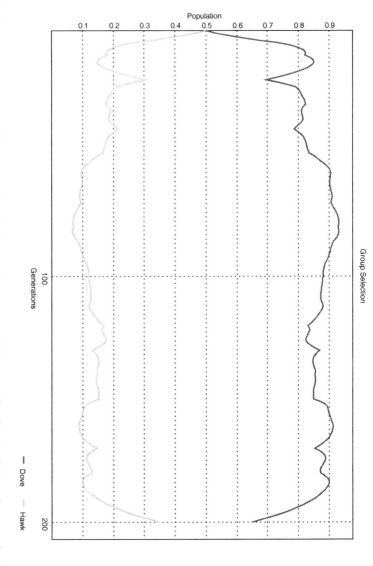

Figure 4.17: In a group selection model even genuine altruism can be a successful strategy. For this simulation of group selection the population was divided into 25 demes which are reshaped randomly every 10 generations.

high fraction of *Dove* players increase their population share at the cost of demes with a high fraction of *Hawk* players. With the chosen simulation parameters this increase of the population shares of demes with a high amount of *Dove* players outweighs the decrease of the amount of *Dove* players within the demes. Therefore, the overall population share of *Dove* players increases. This process depends crucially on the fitness differences between the demes, which in turn is due to the difference of *Dove* - *Hawk* ratios between the demes. Now, since inside all demes the fraction of *Dove* players gradually converges to zero (because selection inside the demes strongly acts against the *Dove* players), the fitness differences between the demes will also gradually decrease over time, thus diminishing the *Dove* player's advantage through interdeme selection. This is where the exchange of group members between different demes, which in our simulation is modeled as a reshaping of demes, comes in: Through the reshaping of demes the fitness differences between the demes are reestablished. On the graph the reshaping of demes can be discerned by the sharp edges that occur in every 10th generation. Usually, before reshaping takes place the aggregated population share of *Dove* players decreases and it increases again after the reshaping took place. The slope of the curve between two reshaping intervals, however, is always decreasing, which is due to the fact that the fitness differences between the demes, from which *Dove* profits, is continually diminishing.

The decisive difference of the reshaping of demes is further emphasized by a look at figure 4.18. Here, the same simulation is run without periodic reshaping of demes. In the beginning *Dove* profits from the interdeme competition. But the group selection effect that gives *Dove* an advantage over *Hawk* remains temporary. In the long run the result is exactly the same as without any group selection.

What the results of the original group selection simulation (figure 4.17) demonstrate is first of all that group selection is possible. While a numerical simulation that does not represent any specific empirical situation cannot tell us whether something is the case or not, it can still tell us something about theoretical possibilities. This simulation demonstrates that group selection is theoretically possible. A line of purely theoretical reasoning as it has been presented on page 129 is therefore not sufficient anymore to reject group selection. Whether the mechanism of group selection is of any empirical importance is ultimately up to empirical science to decide, but it is certainly a mechanism that deserves seriously to be considered.

With respect to the evolution of altruism, another important result is that through group selection even the evolution of genuine altruism is possible. While the other two types of altruism that have been discussed

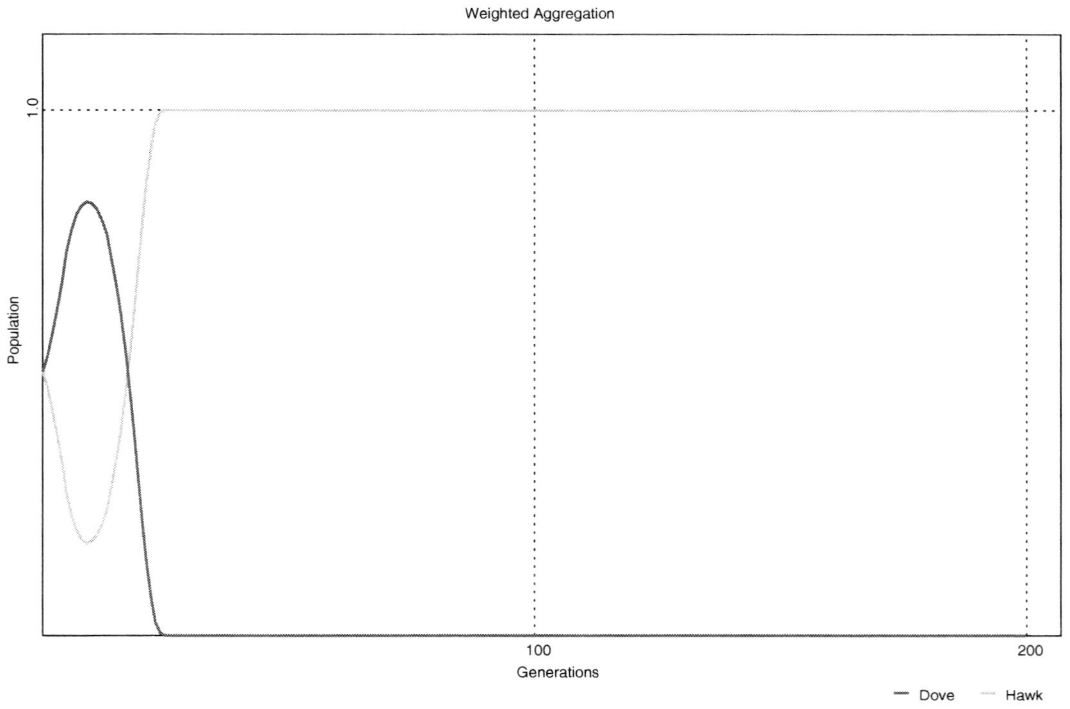

134

Figure 4.18: If the demes are completely isolated, any group selection effect remains transitory. Again, the population was divided into 25 demes in this simulation (with every deme containing at least some members of each species). But this time the demes were never reshaped.

in this chapter (reciprocal altruism and altruism through kin selection) could appear somehow tainted to a moralist observer, because reciprocal altruism could be interpreted as merely a deferred type of egoism and kin selection seems to be just egoism of the gene, group selection even allows for the evolution of genuine altruism, i.e. a kind of altruism where the altruist is not compensated for the benefits he or she bestows. It is true that in the massive simulation of reciprocal altruism (chapter 4.1.4), the evolution of genuine altruism appeared as a marginal though noticeable phenomenon in the "slip stream" of reciprocal strategies or as the "laughing third" if badly coordinated reciprocal strategies impeded each other. But this was the exception rather than the rule and at any rate genuine altruism is not evolutionarily or collectively stable in the repeated Prisoner's Dilemma. In the group selection simulation presented here, genuine altruism has a much stronger foothold than in the simulation of the reiterated Prisoner's Dilemma. If we interpret the game underlying the group selection simulation as a one shot Prisoner's Dilemma then there are no strategies other than *Dove* and *Hawk*. And since *Hawk* is – save for a very small probability with which the randomized reshaping process could diminish instead of increase the fitness differences between the demes – obviously not able to invade a population of *Doves* up to more than roughly 10% or 20%, the strategy *Dove* is a stable strategy under the conditions of the simulation.

Group selection as an impediment to the evolution of altruism

The recent discussion about group selection that has been triggered by Sober's and Wilson's "Unto Others" (Sober and Wilson, 1998) has been mainly centered around how group selection promotes altruism. This and the fact that models of group selection do – as has just been demonstrated – indeed reveal some very astonishing results with respect to altruism may easily lead to the conclusion that group selection mechanisms always strengthen altruistic behavior. But just as it has been demonstrated with a simple computer model that group selection is – despite the reasonable objections against it – theoretically possible, it can also be shown with a computer simulation that it is not generally true that group selection promotes altruism.

In order to disprove the presumption that group selection always promotes altruism, it fully suffices to draw up a numerical simulation where under the condition of group selection non altruistic strategies are successful while altruistic strategies are successful under the absence of group selection, all other simulation conditions being the same. Figure 4.19 shows the results of a simulation where group selection acts against

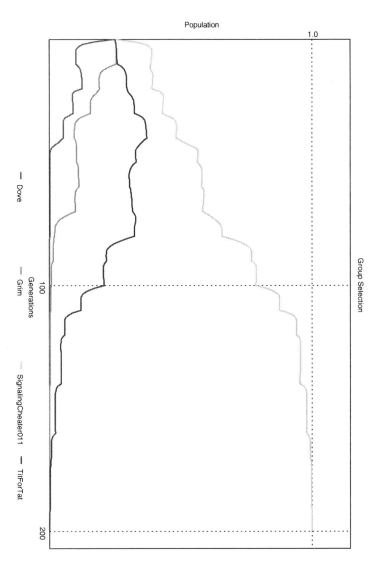

Figure 4.19: Under certain conditions group selection can work against the evolution of altruism. To produce this result the payoff parameters have been set to T=5.9, R=3, P=1, S=0. The population was divided into 10 demes which contain either one, two or three strategies and which were reshaped every 10 rounds.

the evolution of altruism. In this simulation the strategies *Dove*, *Tit for Tat*, *Grim* and *Signaling Cheater 011* take part. *Signaling Cheater* is a strategy that plays a predefined sequence of cooperative and defective moves in the first n rounds of the repeated Prisoner's Dilemma. If the opponent player starts with exactly the same sequence of moves, *Signaling Cheater* assumes that it has met another *Signaling Cheater* and cooperates unconditionally for the remaining rounds of the repeated game. Otherwise *Signaling Cheater* defects for the rest of the game. Thus, *Signaling Cheater* is a strategy that is designed to cooperate only with its own kind (that is other *Signaling Cheaters* that use the same starting sequence as a signal) and not to cooperate with any other strategy. *Signaling Cheater* is here understood as a non altruistic strategy as in general it does not bestow any benefits unto others nor does it reciprocate benefits it receives from others unless the other player is also a *Signaling Cheater*. At best it could be understood as representing a type of very restricted kinship based altruism, but then it is still much less altruistic than *Tit For Tat* or even *Grim*.

In the simulation that is depicted in figure 4.19 the population of these four strategies is spread over 10 demes that contain from one up to three strategies. Reshaping takes place every 10 rounds. The payoff parameter T (= temptation, the payoff for successful cheating) has been set to 5.9 instead of 5. With these parameters the simulation sometimes[32] exposes the results that are depicted in figure 4.19. Here, *Signaling Cheater* emerges as the winner and, as can be observed, every reshaping of genes, gives *Signaling Cheater* another boost. This means that the most uncooperative of the four strategies directly profits from group selection. If under the same configuration the simulation is run without group selection, the reciprocal altruists *Grim* and *Tit for Tat* fare much better and even *Dove* can survive in the slip stream of the reciprocal strategies.

It should be mentioned, however, that with this type of simulation it is not very easy to find a configuration, where group selection works against the evolution of altruism. Even with this simulation the effect depicted in figure 4.19 is rather untypical and does occur only in about one third of the simulation runs. Still, this should warn us that the effect of group selection on the evolution of altruism must not necessarily consist in promoting altruism or even genuine altruism.

---

[32]Whether it actually does, does depend on the random factors in the simulation.

138

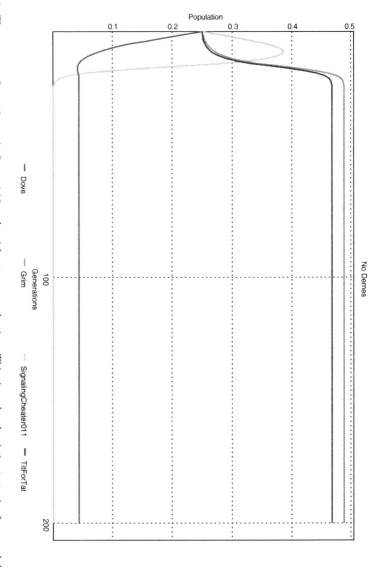

Figure 4.20: The same configuration as in figure 4.19, only without group selection. This time the altruistic strategies fare much better.

4.3.2 Extending the model?

The computer model of group selection just described has demonstrated two important results about group selection: 1) Group selection is possible and can lead to the evolution of a very strong kind of altruism, namely genuine altruism, where otherwise altruism would not evolve at all. 2) At least theoretically there are exceptions to the rule that group selection typically strengthens altruism. Nonetheless, these results remain, so far, purely theoretical and the simulation by which they have been obtained can at best be called a toy simulation, because it has intentionally been kept extremely simple and it is in no way related to any empirical "real-world" problem. Nothing would of course be easier than to develop the simulation further on into a massive simulation, just as it has been demonstrated before for the simulations of reciprocal altruism. But what would be the point of such an exercise? While further and more "massive" simulations can help to obtain a better "feel" for the simulated mechanisms, it is doubtful whether a massive simulation of group selection would lead to any new insights other than those that can be obtained by simple toy simulations. In the case of reciprocal altruism we have seen that it is almost impossible to obtain any generalizable results from the simulations, because for any candidate of such a result it seems that another simulation can be constructed where just this supposedly general result does not hold (see section 4.1.5). Of course, if this is the case then it will be equally impossible to derive any general results by mathematical reasoning, because the counterexamples already exist in form of simulations.[33] But if no or only few general conclusions can be drawn from the computer simulations alone then this means that the question which of the results are important can only be determined by empirical research.

4.3.3 Group selection in cultural evolution

The concept of group selection, the working mechanisms of which have just been demonstrated by a simple computer simulation, was originally developed for biological contexts. It remains to indicate how the concept of group selection can possibly be applied to a cultural context. Just as in the case of kin selection, different ways are imaginable as to how group selection could appear in a social context. Here, only one such scenario will briefly be outlined to show what kind of selection processes can possibly be interpreted as group selection in a social context: If,

---

[33]Therefore, the problem is not – as it is sometimes believed – that the working mechanisms of computer simulations are often not well enough understood analytically (i.e. mathematically).

for example, we assume that people tend to choose the social groups that they want to become members of by the average success of group members and if we furthermore assume that when entering a new group, people start by following (or "copying") the behavioral rules that are common standard in the group, then group selection can take place in the following way: Suppose, there are different groups with different levels of altruism in a society. As the groups with a higher proportion of altruists will be more successful people will move from the less altruistic groups to the more altruistic groups, that is, between-group selection takes place by the movement of people from low performing groups to high performing groups. At the same time, in-group selection can be assumed to take place by the less successful group members copying the behavior of the more successful members. A similar scenario has indeed been designed in an experiment on economic behavior which will be discussed in detail later (see chapter 5.2.1).

Similarly as in the case of kin selection, the question remains how much empirical impact the concept of group selection has in a cultural context. One factor which group selection models such as the one presented here do not (yet) take into account ist that alturistic or eogistic behavior may be conditioned on whether the potential recipients of the altruistic acts are members of one's own group or not. This in-group or out-group behaviour is a most salient feature of group psychology and has also been confirmed in behavioural experiments (Bernhard et al., 2006). It stands to reason that group selection pressures strengthen the difference between in-group altruism and out-group egoism and do in this way also lead to the evolution of an, albeit qualified form of altruism. Attempts to apply the concept of group selection to the social sciences in a very broad sense have also been made. But so far, none of these has been wholly convincing.[34] It is probably more promising to link group selection models to certain recurring modes of human behavior than to try to interpret cultural or religious history on the basis of groups selection.

4.4 Summary and conclusions

In this chapter the three basic explanations for evolutionary altruism (i.e. altruism that results from some Darwinian evolutionary process

---

[34]Wilson's seriously flawed "Darwin's Cathedral" (Wilson, 2002) has already been commented on earlier. In their book on altruism "Unto Others" (Sober and Wilson, 1998) Sober and Wilson exemplify group selection mainly with biological thought experiments. For the discussion of human altruism in the second half of their book, they rely on psychology and only vaguely refer to group selection (Sober and Wilson, 1998, p. 296ff., p. 345ff.).

in contradistinction to altruism that has other causes) have been presented. Each type of altruism has been described by a simple inequation or a computer simulation or both. The tool of computer simulations in particular can serve the following purposes for the investigation of altruism:

Merits of computer simulations

1. Computer simulations allow proving theoretical possibilities; for example the possibility of the evolution of altruism in dilemma situations (section 4.1.2).

   Sometimes, however, the demonstrated theoretical possibilities do not go beyond mere trivialities that can immediately be derived from the mathematical background theories. For example, the mere fact that reciprocal altruism can evolve in the repeated Prisoner's Dilemma is a trivial consequence of the folk theorem (see page 77 and 83).

2. Computer simulations allow disproving assumed theoretical necessities, like the assumption that group selection necessarily strengthens altruism (section 4.3.1).

3. Because they are often easier to handle and more flexible than purely mathematical models, computer simulations allow easy investigation of the most diverse and variegated constellations under which altruism might possibly evolve. Whether the investigation of these purely theoretical settings is of much scientific relevance is then of course a different question.

4. Computer simulations can expose "new" phenomena in the sense of theoretical possibilities never thought of before (like the phenomenon of "slip stream altruism" described in section 4.1.4). For this purpose, series of simulations ("massive simulations") might be employed to detect such phenomena.

5. Just as mathematical models, computer simulations may help the theorist to understand his or her own theory better, because they force the theorist to cast the theory in clear and unambiguous terms. When formulating a theory as a computer program, possible misconceptions, contradictions or logical gaps become apparent.

But apart from these merits also some severe limitations of the use of computer simulations for understanding evolutionary altruism have become apparent:

Limitations of computer simulations

1. It is not possible to draw general conclusions about the evolution of altruism from computer simulations of the evolution of altruism. Any such simulation respresents just a highly contingent sample calculation (see section 4.1.6). Conducting series of simulations can only slightly remedy this limitation, which represents a fundamental limitation of computer simulations in general.

2. For almost all general conclusions that computer simulations of the evolution of altruism suggest, it is easy to draw up another simulation of the evolution of altruism, where the conclusion does not hold any more (see section 4.1.5). It is therefore hardly possible to take the general conclusions that specific simulations of the evolution of altruism suggest as a first step towoards constructing a general theory of altruism. For, one cannot tell on on *which* of the diverse and contradicting conclusions that different computer simulations suggest the theory should be based.

3. Therefore, *it is not possible to obtain any scientifically tenable results about the evolution of altruism by the analysis of computer simulations alone!*

4. Indulgence into pure model research can lead to fundamental misconceptions about the subject matter. In the worst case, these misconceptions can take the form of myths that are hard to redress (Examples: The "Tit for Tat bubble" (Binmore, 1998, p. 317), the "skew towards reciprocal altruism in theoretical literature" (Dugatkin, 1997, p. 167)).

The third of these points, which has been highlighted above, may sound like a mere triviality, but in fact it is not. If the problem of understanding the evolution of altruism had been primarily theoretical, that is, if there was only one reasonable way in which the evolution of altruism could be conceived and modeled then the analysis of computer simulations might indeed have yielded substantial results about the evolution of altruism. But, unfortunately, there are innumerable ways how the evolution of altruism can be modeled. And then the question inevitably arises why one should give preference to one model rather than to another. The only reasonable answer to this question is that the decision must be taken on empirical grounds. The empirical research on the evolution of altruism is what we turn our attention to now.

Chapter 5

Empirical research on the evolution of altruism

The last chapter closed with the conclusion that substantial scientific results about the evolution of altruism cannot be obtained by looking at computer simulations alone. The situation would be different if there were only one right way to model altruism. But because there are so many plausible ways to do it only a look at the empirical examples can tell which one is the right one. In the following we will therefore examine some of the empirical research on altruism. We will first look at biology and then at the social sciences. When surveying the research in these fields, there are two questions that are important for us: First of all, we do of course want to find out whether, how and why altruism evolves in nature and among humans. Theoretical models and computer simulations demonstrate how it *could* evolve. Empirical research, hopefully, can tell us something about how, why and where it *does* evolve. The second question concerns the method and research strategy. Already in the previous chapter there has been opportunity to raise some doubts concerning the usefulness of the tool of computer simulations for the understanding of reciprocal altruism. Now we want to know how these simulation models live up to the empirical research, that is whether they are helpful for conducting such research and whether they prove valuable for the explanation of the results of the empirical research.

A survey of empirical research on the evolution of altruism raises certain methodological issues by itself, which shall briefly be discussed, before entering into the discussion of the empirical material. First of all, there is the question of the selection of the material. As the research on altruistic behavior is a wide and varied field both in biology and in the social sciences and as the focus of empirical scientists and the categories they employ are often not the same as those the theoreticians develop, a selection of materials is unavoidable. In the following, I have tried to choose examples that are most closely linked to the theoretical models and to the concepts of reciprocal altruism, kin selection and group selection described earlier. This criterion of selection also has advantages for addressing our second question, the question of the usefulness of simulations as a method. For, if this method fails in those cases that we would assume it is best suited to deal with, then we have good reason to assume that it is a bad method (at least in the way it is applied today) without worrying that we might have been unfair. Still, it must be admitted that the following selection of empirical example cases is quite eclectic. This is unavoidable given the sheer extent of this field of research, but – as should frankly be admitted – it is also partly due to the fact that I am neither an expert in biology nor in experimental game theory.

Another methodological issue when surveying research, concerns the question as to whether one should give a broad overview covering as much of the research as possible or whether one should rather pick out a few examples and discuss them in depth in order to demonstrate how the respective kind of research works and what degree of credibility can be attributed to it. Regarding the biological examples, I have tried to combine both approaches. First, an overview of a larger number of empirical studies on reciprocal altruism will be given to convey an idea of where this research stands. Then, one example will be picked out and discussed in depth to see how reliable the results of this research are and especially how well the theoretical models do when submitted to the "on-road test". For the social sciences I confine myself to the discussion of a few select examples. The reason for this is that while there exists a lot of empirical research on cooperation dilemmas of one kind or other, there are hardly any empirical studies that are closely attuned to the kind of models that have been discussed before.[1] It would be spurious to present a summary of research on behavioral economics that mostly falls outside the narrower topic of this book.[2] But just as in the case of biology, one of the examples from the social sciences will be discussed in depth. For the in depth discussion I have in both cases picked examples that were by their authors intended as show cases for the application of reiterated Prisoner's Dilemma models. Therefore, these examples should be best suited to assess the possible merits and defects of this

---

[1]This is even true for Axelrod's popular model of reciprocal altruism, which has spurred myriads of further model studies (Dugatkin, 1997, p. 24ff.), but remained quite infertile for the empirical research.

[2]A fairly recent overview of the research on altruism in experimental economics can be found in (Fehr and Fischbacher, 2003). The bulk of this research is concerned with the question how altruism works among humans. While this has some bearing on which kind of evolutionary explanations are more plausible than others, only few evolutionary models seem to be have been put to the empirical test directly.

type of modeling.

5.1 The empirical discussion in biology

5.1.1 Altruism among animals

As in any other field of science the specialist literature on altruism in biology comes in two different brands. First of all, there are articles in different biological journals. Then, there are books on the topic written by specialists that usually present the results of the research published in articles in a condensed and simplified form. For a non-specialist it is advisable to stick to the latter kind of literature, for otherwise there exists a considerable danger of misunderstanding and of giving too much weight to unimportant details and too little weight to important ones. Luckily, there exists a treatment of the subject in book-form by an author who is strongly committed to a game theoretical approach to the study of altruism. This treatment is Lee Allan Dugatkin's already afore mentioned "Cooperation Among Animals" (Dugatkin, 1997). In what follows I therefore present mostly examples from Dugatkin's book. Unfortunately, the book was issued in 1997 and therefore does not cover the latest research. For this reason, later on I also discuss an example of a study that has been published on the topic since.

The empirical research which Dugatkin reviews, cannot always be sorted neatly into different categories of altruism like reciprocal altruism, kin selection or group selection. The reason for this is that when scientists set out to research altruistic behavior in certain animal species they usually are not sure beforehand what kind of altruism is concerned. And quite often the data they are able to obtain does not allow making the distinction afterwards. Often it is not even clear whether the behavioral trait in question is altruistic at all or merely some kind of byproduct mutualism.[3] In the following, different examples of cooperative and potentially altruistic animal behavior that are described in Dugatkin's book will be presented. The main aim is to clarify whether the theoretical categories for altruistic behavior (reciprocal altruism, kin selection and group selection) can be identified empirically and to what degree assumptions about the type of altruism can be ascertained. Also,

---

[3]The difference between altruism and byproduct mutualism is that while both entail benefits for some other individual, it must in the case of altruism at least be possible to cheat, while in the case of byproduct mutualism cheating is impossible in principle that is, an exchange of benefits still may or may not take place, but if it takes place cheating is not an option. An example to illustrate this might be two people warming each other in winter by moving closer together. None can enjoy the warmth of the other without giving warmth him- or herself, which means that there is no way to cheat.

it will be asked in how far models such as those presented in the previous chapter can be validated empirically and whether and in how far these types of models have been useful to empirical research.

Cooperative behavior as it occurs in nature

Egg Trading   An often quoted example of reciprocal altruism in particular is that of egg trading among hermaphroditic fish. According to Dugatkin it is best documented for sea bass (Wolfsbarsch) (Dugatkin, 1997, p. 46). Sea bass (as well as many other egg trading fish species) parcel their eggs into small packages. When mating, one fish starts by releasing a parcel of its eggs, which typically consists of only a small fraction of the eggs it has. At the same time the partner releases sperm. Then they switch roles and regularly alternate the release of eggs subsequently. These cycles of alternating egg spawning suggest an interpretation of this process as a repeated game. But is the game a Prisoner's Dilemma and do the sea basses use a reciprocal strategy, i.e. would they retaliate if being cheated? Dugatkin's answer is that it can loosely be interpreted as a repeated Prisoner's Dilemma if the release of one parcel of eggs by one partner and the following release or failure of release by the other partner is interpreted as one round of the repeated game and if it is assumed that producing eggs is more expensive than producing sperm. Although it is difficult to quantify the costs, the latter assumption is almost certain to be true (Dugatkin, 1997, p. 48). A problem is that due to the lack of quantitative data (and – as of now – the lack of measurement techniques to obtain such data), it is impossible to fill in the payoff matrix of the game other than by rough estimates. But then it is not even sure whether *Tit for Tat* is a suitable equilibrium strategy. Regarding the question whether fish engaged in egg trading do in fact play *Tit for Tat*, there exists, according to Dugatkin, some anecdotal evidence (i.e. non-systematic evidence from incidental observations) for certain types of fish that they do in fact play some deviant version of *Tit for Tat*. It is reported that black hamlets and chalk basses retaliate by waiting much longer to parcel out eggs if a partner failed to reciprocate before. But sometimes they omit retaliation, which suggests that they are really using a *Generous Tit for Tat* strategy (Dugatkin, 1997, p. 48).

The repeated Prisoner's Dilemma model of Axelrod and Hamilton (Axelrod, 1984) which assumes a fixed number of rounds or at least a fixed termination probability is not the only model that can potentially be applied to the egg trading behavior among fish. Dugatkin also describes another interpretation of the egg trading behavior by R.C. Conner that is related to a species of plycheate worms and according to which there is no fixed termination probability but each partner decides continuously whether to continue or to break off the interaction. For Connor this is simply a matter of whether the benefit of staying[4] exceeds the benefit of leaving and, given his interpretation is right, he justly speaks of "pseudo-reciprocity" instead of reciprocity (Dugatkin, 1997, p. 49). However, without more precise quantitative data it is not possible to decide this question.

Alloparenting   Another type of potentially altruistic behavior is that of *alloparenting*, which according to Dugatkin means "the dispensing of 'parental' behavior to young that are not one's own" (Dugatkin, 1997, p. 101). "Alloparenting" concerns sexually mature individuals that *could* also produce offspring of their own. From an evolutionary point of view such a behavior demands explanation because animals that want to spread their genes should primarily be interested in raising their own children not those of others. Nonetheless *alloparenting* is quite widespread and found among various kinds of mammals, birds and fish. *Alloparenting* among fish has been studied for *Lamprologus brichardi*, a type of perch (Barsch) found in the Lake Tanganyika in East Africa. For this species it is typical that the young stay at the nest for a while even after they have grown sexually mature and help cleaning eggs and maintaining and defending the territory. That this kind of helping activity is costly is illustrated by the fact that the young that stay at the nest have a slower growth in comparison with young that do not stay at the nest. The benefits that mature young derive from staying and helping at the nest include relative safety from predators and rearing kin that is at least closely related even if it is not their own. (Other suggested benefits were not confirmed or at least not measurable by experimental research.) This suggests that both byproduct mutualism (safety from predators) and kin selection are involved in the *alloparenting* behavior of *Lamprologus brichardi*. But according to Dugatkin there is also a reciprocal element present because when the mature young start to reproduce themselves they are expelled from the nest by their parents.(Dugatkin, 1997, p. 50) The only factor promoting altruism that could strictly be measured was that of kin selection, which of course is relatively easy to measure. The assumption that byproduct mutualism and reciprocal altruism are involved as well can, according to Dugatkin, be confirmed by observation but it is not possible to actually measure the payoff parameters of the game matrix and apply any of the game

---

[4]Although Dugatkin does not say anything about this in his report of Connor, one should assume here that what is meant is the *expected* benefit of staying, as the possible future benefit also varies according to when the other partner decides to break up the interaction.

theoretic models, let alone computer simulations in any strict sense. In other species the *alloparenting* behavior naturally takes a different form. A type of *alloparenting* common among many mammals is *allonursing* by giving milk to unrelated conspecifics. It has been researched in some detail for the evening bat *Nycticeius humeralis*, where "approximately 20% of nursing bouts involved females feeding unrelated pups" (Dugatkin, 1997, p. 109). Among the discussed benefits are the decrease of weight during foraging bouts following the nursing and the decrease of chances of infection as a consequence of not storing surplus milk in the mammary glands. Both of these advantages would fall under the category of byproduct mutualism (which is according to our definition of altruism in chapter 2.2 not altruistic). But there could be more to it. According to Dugatkin, who relates to a study by G.S. Wilkinson, females are more likely to nurse unrelated female pups than unrelated male pups (Dugatkin, 1997, p. 109), which may be due to the fact that the males disperse. If this is true then this means that some degree of reciprocity is also involved. Another variant of *alloparenting* which has been described for Rodriques fruit bats consists in the provision of assistance in the birth process by unrelated females ("midwives") (Dugatkin, 1997, p. 109). Though it has not been determined how the altruistic behavior has evolved in this case, it is reasonable to assume that it is somehow connected with the extremely social nature of the long-lived individuals of this bat species. Again, if this is true, bat-"midwives" would at best be described as reciprocal altruists (Dugatkin, 1997, p. 109). Given the social nature of this species, one might – by drawing a somewhat risky comparison – speculate if these altruistic acts may not somehow resemble the sort of friendship altruism among humans that goes beyond the "bookkeeping kind of altruism" that reciprocal altruism is often assumed to be (Silk, 2003). But this is of course just a speculation.

Staying with the bats, one of the classical examples of animal altruism is that of blood sharing among vampire bats (Dugatkin, 1997, p. 113/114). Empirical research indicates that it is a mixture of both kin selection and reciprocal altruism. Again, the precise conditions (i.e. payoffs) cannot be measured, but several indications make the assumption highly plausible that reciprocal altruism is involved: 1) A high probability of future interaction, 2) the relatively cheap cost of providing a meal in comparison to the benefit of receiving one (the latter can be a question of life and death), which means that the threshold to offering an altruistic benefit is low, and 3) the ability of the vampire bats to recognize one another (Dugatkin, 1997, p. 114). *Alloparenting* behavior is also documented for many primate species, though here it typically does not include the provision of food by the allomothers and usually the allomothers are immature animals (Dugatkin, 1997, p. 138) so that they do not fall under the strict definition of *alloparenting* any more.

Alarm Signals   Yet another type of potentially altruistic behavior that has attracted the interest of researchers is that of giving alarm calls or alarm signals. As in many of the other instances of possibly altruistic behavior the empirical data is often too scarce to decide in any specific case whether giving an alarm call really constitutes an instance of altruistic behavior or not. In willow tits the giving of alarm calls seems to be related to the place in the dominance hierarchy and thus probably falls into the category of byproduct mutualism as the benefits derived by the survival of group members as a consequence of giving a call depend on the position of the group member. However, reciprocity has also been suggested in this context (Dugatkin, 1997, p. 86). In other bird species, downy woodpeckers and black-capped chickadees, alarm calls mainly serve the purpose of mate protection, which is demonstrated by the fact that alarm calls are not given in same sexed flocks. Then alarm calls do not provide an example of altruism but of byproduct mutualism. Still, byproduct mutualism sometimes is the first step in an evolutionary history that may eventually lead to altruism. As Dugatkin imparts, byproduct mutualism typically evolves in harsh environments. In this case the "harshness" consists in "the decreased probability of acquiring new mates" (Dugatkin, 1997, p. 86). In terms of chances of reproduction it may pay off to risk one's own survival (by giving an alarm call) in order to increase the probability of survival of a mate. Regarding the different explanations for the same type of behavior in willow tits, chickadees and woodpeckers, it should be borne in mind that it is not necessarily the case that the same type of behavior has the same evolutionary causes if it occurs in different species.

Another species for which alarm calls have been studied quite extensively are Belding's ground squirrels. Here it is quite well assessed that kinship based altruism is the decisive factor for giving alarm calls. For, typically alarm calls are given by females, and in this species females are sedentary and breed near their natal sites, while males leave their natal sites (Dugatkin, 1997, p. 97/98). The hypothesis is further strengthened by the observation "that 'invading' (non-native) females gave alarm calls less frequently than native females." (Dugatkin, 1997, p. 98). A fairly well known example of alarm calls is that of alarm calls in vervets provided by Cheney and Seyfarth in their book "How monkeys see the world". Among other things Cheney and Seyfarth found out that the vervets' alarm calls vary depending on whether the approaching predator is a leopard or an eagle or a snake, with a different reaction elicited by the respective alarm call in each case. With respect to altruism the important question is whether the alarm call is really given with the intention to warn other conspecifics as opposed to the possible intention to signal to the predating animal that it does not need to bother because it has been detected (Dugatkin, 1997, p. 136/137.). But the former is obviously the case as different alarm calls elicit different escape reactions. As alarm calls are given with a higher probability either if offspring is present or if mates are present (in the latter case there exists again a further dependency on the dominance hierarchy), kinship and byproduct mutualism provide the most plausible explanations.

That giving alarm signals does not necessarily need to be an instance of altruistic behavior and not even a form of byproduct mutualism is illustrated by the stotting behavior that occurs in Thomson's gazelles (and also in some other less well studied species), a curious kind of behavior "wherein individuals take all four legs off the ground simultaneously and hold them straight and stiff in the air" (Dugatkin, 1997, p. 94). From numerous hypotheses that have been put forth to explain stotting only two could be confirmed according to Dugatkin, namely that stotting is meant to inform the predator of the health of the stotting animal (which means that the predator will know that the stotting animal will be difficult to catch and will rather "lock on" some other individual) and that young animals stott to attract the attention of their mother in dangerous situations (Dugatkin, 1997, p. 95). In both cases altruism or cooperation is not involved.

Grooming Most of the examples of cooperative or altruistic behavior among animals so far have been examples of kin selection or byproduct mutualism, but in spite of the fact that there is a strong "skew towards reciprocity in the theoretical literature" (Dugatkin, 1997, p. 167) there have been very few clearcut cases of reciprocal altruism, let alone of group selection. One kind of behavior that from its very appearance seems to fit the conception of reciprocal altruism quite well and is often mentioned as a kind of role model in this context is that of grooming. Dugatkin relates several studies about grooming in primates as well as other mammal species. One non-primate species where grooming has been studied are impala, an antilope species. It is at the same time one of the rare examples that really fits the model of a repeated game – at least on a qualitative level. According to Dugatkin who refers to two studies from Hart and Hart and Mooring and Hart, impala exchange bouts of grooming, each bout consisting of a repeated "upward sweep of the tongue or the lower incisors along the neck of the partner" (Dugatkin, 1997, p. 91). These exchanges of grooming bouts expose several striking features which strongly suggest that grooming in impala is an instance of pure reciprocal altruism: 1) There is an almost perfect match between bouts of grooming received and bouts delivered; 2) the exchange of bouts ends after one partner stops allogrooming. This rules out the possibility of byproduct mutualism, which could otherwise offer an explanation if it is assumed that ticks provide some extra nutrition for the impala; 3) there is no correlation with the rank in the dominance hierarchy (Dugatkin, 1997, p. 91-94). All in all, this finally seems to be a clearcut example for the kind of reciprocal altruism that is described by the repeated Prisoner's Dilemma model. However, even in this case the match between model and empirical reality can be ascertained only on the basis of qualitative similarity because a quantitative measurement of the payoff parameters has not been done.

Grooming is also one of the most salient behavioral features of our closest relatives in the animal world, the primates, and therefore has caught a lot of attention by researchers. The patterns of grooming exchanges among primates are much more complex than among the impala just described. In primates, grooming can serve many different functions next to the purpose of removing ectoparasites. Among these are the reduction of tension (which could otherwise result in conflicts), coalition formation, where grooming serves as a means to "bribe" others to become allies, and, more general, grooming as an "exchange currency" to gain other favors in return. While all these describe possible benefits of grooming, Dugatkin notices that in most studies very little is said about the costs of grooming (Dugatkin, 1997, p. 117). But certainly there are costs. Apart from the time and energy spent, it has been recorded that the lowered attention of mothers engaged in grooming activities results in their unattended offspring being significantly more often being harassed by other animals (Dugatkin, 1997, p. 117/118). There is good evidence that grooming is to a certain degree reciprocal in chimpanzees, though the reciprocal nature of grooming is not as clear cut as in the case of impala. In vervets (Meerkatzen) the relation of grooming and coalition forming has been studied. Here grooming does increase the probability of responding to solicitation calls for unrelated animals but not for related animals (where the probability of responding is high, anyway). These results are not completely undisputed (Dugatkin, 1997, p. 120), but if they are true, then it appears to be a case of reciprocal altruism because kinship can be ruled out and, as there exists an opportunity for cheating (groomed animals could fail to respond to solicitation calls), byproduct mutualism can be ruled out as well. Further kinds of grooming in exchange for "goods and services" have been documented in chimpanzees and macaques. In chimpanzees grooming sometimes is related to food exchange (Dugatkin, 1997, p. 123). In an experiment conducted by Stammbach, a single subordinate member of a group of macaques was trained to operate a complex lever mechanism for food release (from which all group members could eat). While the subordinate "specialist" did not rise in rank, it received significantly more grooming than before by other group members. The acts of grooming did, however, not take place in strict connection with acts of operating the mechanism (Dugatkin, 1997, p. 124). So, if any kind of reciprocity is involved here, it is not the strict type of "bookkeeping reciprocity" that the repeated Prisoner's Dilemma model suggests. Quite a lot of studies on primates emphasize the factor of kinship in grooming (Dugatkin, 1997, p. 124).

Eusociality   The most astonishing example of cooperation in the animal kingdom is that which is found in bee hives or ant hills, where a large state of insects operates in what appears to be an extremely cooperative and coordinated manner. Biologists call these kinds of insects *eusocial insects*, where *eusociality* is defined by three criteria: 1) Reproductive division of labour, 2) communal care for the young and 3) overlapping generations of workers in the colony. Eusociality is not only found in insect species like bees, wasps, ants, termites but also in certain vertebrates like naked mole rats and Darmland mole rats. When one compares the forms of cooperation that take place in eusocial animals with the other instances of cooperative behavior that have been described in this chapter one cannot help but notice the extraordinary qualitative difference that eusociality makes for cooperation and altruism. Eusocial animals do not just cooperate with respect to a single function (like grooming in mammals) but they seem to cooperate in any possible form and manner. Of the many possible examples of cooperative behavior among eusocial insects, Dugatkin describes in more detail the cooperative behavior of honey bees in foraging, hive thermoregulation and anti-predator behavior. When foraging, honey bees cooperate in different ways. They inform each other about the location of food resources via the famous "waggle dance" and they coordinate their foraging activity with regard to the level of food supply in the hive in a complex manner (Dugatkin, 1997, p. 152/153). Hive thermoregulation is achieved by the bees behaving in such a way as to keep the temperature inside the bee hive at an ideal 35 degrees Celsius. As the temperature of the whole hive only marginally depends on the activity of a single bee, this raises a typical collective goods problem, where one would expect that the individual bees are encouraged to cheat. But in fact they do not (Dugatkin, 1997, p. 154/155). Even more admirable is the self sacrificial behavior of honey bees for the defense of their colony. Because honey bees die when stinging, this behavior appears to be an extreme case of altruism to the advantage of the colony.

How is the astonishing variety of forms of cooperative behavior as well as the intensity that altruistic behavior reaches in eusocial animals to be explained? The best known explanation is that by inclusive fitness. It has been found out that eusocial insects are haplodiploid species, where the males carry only a single (haploid) set of chromosomes while the females have a double (diploid) set of chromosomes. The female descendants of the queen all share the same genes from their father and on average 50% of their mother's genes. In consequence, the worker sisters are on average 75% related to each other. Thus cooperation in eusocial insects is easily explained by kinship, one should think. But there are problems with applying the inclusive-fitness-theory to eusocial animals. One problem is that there exist eusocial species where the queen has multiple matings and others where there are several queens in one colony (Dugatkin, 1997, p. 144). Therefore, kinship cannot be the only explanation for eusociality. Dugatkin discusses in this context a number of alternative hypotheses on eusociality (Dugatkin, 1997, p. 144-149). But rather than entering into the complex debate about these hypotheses, which for a layman would be difficult to present accurately anyway, I confine myself to a few general reflections on eusociality as an example for the evolution of cooperation.

In order to do so, I distinguish between two different questions: 1) Why do the workers in the colonies not reproduce? Or in other words, why did centralized reproduction evolve and how is it maintained? 2) Given that the workers cannot reproduce, why do they cooperate? I am going to answer the second question first because it seems to be an almost trivial question. If, for whatever concrete reason, the workers really cannot reproduce individually, then it follows that the best thing they can do to spread their genes is to cooperate as well and as completely as possible with the rest of the colony. For, imagine that due to a mutation some of the worker ants hatching in an anthill were lazy ants that did nothing to contribute to the colony. Then although the lazy ants would greatly profit from letting the others do all the work, they would not be able transform this advantage into greater reproductive success within the hive simply because they cannot reproduce themselves. At the same time the anthill as a whole would suffer increased selection pressure from other anthills without lazy ants. One could say that the scenario that explains the cooperation within eusocial species is that of group selection, only that the within-group selection that counteracts the evolution of altruism in group selection models is inhibited. Therefore, in order to produce altruism, evolution only has to solve the technical problem of coordinating the behavior of the eusocial insects as well as possible but evolution does not have to resolve a conflict of reproductive interests any more, which in non-eusocial species acts against the emergence of altruism. This explains both the extraordinary intensity of altruistic behavior (up to self-sacrifice!) as well as the great variety of cooperative behavior in eusocial species. Strictly speaking, however, our definition of altruism in chapter 2.2 would preclude calling the cooperative behavior of eusocial insects altruistic if the "benefits" in the definition are understood in terms of reproductive fitness. Because the workers in a colony do not reproduce, no fitness costs are incurred by them by acting altruistically.

Given that the altruistic behavior of eusocial animals is easily explained by (uninhibited) group selection, the remaining question is, how did the workers ever become so altruistic as to stop reproducing individually and why do they remain so? It is in answer to this question that other mechanisms like inclusive fitness or byproduct mutualism come into play. In mole rats, Dugatkin maintains, it was byproduct mutualism forwarded by harsh environmental conditions such as successive prolonged droughts in the evolutionary history of certain mole rat species that caused the evolution of eusociality:

> ... at the evolutionary onset of cooperation in naked mole rats, when reproductive division of labor was likely minimal, a "harsh environment" central to byproduct mutualism, rather than kinship per se, may have been the predominant selective agent. (Dugatkin, 1997, p. 106)

Differently from typical eusocial insect species, mole rats have a diploid set of chromosomes, which once more shows that eusociality does not by necessity depend on the genetics of a haplodiploid set of chromosomes. Still, it is plausible to assume that the close kinship ties in haplodiploid species facilitate the evolutionary transition to a reproductive division of labor because the fitness cost of giving up individual reproduction in favor of centralized reproduction in a colony is much lower if the relatedness is close. The mechanisms by which the reproductive division of labor is maintained do – as one should expect – also vary from species to species. For honeybees, for example, a mechanism called "worker 'policing' " has been described, where the males that hatch from worker laid eggs[5] are killed by other workers. The behavior is probably best explained by kinship. (If the queen has multiple matings, workers are more related to their brothers than to their nephews (Dugatkin, 1997, p. 150).) But Dugatkin also suggests that group selection may play a role "in that without policing a much greater degree of within-colony aggression would exist, and this, in turn, could decrease group productivity" (Dugatkin, 1997, p. 151). Another obvious way to ensure the monopoly of reproduction is aggression on part of the queen by which the workers are coerced into their role. This has been reported for the previously mentioned mole rats (Dugatkin, 1997, p. 106).

If the alleged altruism of eusocial species is easily explained by the reproductive division of labor, then the cooperation of several queens in one colony must still be explained by the other mechanisms of the evolution of altruism. And indeed, here we can find some striking cases of reciprocal altruism and even group selection. One such case is the "social contract" that is found in paper wasps (*polistes fuscatus*) (Dugatkin, 1997, p. 157/158). In paper wasps dominant queens tolerate other, subordinate queens in their nest. Both dominant and subordinate queens lay queen-destined as well as worker-destined eggs. But subordinate queens disappear by the time the workers emerge. Cooperation between dominant and subordinate queens requires that they leave each other's eggs unharmed. Experimental research has shown that subordinate queens reacted aggressively to simulated oophagy on queen destined eggs, but not on worker destined eggs, while the dominant queen did not show such a reaction. This strongly hints to reciprocal altruism on part of the subordinate queens. The suggested reason why dominant queens do not react to simulated oophagy at all is that they can still produce queen-destined eggs after the subordinates are gone, while the subordinates themselves do not get a second chance. For the dominant queen it is a different deal, so to speak.

An example of cooperation between colony founding queens that is probably due to group selection can be found in desert seed harvester ants (*Messor pergandei*) (Dugatkin, 1997, p. 159). For some populations of this species it has been observed that the queens jointly produce workers when founding a colony. Once the workers have emerged, the queens fight to the death until only one queen is left. Another feature of the desert seed harvester ant is that different colonies are engaged in brood raiding against each other. According to Dugatkin's account, the

---

[5]In honeybees workers lay eggs, but these are unfertilized and only develop into males, whereas the queen can control which of her eggs are fertilized and thus develop into females and which are not fertilized and develop into males.

following holds:

> In the case of *M. pergandei*, the trait of interest is the pro-
> duction of workers, which, although selected against within
> groups (via the cheater problem), may be selected for as groups
> with many cooperators survive brood raiding (i.e. differential
> productivity of groups). (Dugatkin, 1997, p. 160)

As the relative isolation of groups is a vital requirement for group selection to operate towards the evolution of cooperation, it is no surprise
that the cooperative behavior only occurs in populations of *M. pergandei* "where environmental factors aggregate starting colonies, which
occur only in the sandy ravine bottoms where soil moisture is available" (Dugatkin, 1997, p. 160). Other populations of the same species
that live in different habitats do not display cooperative behavior in the
founding phase of a colony, but here queens react aggressively to any
rival right from the beginning (Dugatkin, 1997, p. 160/161). The conclusion that cooperation in *M. perganei* is a result of group selection has
not gone completely undisputed however. As in this case – just as in
any other of the empirical instances of the evolution of cooperation in
biology described so far – no quantitative measurement of payoffs could
be made, it is of course difficult to assess these findings beyond what
can be deduced from the mere phenomenology of this instance of cooperation. Still, similar results have also been obtained for another ant
species, *Acromymes versicolor* (Dugatkin, 1997, p. 161), which bestows
the explanation by group selection in this case with some additional
credibility.

**Discussion: Do the computer models of altruism live up to the empirical
research in biology?**

The list of examples of cooperative and altruistic behavior among animals that has just been given is, of course, far from being complete.
Still, it shows how far reaching and varied the forms of cooperative
behavior that exist in nature are. But apart from this scientific fact,
which is certainly interesting in its own right, our main concern here is
to find out in how far the kind of modeling of altruism that has been
demonstrated in the previous chapter proves to be helpful for the understanding of the empirical instances of altruism and, if not, what are
the causes for this failure. In order to tackle these questions we must
distinguish different levels of the application of formal models and in
particular of computer simulations to the empirical problem:

1. *Conceptual Level*: On this level the model is merely meant to demonstrate how a certain mechanism works in principle. For this purpose it is not necessary that the model is empirically very adequate or that the parameter values used in the model are based on more than plausible assumptions. Still, the model cannot be arbitrary. It must at least give us some indication of how the empirical phenomenon can be identified as one that falls within the class of phenomena which the model describes. For example, repeated Prisoner's Dilemma models of reciprocal altruism indicate that there must be repeated interaction and that the situation should be a (repeated) dilemma situation, not just one where the participants profit from their interaction anyway, as in byproduct mutualism. This alone – as the previous brief survey of empirical examples has shown – can already be difficult to determine.

2. *Application Level*: At this level we require that there is a close concordance between the model itself and the empirical phenomenon or class of phenomena that the model describes (or "models"). The concordance must be close enough so that we can empirically determine 1) whether the model applies to the empirical phenomena in question and 2) whether it describes them correctly. If the model contains quantitative magnitudes as input or output values then this implies that we must be able to measure these magnitudes in some way or other.

We will elaborate on these two categories of models a little more in chapter 6. Here the distinction is made mainly to preclude a certain defense strategy that is often used to excuse spurious modeling. This defense strategy consists in replying, whenever somebody calls into question that the model fits empirical reality, that it is just a model and that from a model, being by definition a strongly simplified representation of reality, one cannot expect a representation of the modeled empirical situation that is accurate in every possible respect. However, as not every model can be a model for anything, there must be a limit up to which this excuse is acceptable. And this limit certainly depends on what claim is connected with the model. If the claim is that the model can actually be applied, the requirements are certainly higher than when it is just meant to give expression to a certain idea or concept.

Regarding the empirical examples from biology that have been presented so far, it can safely be concluded that *not a single one* of the simulation models of the kind that have been presented in chapter 4 proved to be applicable in a strict sense. In the beginning of his book on "Cooperation among Animals" (Dugatkin, 1997) Dugatkin lists a whole array of such models. But even though he is extremely sympathetic towards this approach, he almost nowhere in his book refers to any of these models. There is no instance – except one which ultimately turned out to be a failure (see chapter 5.1.3) – where the empirical research he presents is related or can be related to any of the theoretical simulation models. The reasons for this are hinted at by Dugatkin himself in the last chapter of his book: Save for one exception, Dugatkin was not able to present a single empirical study where the payoff parameters, which are crucial for the application of any game theoretical model, have been or could be measured. The one exception concerns an experimental study on blue jays, where blue jays could trigger a "cooperate" or a "defect" button (Dugatkin, 1997, p. 80/81) and thereby release food according to a Prisoner's Dilemma game matrix or – in a second experiment – according to a stag hunt game matrix (which is one way to circumscribe byproduct mutualism in game theoretical terms). The result was that blue jays never cooperated in the Prisoner's Dilemma, even though it was repeated, and always cooperated in the stag hunt game. The authors of the experiment concluded that no strategies for interaction in the repeated Prisoner's Dilemma have evolved in blue jays, which leads them to doubt the "general significance of the Prisoner's Dilemma as a model of non-kin cooperation." (Dugatkin, 1997, quoted p. 80). Notwithstanding this skeptical conclusion about the Prisoner's Dilemma as a proper model for non-kin cooperation, Dugatkin regards it at least as a serious attempt to address the issue of quantifying the payoff matrix (Dugatkin, 1997, p. 165). This can surely be granted, but it is still a long way until a satisfatory mode of quantification will be reached. For, in order to quantify the payoff matrix we would need to know the payoff values in terms of reproductive fitness and not merely in terms of food release, which does most probably not transform proportionally into relative numbers of offspring.

If this was the only example where the empirical research was approaching the measurement of payoff paramaters and if – as we have seen in chapter 4 – the computer models of altruism crucially depend on the values of the payoff parameters then this means that the level of empirical applicability of these models has not yet been reached – at least not at the time when Dugatkin compiled his surveying study on "Cooperation among Animals" (1997).[6]

But what about the conceptual level? If the computer models are not (yet) really applicable, do they perhaps help us to form sound concepts and provide us with categories of analysis? Even on the conceptual

---

[6]This still seems to be true today (see the following section).

level, it has in many cases been difficult to decide which type of altruism is at work in a specific case and whether it is altruism at all and not merely byproduct mutualism. At the same time, game theoretical models (though not game theoretical models alone) allow for a relatively sharp conceptualization of different types of altruism, which is helpful even if these types do in many instances not appear in a pure form in nature (grooming among impala being one of the few exceptions). One could say that on this level they serve a similar function as the "ideal types" do in the social sciences according to Max Weber: Even though they contain very strong abstractions they can help to get a better grip on empirical reality. The heuristic benefits of game theoretical thinking for the understanding of altruism become apparent in the case of grooming among primates. Here, as Dugatkin notices (Dugatkin, 1997, p. 117), behavioral ecologists have mostly focused on the benefits of grooming but not often asked the question of the costs of this type of behavior. This is quite understandable from the point of view of behavioral ecologists because from its very appearance the grooming behavior does more strongly suggest to ask the question of what it is good for than the question of its costs (which even might seem quite negligible at first sight). But from the theoretical perspective it is clear that the question of why this kind of potentially altruistic behavior evolved is a question of benefits *and* costs. Thus, theoretical reflection on models of altruism, even if they are toy models, may help to direct the empirical research in a useful manner.

This said, there is of course an important caveat that has to be mentioned right away. The benefits just described of modeling on the conceptual level (clarifying and sharpening our concepts, directing empirical research) only hold for the most elementary and simple models, but not for complicated models, massive simulations and in general the whole baroque richesse of theoretical models and simulations that can be derived from any simple model by changing parameters, adding further "plausible" conditions etc. Judged against the background of the empirical findings that are summarized in Dugatkin's book (which, after all, is the book of an author who is very sympathetic towards the modeling approach), simulations in the fashion of those of which a small sample has been discussed in chapter 4.1.5 and of which a role model has been presented in detail in chapter 4.1.4 have turned out to be as good as completely useless. Neither did they provide us with important insights on the conceptual level that went beyond what can already be demonstrated by much simpler toy models, nor was any simulation of this type empirically applicable in the sense described above.

Given that the simulation models turned out to be largely useless for the explanation of the evolution of altruism in nature, the question is, of course, what are the reasons for this deplorable state of affairs. One possible explanation could be that most of the empirical research surveyed in Dugatkin's book was not designed to put any particular models of altruism or cooperation to the test, but that the behavioral ecologists conducting such research had other research interests. This might be especially true for the field research on cooperative behavior as opposed to the experimental research. Usually, there exists a time lag with which newly invented concepts and methods pervade a whole science. If this was true then maybe the only problem was that Dugatkin wrote his book too early, at a time when only a small part of the empirical research was informed by the latest models of the evolution of altruism? But then we should expect to find more usage of simulation models in the empirical research on altruism that has been published since. In order to check whether this is the case we will briefly examine a more recent example of the empirical research on altruism in the following section (section 5.1.2). It will turn out that just as little use could be made of simulation models as in any of Dugatkin's examples. In order to further pinpoint the difficulties that prevent the application of simulation models, or, more precisely, the brand of simulation models that has dominated the modeling of the "evolution of altruism" for a long time, I finally discuss in depth one of the few examples where biologists set out with Axelrod's and Hamilton's concept of reciprocal altruism but soon became aware of the limits of this theoretical background (see chapter 5.1.3).

5.1.2   A more recent example: Image scoring cleaner fish

The discussion of Dugatkin's survey on "Cooperation among Animals" has shown that there is a wide gap between the modeling of altruism and cooperation on the one hand and the empirical research on cooperative behavior among animals on the other hand. While the theoretical models did allow formulating certain concepts of altruism, it was not possible to relate the simulation models of altruism to the empirical instances of cooperative behavior in any more than a metaphorical sense. But is this limitation due to systematic difficulties of applying abstract simulation models or is it, maybe, just an interim problem that can ultimately be overcome by more refined empirical research methods? Since Dugatkin's survey dates from 1997 it is reasonable to ask whether the situation has changed till then. Therefore, we will look at one recent example of empirical research on altruism in biology. Again, the purpose of the discussion of this example is primarily epistemological. No claim is made that the examples discussed in the following, concern very important or representative types of altruism in nature (although they fit well into the overview of animal altruism given previously). We want to find out, how much use is made of theoretical models of altruism in typical empirical research studies.

The study concerns "Image scoring and cooperation in a cleaner fish mutualism" (Bshary and Grutter, 2006). *Image scoring* is variant of reciprocal altruism, where cooperation depends on whether the partner has been seen to cooperate with others. Image scoring is thus a type of indirect reciprocity because it is the altruistic act that has been bestowed unto someone else that is being reciprocated. The rationale behind indirect reciprocity is that someone who has behaved cooperatively towards someone else may also behave cooperatively to oneself. Another type of indirect reciprocity that does only occur among humans is reputation based cooperation, where one gains reputation by cooperating with people that have a high reputation. Differently from mere image scoring, reputation can be passed on by telling about it. Image scoring only requires that the partner's behavior is observed in a similar situation. In contrast to reputation based cooperation the cognitive requirements for image scoring are therefore only comparatively low. In fact they may be even lower than the cognitive requirements for the evolution of altruism in repeated Prisoner's Dilemma situations because for image scoring no bookkeeping or partner recognition is required so that it does not come as a surprise that image scoring behavior can be found even among relatively "primitive" animals.

In the cleaner fish *Labroides dimidiatus* (also known as Striped Cleaner Wrasse, or in German: "Putzerlippfisch") that Bshary and Grutter experimented with, the clients "invite" the cleaner fish for inspection. The cleaner fish then usually feed upon the ectoparasites of the client. But they could also feed on the mucus of the client and there is evidence that the mucus is actually their preferred nourishment. Thus, the cleaner fish can either cooperate by removing the ectoparasites or cheat by munching the client's mucus. The client on the other hand cannot cheat the cleaners. Due to the asymmetry of the situation, cooperation could not have been evolved via direct reciprocity. That image scoring is a potential candidate for the explanation of cleaner fish cooperation is suggested by field research on cleaner fish according to which: "Client fish almost always invite a cleaner's inspection if they witnessed that the cleaner's last interaction ended without conflict, invite less if they do not have such knowledge, and invite the least if the last interaction ended with conflict." (Bshary and Grutter, 2006, p. 975).

In order to test the image scoring hypothesis Bshary and Grutter conducted two experiments, one on the client behavior and one on the behavior of the cleaner fish. In the first of these experiments a client was placed in the middle of an aquarium divided by one-way mirrors into three basins. In one of the side basins a group of cleaner fish fed on prawns attached to a model client fish. In the other side basin a group of cleaners was placed without a model. The result of this experiment was that the client spent significantly more time near the group of cleaners that was engaged in cleaning activity. This result suggests the conclusion that clients prefer cleaners that can be observed to be cooperative over cleaners with an unknown cooperation level.

The second experiment was more complicated. This time the cleaners were placed in either an image scoring or a non image scoring scenario. In both scenarios the client fish was simulated by plates to each of which two different types of food items, fish flakes and prawn items, were attached. *Labroides dimidiatus* prefers prawns to fish flakes just like it prefers mucus to ectoparasites. The question that the experiment was intended to answer was whether the cleaner fish would cooperate by feeding against their preferences in the image scoring scenario. In both the image scoring and the non image scoring scenario the cleaner fish could feed from two identical plates. In the image scoring scenario both plates would be removed immediately after one prawn item was eaten from one of the plates, while in the non image scoring scenario only the plate from which the prawn item was eaten was removed. To make sure that the cooperative or non cooperative behavior did not merely depend on the sheer amount of nourishment available a third scenario was tested, where the cleaner fish could feed only on one plate which was also removed immediately after a prawn item was eaten. The result was that in the image-scoring scenario the cleaner fish fed significantly more often against their preference when feeding on the first plate than when feeding on the second plate or a single plate or when feeding on the first plate in the non-image-scoring scenario.

The experimental results thus strengthen the assumption that cooperation in cleaner fish is due to image scoring. It is noteworthy that the cleaner fish do not merely react to the presence of another client, a condition which was fulfilled in the image scoring and the non image scoring scenario, but to the reaction of the other client that is present. This means that the cleaner fish do only cooperate if the clients actually engage in image scoring.

Now the crucial question for our purpose, the assessment of the value of theoretical models for the empirical research, is whether and to what level Bshary and Grutter could draw upon theoretical models of the evolution of cooperation. Bshary and Grutter do not make more than passing mention of the mathematical models and computer simulations on image scoring (Bshary and Grutter, 2006, p. 975). Not to enter upon a discussion of these models is quite reasonable for them as the specific features of these models remain completely irrelevant for their empirical research. It is only the basic concept of indirect reciprocity that Bshary and Grutter draw upon for their empirical research. The concept of simple indirect reciprocity requires "image scoring by clients and an increased level of cooperation by cleaners in the presence of image-scoring clients" (Bshary and Grutter, 2006, p. 796). Both these requirements have been tested experimentally by Bshary and Grutter. Again, we find a concordance of theoretical modeling and empirical research only on a basic conceptual level.

5.1.3 An in-depth example: Do sticklebacks play the repeated Prisoner's Dilemma?

In order to show what difficulties the attempt to apply the models of reciprocal altruism meets in practice, I discuss in the following an example where biologists tried to apply the theory of the "evolution of cooperation" of Axelrod and Hamilton (Axelrod, 1984) (which is based on computer simulations that have been a role model to the ones presented above) to a case of altruistic behavior in nature. The example concerns a behavioral trait called "predator inspection" that is found in certain types of shoal fish like sticklebacks. The behavior of "predator inspection" has among others been examined in two empirical studies by Manfred Milinski and Milinski and Geoffrey Parker. The earlier of these two studies (Milinski, 1987) still draws heavily on Axelrod's and Hamilton's model of the repeated Prisoner's Dilemma. The other study that has been described in a paper that appeared ten years later (Milinski and Parker, 1997) and employs a totally different theoretical interpretation of the results. As I try to demonstrate in the following, both studies taken together show that the choice of an appropriate formal description of reciprocal altruism (or cooperation) raises very difficult and often by no means unambiguous questions of interpretation and measurement. Against this background any game theoretical model research that is not closely linked to empirical questions must appear like a pure "Glasperlenspiel".[7]

"Predator inspection" is a behavior that is found (among other

---

[7]That this has nothing to do with the usual gap between theory and practice or between theoretical and empirical research but reflects a specific impasse of the modeling approaches in evolutionary game theory will have become clear at the end of this section and will be discussed again in chapter 6.

species) in sticklebacks. Sticklebacks are small fish living in shoals. If a predator (a pike for example) comes within a certain range of the shoal, it can be observed that either a single stickleback or a pair of sticklebacks leaves the shoal and carefully approaches the predator. The sticklebacks do so in order to inspect the predator, presumably to gain information about the type, size, location and movement of the predator. Typically, a pair of sticklebacks gets much closer to the predator than a single stickleback. If the sticklebacks approach as a pair, it can be observed that they advance with characteristic jerky movements in such a way that one stickleback swims a short distance ahead and then "waits" for the other, who follows in a similar jerky movement (Milinski, 1987, p. 433). This suggests interpreting the sequence of jerky movements as a repeated Prisoner's Dilemma, where the sticklebacks play *Tit for Tat*. In his earlier paper Milinski tried to confirm this assumption by simulating the partner stickleback with different types of mirrors so that the mirrored fish either appeared at the same distance from the predator (simulating a cooperative partner) or a little bit further behind (simulating a non cooperative partner). The result was that the sticklebacks advanced much closer to the predator when they were accompanied by a cooperative partner. Milinski interpreted this result as an empirical confirmation of Axelrod's and Hamilton's theory of cooperation. By and large this seems correct if we ignore for a moment the fact that the results of Axelrod's and Hamilton's simulations were more contingent than was known at that time. But there exists a problem in so far that Milinski confines himself to assessing that the two inequalities $T > R > P > S$ and $2R > T + S$ hold. Now, as the simulation results above show, the simulation is sensitive to changes in the concrete values of the payoff parameters, and unfortunately these would be very hard to measure in the case of the sticklebacks.

After much further experimental research on sticklebacks in the later paper, Milinski and Parker offer quite a different formal description of the same behavioral trait of "predator inspection". There is not much talk about the repeated Prisoner's Dilemma any more. While it is still true that the situation of two sticklebacks approaching a predator can (at a certain distance range) be interpreted as a Prisoner's Dilemma, this assertion alone does not shed much light on the problem. Instead of meddling with the Prisoner's Dilemma, Milinski and Parker therefore examined the possible utility calculus that controls the behavior of the sticklebacks.[8] According to Milinski and Parker, even a single stickle-

---

[8]In the following Milinski's and Parker's construction will only be described in general terms. For the mathematical details see Milinski and Parker (1997). A major problem of this construction, which is also the reason why Milinski and Parker only reach an ambiguous conclusion, is that the fitness benefits of

back will approach a predator up to the point where the advantages (of gaining information about the predator) are balanced by the risk of being eaten (Milinski and Parker, 1997, p. 1241/1242). For the case when two sticklebacks jointly approach the predator, Milinski and Parker offer two alternative descriptions one that assumes cooperation (Milinski and Parker, 1997, p. 1242) and another one that does not necessarily presuppose cooperation (Milinski and Parker, 1997, p. 1242-1245). Milinski and Parker do not ultimately reach a decision which of these descriptions is the right one. For, even if one does not assume cooperation, two fish will – according to their model description – move closer to the predator than a single fish. The reason is this: The distance to the predator can be divided into three zones, the "far zone", the "match zone" and the "near zone". In the "far zone" that is, when the distance to the predator is still very great, each of the two fish gets an advantage from moving closer to the predator, even if the other fish stays back. In the "match zone" (medium distance to the predator) a partner that has fallen behind will try to catch up with its forerunner, although neither of the two partners gets an advantage from taking the lead (from which it follows that both fish can only advance synchronously if one does not assume at least a minimum of reciprocal altruism). Finally, in the "near zone" the "best reply" of each fish is to stay back behind the other one.

If there are two different theoretical descriptions of the behavior of a pair of "inspecting" sticklebacks, one that assumes cooperation between the sticklebacks and one that does not, then this raises the question which of these is true or whether the sticklebacks in reality cooperate or do not cooperate when jointly inspecting a predator. At the time of writing the second paper Milinski and Parker come to the conclusion that the current state of research does not allow to decide this question: "However, it is not yet possible to analyze quantitatively whether pairs are conforming to the cooperative or non-cooperative ESS [Evolutionary Stable Strategy, E.A.]." (Milinski and Parker, 1997, p. 1245) How can this result be reconciled with their earlier study that seemed to confirm Axelrod's and Hamilton's theory of the "evolution of cooperation"?

---

inspection can only be guessed. While it is plausible to assume that the benefits decrease with decreasing distance from the predator, there exist no exact measurement procedures for the benefits. Therefore, both the type of the function (Milinski and Parker present two alternatives, an exponentially decreasing and a linearly decreasing function) and its parameter values can only be guessed. – In response to a criticism that appeared slightly earlier, Dugatkin, who worked theoretically and empirically on the same topic as Milinski, still defends the notion that predator inspection behavior is best understood as a *Tit for Tat* strategy (Dugatkin, 1996). But he misses out the problem that the respective Prisoner's Dilemma models are notoriously unstable and he seems to assume that there exist only the two alternatives to explain the behavior of predator inspection either as the outcome of a reiterated Prisoner's Dilemma or as byproduct mutualism. But as the later paper from Milinski and Parker (Milinski and Parker, 1997) suggests, these are not the only alternatives to conceive of predator inspection (see the main text below).

The answer is that obviously the earlier conclusions have been drawn too rashly, probably due to a subtle misconception in the earlier experiment's setup: An uncooperative fitness maximizing fish would never have behaved as the uncooperative fish simulated by the mirror did. Therefore, the reaction of the real fish that stopped at a specific distance from the predator does not necessarily need to be interpreted as a "punishment" which is part of a *Tit for Tat* like strategy. The distance at which the real fish stopped may just have been its optimal distance (from a purely "egoistic" point of view) given the presence and distance of the simulated partner fish.

The result shows how difficult it is, even in a biological context, to apply simulation models of reciprocal altruism such as those described above. The repeated Prisoner's Dilemma does not seem to be an appropriate model for the sort of behavior Milinski examined. As has been shown previously, other examples for reciprocal altruism from biology meet the same difficulties. The same conclusion is confirmed by other biologists that work in the field of evolutionary game theory. An expert in this field, Peter Hammerstein, writes: "Why is there such a discrepancy between theory and facts? A look at the best known examples of reciprocity shows that simple models of repeated games do not properly reflect the natural circumstances under which evolution takes place. Most repeated animal interactions do not even correspond to repeated games." (Hammerstein, 2003a, p. 83) In face of the vast multitude of models of reciprocal altruism and the "evolution of cooperation" this is a rather sobering conclusion. Yet, it must be taken seriously. And if it is taken seriously, it strongly confirms the skepticism towards purely theoretical simulations that has already been expressed earlier. As it appears, "blind modeling" (that is modeling that is not informed by empirical research but relies only on plausible assumptions alone) is not a proper research tool that allows us to find anything out about reciprocal altruism beyond the merest truisms.

Is there really nothing that can be done about it? In a critical appraisal of the game theoretical computer simulations in biology, Dugatkin described the situation roughly as follows: In order for the models to contribute to scientific progress, models and empirical research must be part of a feedback loop that is, theoretical models may help to direct empirical research but then the insights and results of the empirical research must be "fed back" into the construction and refinement of models (Dugatkin, 1998, p. 54ff.). Obviously, the feedback loop was not closed, insofar as the bulk of simulations on the evolution of cooperation did never really take into account the restrictions and conditions of the empirical research on the subject. The question of the relation between empirical research and theoretical modeling will be elaborated a little more in chapter 6, where a *build to order principle* of computer modeling will be proposed, according to which models that aim to go beyond a merely conceptual level should always be constructed around empirically measurable quantities. That the burden of accommodation is thus laid on the theoreticians finds its justification in the fact that much stronger restrictions apply when devising measurement procedures (including the restriction that only certain quantities can be measured at all) than for the design of models which has become comparatively simple with the advent of computers.

5.2 Empirical findings in the social sciences

Empirical research on cooperation and altruism in the social sciences falls roughly into two different categories. One part of the empirical research consists of laboratory experiments, where the predictions of game theory are tested by letting subjects play different types of cooperation games. For this type of research subjects are placed in highly stylized and artificial laboratory situations. This allows creating situations which are somewhat similar to the highly abstract settings presupposed by mathematical models or computer simulations of cooperation. Although the laboratory experiments are usually not designed to match a particular model[9], they allow for some degree of comparison between theoretical results and empirical reality. Following as before the pars pro toto approach, I discuss two selected examples of this type of research and highlight the epistemological issues involved.

The other and more important part of empirical research on cooperation would be real world examples that potentially expose the patterns of cooperation predicted by the theory. In spite of the extreme popularity of Axelrod's book on the "Evolution of Cooperation" (Axelrod, 1984), there exist only relatively few empirical field studies that make use of the theory of the evolution of cooperation which is based on the repeated Prisoner's Dilemma.[10] Usually, such studies rather draw a sort of general inspiration from the ideas related to the repeated Prisoner's Dilemma model than relate to any simulation models in particular. But then – as has already become apparent in the biological case – the respective computer simulations are not really suitable for empirical application. For, it is often close to impossible to measure the relevant parameters, to exclude interferences of coefficients not captured by the theory or just to ascertain which kind of game is played in a given situation. In order to show what difficulties are involved when one tries to apply the results of computer simulations to real world problems, I discuss the application of the reiterated Prisoner's Dilemma model of the evolution of altruism to the "live and let live" system that evolved in the First World War among soldiers of opposing armies. This example is particularly well suited for demonstrating the epistemological

---

[9]They are rather designed with certain research questions in mind, taking into account the pragmatic restrictions of the laboratory and not always strictly relating to theoretical results.

[10]For an overview of the literature that relates to Axelrod's theory see (Axelrod and D'Ambrosio, 1994), (N.M.Gotts et al., 2003) or (Hoffmann, 2000). It is characteric that the the only empirical application scenario that the latter quotes is the ultimately failed attempt of Milinski to interpret the predator inspection behavior of sticklebacks in terms of the repeated Prisoner's Dilemma (see also chapter 5.1.3). All three surveys strengthen the impression that the modeling business is mostly self-contained and quite detached from the empirical research.

issues involved in the use of simulation models in the context of empirical research because it has originally been advanced as a showcase to demonstrate the power of the simulation based approach to the study of the evolution of altruism (Axelrod, 1984, p. 67-79). The example will be discussed in depth and it will be demonstrated that far from being a showcase for the use of simulation models it exposes some severe limitations of this method. The criticism will be elaborated thoroughly in the final chapter (chapter 6).

5.2.1 Laboratory experiments

The evolution of institutions

Laboratory experiments usually center around simple "standard" dilemma situations like the Prisoner's Dilemma or a public goods problem. One particular question that has been examined experimentally is that of how punishing institutions can evolve. The evolution of punishing institutions is a riddle because in those situations where a punishing institution would be needed to solve a dilemma, a new dilemma arises that precludes the evolution of punishing institutions. One such constellation has been examined experimentally by Gürerk, Irlenbusch and Rockenbach (Özgür Gürerk et al., 2006). They set up an experiment where subjects interact anonymously in a public goods dilemma for 30 rounds. Each subject can decide which amount of its income to donate for the provision of a public good. The return value was such that each subject profited strongly from the overall contributions, but still had an incentive to let the others pay the public good and not to contribute himself or herself. Typically, the provision of public goods degrades in such a situation after only a few rounds.[11] To make matters more interesting, the subjects could choose to join either of two groups, one group that was provided with a sanctioning institution and one that was sanctioning free. After each round, subjects could choose to change groups. The sanctioning institution worked in the following way: In the group with sanctioning, each participant was allowed to punish or reward other participants within the same group. Both punishment and rewards cost the punishing or rewarding subject one monetary unit. Persons punished would lose three monetary units, while persons rewarded would gain one monetary unit. (Punishments and rewards were issued in the same round after the contributions were made.) The de-

---

[11]It should be remembered that the provision of a public good is an N-person dilemma. In an N-person dilemma the evolution of reciprocal altruism faces much stronger barriers than in the 2-person dilemma, though it has indeed been demonstrated that there exists a theoretical possibility for conditional cooperation to be stable even in an N-person game (Taylor, 1997, p. 82ff.).

cision to punish or to reward was left entirely at the discretion of the participants. Since punishment was costly, the provision of punishment therefore constituted a second level free rider problem.

Although the authors of the experiment were not primarily concerned with studying evolutionary social processes, their experimental setup does in fact resemble a kind of group selection scenario with two levels of selection. On the within-group level selection takes place between a cooperative and a non cooperative strategy, both of which – as one could say – compete for players adopting them. At the same time a between group selection process takes place between the sanctioning and the non sanctioning group, which compete for group members. (See also chapter 4.3.3.) However, the situation does not exactly reflect the group selection model presented earlier, insofar as the groups do not merely differ in the composition but also by the presence or absence of the sanctioning institution and because – as will be seen – the selection pressure within the sanctioning group does not counteract the between-group selection pressure as it is assumed in the theoretically most interesting case of group selection (see chapter 4.3).

The result of the experiment was that after 30 rounds almost everybody had joined the group with the sanctioning institution and almost everybody cooperated almost entirely (i.e. donated almost all of the income to the provision of the public good). About 3/4 of the subjects in the sanctioning group did exert punishment. (Rewards proved to be far less effective, since they even had a slightly negative influence on cooperation, supposedly, because subjects thus rewarded conclude that they have given too much.) Interestingly, subjects that changed the group quickly adopted the behavior common in their new group, both with regard to cooperation and non cooperation and with regard to punishment and refraining from punishment. The main question that this experiment raises is why punishing behavior did not erode as did cooperation in the non sanctioning group. Given that punishment is a second order public good and that it thus raises a free rider problem that is structurally similar to the original social dilemma situation simulated in the experiment, this appears quite surprising. Several explanations are possible[12]: 1) Human beings are just not so rational as the theory of public goods assumes. Therefore, in some instances (second level problems) they provide goods, even though they would be better off cheating. But then, why didn't a more rational mode of behavior evolve if this would entail greater revenues? 2) The subjects come from a society where certain modes of behavior including punishment, revenge etc. have –

---

[12]Only some of these are discussed in Gürerk's, Irlenbusch's and Rockenbach's paper.

for whatever reason – already evolved and are now transferred by them to the game. 3) There exists a certain amount of conformism. That is, people imitate other people's behavior and only deviate if they have a strong incentive to do so. As the necessity of punishment decreases over time because people that tried to cheat and were punished have learned their lesson, conformism suffices to uphold punishing behavior before it can deteriorate (in the end the payoff disadvantage of punishers is about 2% compared to non punishing cooperators). In other words, the costs of punishment become small enough to fall under the conformism threshold. 4) There is also a possibility that the second level public goods problem falls into a category where it may even pay for a participant to provide the good all on his or her own even though nobody else is willing to share the cost. In order to find out whether the problem of providing costly punishment falls into this category of public goods problems, it would be necessary to measure the gain in the provision of the first level public good that is effected by the successful betterment of reluctant cooperators.

Having thus briefly discussed the results of a typical study of experimental economics, the question shall now be considered, how this can be related to simulation models of the kind that have been presented previously (chapter 4). There are a few things to say regarding this question: The setup of the experiment does not precisely fit any of the simulation models presented earlier, neither does it closely resemble any other particular simulation study that has been published on the evolution of cooperation. It follows the common pattern of public goods problems as they are also expressed in the respective models that illustrate the theory of public goods. Of course it would be easy to draw up a computer simulation that more or less resembles the experimental setup. But what could the goal and possible benefit of such an endeavor be? As experiments provide *prima facie* stronger evidence than any simulation, why would anything need to be demonstrated by a computer simulation that has already been shown experimentally? One might reason that computer simulations could be helpful for deciding between the four possible explanations given for the punishment cooperation above. But this would only be the case if the decision between these alternative explanations were one that did on one point or other rest on the question of the mere theoretical possibility of any of these and this is not the case, except perhaps for the last alternative for which, however, a simple calculation should suffice. In order to decide between the other three alternative explanations, further experiments or further measurements would be required, but not more models.

Still, experiments of economic behavior provide a type of empirical research where a close fit between model and empirical reality is comparatively easy to achieve. If indulging in computer simulations of the evolution of altruism appears so little rewarding because it is so far removed from any empirical problem of cooperation or altruism – an impression that was very much strengthened by the earlier discussion of the empirical literature on the evolution of altruism in biology – , experimental economics finally offers a basis where simulation models of the evolution of altruism and empirical research can be linked together in a more than merely metaphorical and story telling way. One might wonder why this should work in economics but not in biology. The probable reason is that for the simulations to be applied in biology it would be necessary to measure the reproduction relevant fitness payoff of certain types of behavior, which obviously is a task that is extremely difficult to accomplish in most cases. The one exceptional example given in Dugatkin's comprehensive empirical meta-study (Dugatkin, 1997) where payoff parameters were actually measured, was an experimental study about blue jays. And even in this case the measured payoff parameters did not resemble a payoff in terms of the reproduction rate (see page 160).

Experimental studies such as the one outlined above can potentially be linked to computer simulations because they take place in an artificial laboratory setting that is streamlined and simple enough to reproduce it in a mathematical model of a computer simulation. But at the same time experimental laboratory studies raise certain epistemological concerns of their own, which are similar to those of computer simulations. Regarding computer simulations of the evolution of cooperation, there exists the problem of transferring the results of the computer simulations to empirical situations. As has been demonstrated in the case of biology (see chapter 5.1) this can be a very difficult problem to solve, especially if the simulations are not designed to fit empirical problems but merely express more or less plausible theoretical assumptions. Now, a similar transfer problem exists for experimental research in economics. For, how are we to know if the behavior of participants in a laboratory experiment is the same as the behavior of people in "real" life? Typically, the laboratory situations are very much simplified compared to the real life situations they are supposed to resemble. Interfering factors such as the psychological factors that drive our behavior in small group interactions are deliberately excluded by putting the participants into small closed boxes, where they sit in front of a computer screen and only receive information about the other participant's choices without ever getting to see their faces or being able to talk to them. Furthermore in many of the experimental studies the participants are university students and not a representative sample of the population. These few remarks should suffice to indicate that there exists a transfer problem in the case of experimental economical research as well. It seems that when the explanatory gap between models and reality is closed by designing experiments which resemble the models, another gap is opened between experiments and the empirical world outside the experiments.

Trust and cooperation in internet auctions

Can the just mentioned dilemma ever be solved? In fact the dilemma can be solved in certain special cases. It can be narrowed or closed if 1) either, we are lucky and find some empirical setting that is indeed simple enough to be easily compared to laboratory setups, or 2) in cases where economic institutions have deliberately been designed to match a previously tried experimental setup. (For example, in order to exploit a certain experimentally proven effect.) A very prominent example that fits these conditions is provided by the economic research on the behavior of buyers and sellers in internet auctions. Internet auctions provide by their very nature a simple and streamlined setting that strongly resembles that of laboratory experiments. Furthermore, some of the economists that have studied the behavior in internet auctions also work as consultants for internet auction companies like eBay. Therefore, we can also expect that the concrete procedures of such auctions are to some degree designed according to precepts learned from economic experiments.

In the following I describe one series of experiments on the behavior of internet traders that was conducted by Gary E. Bolton, Elena Katok and Axel Ockenfels (Bolton et al., 2004). The problem that their series of experiments is centered around is that of why internet traders trust each other. Described in game theoretical terms an internet auction is an asymmetric one-shot and non zero-sum game. It is asymmetric because it is the rule that first the buyer sends the money and upon receiving the money the seller sends the product to the buyer. This means that the seller can cheat, but not the buyer. If the buyer enters upon the interaction, the buyer must therefore trust the seller. The game is one-shot because typically neither the buyer nor the seller have met before, nor will they be trading partners after the trade has taken place. Finally it is a non zero-sum game because both the buyer and the seller profit from the interaction. If they did not, then either the buyer would not bother to enter upon the interaction or the seller would not offer his product. Bolton, Katok and Ockenfels model these conditions by assuming that both buyer and seller retain a payoff of 35 if no trans-

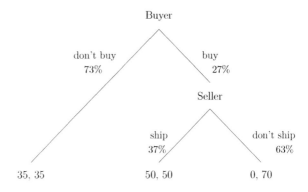

Figure 5.1: The original trust game used in the experiments by Bolton, Katok and Ockenfels. Source: (Bolton et al., 2004). The percentage values indicate how many subjects chose which course of action in the experiment.

action takes place. If the transaction takes place, both buyer and seller receive a payoff of 50. And if the seller cheats that is if the seller takes the money but does not send the product to the buyer, then the seller receives a payoff of 70 while the buyer ends up with a zero payoff. (See figure 5.1.) Except for the asymmetry the situation is thus the same as in the Prisoner's Dilemma game. Theoretically, no interaction should take place. For, if both trading partners were rational egoistic utility maximizers, then the seller would be sure to cheat if an interaction did take place and the buyer, anticipating the seller's cheating, would not even initiate the interaction (Bolton et al., 2004, p. 188).

Now, everyone knows that people in this world (luckily) are not totally rational egoistic utility maximizers, as classical economic theory assumes, but that they are also driven by normative concerns such as fairness considerations. Bolton, Katok and Ockenfels distinguish three different types of such concerns: Fairness in terms of reciprocity, fairness in terms of equal distribution and, finally, collective efficiency concerns. Reciprocity as a fairness concern[13] does in this context mean that the seller might be induced to send the product to the buyer because he or she feels obliged to do so since the buyer has sent the money. Fairness in terms of equal distribution means that the seller cooperates because

---

[13]This should not be confused with *reciprocal altruism* in evolutionary models of the repeated Prisoner's Dilemma, which does not evolve because of any fairness concern but because it yields the highest payoff in the long run.

otherwise the outcome would result in a very uneven distribution of goods (70 vs. 0 instead of 50 vs. 50). And the seller is driven by efficiency concerns if his reason is that the net result for both players is higher than when cheating (100 vs. 70). The model as it stands does not allow distinguishing between these motives. Therefore, Bolton, Katok and Ockenfels draw up an additional model, where buyer and seller retain 105 and 35 points if no interaction takes place, both end up with an equal payoff of 70 if a trade is made and the seller cheats, and where the buyer earns 120 and the seller 50 points if the seller does not cheat. (See figure 5.2.) From the perspective of rational choice theory this second model is equivalent to the first one: Both trading partners would be better off if the trade took place and the seller did not cheat than if no trade took place at all. At the same time, if the trade is initiated by the buyer, the seller gains most if he cheats, wherefore – anticipating rationality of the seller – the buyer would be best off not to initiate the trade at all. However, with regard to fairness concerns, the buyer would initiate a trade and the seller would cheat if both were driven by a "fairness as equality" ideal, while the seller would not cheat if driven by reciprocity or efficiency concerns (Bolton et al., 2004, p. 191).

In an experiment participants were asked to play one of these two games in either the role of the seller or the role of the buyer (that is no participant played the game twice). While in the first game (where participants receive an equal payoff if the seller cooperates) 37% of the sellers did not cheat, only 7% of the sellers did not cheat in the second game. Interestingly, even though the buyers should expect to be cheated in the second game (just as or even more so than in the first game), they were much more willing to buy in the second game (46%) than in the first game (27%). These results strongly suggest that distributional fairness plays a predominant role in this type of interaction, while efficiency and reciprocity seem to be negligible motives (Bolton et al., 2004, p. 193ff.).

In both games the sellers thus proved to be more trustworthy than their rational self interest would suggest. However, even in the original game the degree of trustworthiness (37%) would not be enough to make the game profitable in monetary terms.[14] Taking the question one step further, Bolton, Katok and Ockenfels proceed to examine how institutional arrangements can influence the development of trust. In the case of online auctions, the primary institution to allow the development of trust is the rating mechanism. To examine the effects of such a mechanism, Bolton, Katok and Ockenfels do, however, start with a setting without such a mechanism. In contrast to the previous experiment the

---

[14]As can easily be verified, the expected payoff of buying exceeds the payoff of not buying only when the probability of meeting a trustworthy seller is greater than 70%.

178

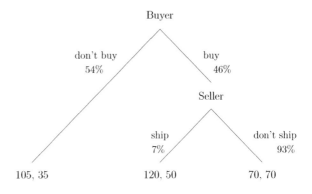

Figure 5.2: A slightly modified variant of the original trust game. Source: (Bolton et al., 2004).

participants play the game repeatedly, but with changing partners and without any information about the previous interactions of the new partner. This setting is called by Bolton, Katok and Ockenfels the *Strangers market* (Bolton et al., 2004, p. 196). The results in the Strangers market are very similar to those in the original experiment (on average 37% of the buyers were willing to buy, while 39% of the sellers actually shipped the product). What the average values conceal is that over time (the participants played the game 30 times) trust collapsed. Obviously, the participants learned that their trust is not sufficiently rewarded in this setting. This was to be expected.

To study the effects of institutional arrangements, Bolton, Katok and Ockenfels contrasted the *Strangers market* with two further settings, the *Reputation market* and the *Partners market*. In the Reputation market, a feedback mechanism was introduced that informed the buyers about all previous interactions of the seller. This is similar to the feedback mechanism in internet auctions such as eBay. Only that in the real internet auctions the feedback consists in a rating by the buyers in previous auctions,[15] while in the experiment the feedback accurately informed about the real behavior of the seller in the experiment. In the Reputation market trust and cooperation did not collapse as in the Strangers market. Instead, 56% of the buyers were willing to enter into

---

[15]As is well known, the ratings by disappointed buyers are not always fair, which in some cases also leads to lawsuits between buyer and seller.

a trade and 73% of the sellers did not cheat. Interestingly, the rate of cooperation of the sellers is very close to the theoretical borderline of 70% where trade becomes profitable in this game (Bolton et al., 2004, p. 198). In the Partners market, which is distinguished from the Reputation market by the fact that the same partners interact throughout the whole repeated game, the rates of buyer's trust and seller's cooperativeness were yet significantly higher than in the Reputation market (83% and 87%). (Again, this result is unexplainable by normative economic theory based on the rational actor model (Bolton et al., 2004, p. 199).)

The experimental setup that Bolton, Katok and Ockenfels used is still in many respects simpler than the real world situation of internet auctions with a rating system. In internet auctions the seller may not only cheat by not shipping the paid product but also by shipping a product of lower quality than advertised, the information propagated through the rating system may not be completely accurate, both buyers and sellers can still take resort to the legal system if they are unsatisfied, which means that cheaters do not only bear the risk of a bad rating but also that of being sued. Still, the experimental setup comes quite close to what happens in internet auctions. Although it has not been done in this particular study, it is well imaginable to compare the data gathered in this or similar experiments with that gathered from real internet auctions. This would in principle allow checking whether such experiments are realistic.

Conclusions

What can we learn from the experimental research in economics for the explanatory validity of results obtained by computer simulations such as those presented in chapter 4? It has already been noted (chapter 4.1.6) that computer simulations which are not tied to specific empirical constellations can at best prove theoretical possibilities, which as such are often not very informative. One way to link computer simulations to empirical constellations would be to create experimental setups which reflect the simplifying modeling assumptions. (Neither of the previously discussed experiments was of course meant to verify any computer simulations,[16] but given the way these experiments work, one could use similar experiments that match the setup of certain computer simulations.) Of course this requires that the computer simulations use

---

[16]In fact, it seems that computer simulations do not play a very important role in this branch of research. In the very issue of "Analyse & Kritik" (1/2004) from which Bolton, Katok and Ockenfels' paper (Bolton et al., 2004) was taken and which was as a whole dedicated to the topic of "online cooperation", not a single simulation study appeared among the 17 articles of the issue.

settings that can at least in principle be reproduced experimentally. For population dynamical simulations of tournaments of the 200 times reiterated Prisoner's Dilemma this might turn out to be a bit impractical.

But when one of the restrictions of the method of employing computer simulations is that in the first instance they only allow us to demonstrate theoretical possibilities, then one of the restrictions of the experimental method is that *prima facie* it only allows us to demonstrate *practical possibilities* and that we still do not know how much impact these practical possibilities have outside the laboratory or – to put it simply – how realistic they are. The gap between the demonstration of theoretical or practical possibilities and empirical reality (outside the lab) can under favorable circumstances be closed, either because we are lucky enough to find a constellation in the real world that is simple enough to match our models, or because we examine social institutions that have been designed according to precepts gained by model research and laboratory testing. (Again, these considerations are somewhat tentative and the previously discussed examples of economical experiments do not suffice to fully warrant such conclusions but they should suffice to show their plausibility.)

The question remains, how many of the empirical questions that are of interest to us in the social sciences are of such a kind that they can be tackled with the help simulation models in the way hinted at above.

5.2.2 A real world example: Altruism among enemies?

It has just been argued that there is some hope to link simulation models with empirical reality via laboratory experiments. Usually, however, when it comes to finding real world evidence for models of the evolution of altruism in the social sciences, things start to get difficult. Of course it is easy to think of many situations which more or less resemble a repeated Prisoner's Dilemma (or some other game): the power game of politics for example, or negotiations between opposing political parties when it comes to decisions that need the full consent of all participants. But the problem is that this "more or less" resemblance is simply not enough to explain the situations in question with sparse models such as those described in chapter 4. Rather than enumerating further examples where our models might apply (or might not apply, as the case may be), I am now going to discuss one such example in depth to highlight the (notorious) difficulties that formal modeling faces in the social sciences outside the field of economics.

The example to be discussed is a sort of "classic" of the theory of the evolution of cooperation. It is the "live and let live"-system that developed at certain stretches of the front line in the trench war of the First World War. The "live and let live" system in the First World War is already discussed in Robert Axelrod's "Evolution of Cooperation" as a prime example for his theory of the "evolution of cooperation" (which is more or less what was here discussed under the heading of "reciprocal altruism"). Because the phenomenon itself is so surprising, it is one of the most stunning examples that have been given for the "evolution of cooperation" in a social science context. Axelrod's exposition of the "live and let live" system has led to much subsequent discussion and criticism most of which centered around the question of whether Axelrod's interpretation of the situation was correct from a game theoretical point of view. Was the situation of the soldiers of the opposing forces really a repeated Prisoner's Dilemma or some other game or, rather, a collective action problem? Were the soldiers of the opposite front lines the players of the reiterated Prisoner's Dilemma or were the soldiers caught in a Prisoner's Dilemma against their own military staff?[17] More important than the problem what kind of game theoretical model can be applied to the "live and let live" system is the question *if* Axelrod's interpretation of the "live and let live" system in terms of evolutionary game theory yields any explanatory power, given that it is by and large correct. Or, to put it more bluntly: Can an explanation in terms of reciprocal altruism give us an explanation of the "live and let live" system that goes beyond what can immediately be inferred from the historical description of the phenomenon alone?

Axelrod's interpretation of the "live and let live" system rests on an extensive historical study of the phenomenon by the sociologist Tony Ashworth (Ashworth, 1980), a debt that Axelrod does, of course, fully acknowledge. Tony Ashworth is neither a game theorist, nor does he try to explain the emergence of the "live and let live" system evolutionarily. Yet, Ashworth does not only describe what happens but also offers an explanation why the "live and let live" system could emerge on a certain front section, how it could be sustained over a considerable period of time and why it eventually broke down again. The crucial question that concerns us here is whether a better explanation for this phenomenon can be given in terms of reciprocal altruism or if at least new light is cast on some of the aspects of the historical events in the First World War that Ashworth has described in his book. In order to answer the question, the explanation that Ashworth offers in his historical treatment must be reconstructed first. For, as it is common in historical literature, description and explanation of the historical events are interwoven

---

[17]For a summary of the discussion of Axelrod's example in the more game theoretically orientated literature see Schüßler (Schüßler, 1990, p. 33ff.).

in one and the same narrative in Ashworth's book.

Let's first look at the descriptive side and ask the question that all studies in history begin with: What has happend? In our collective memory the First World War is commonly remembered as an unusually brutal and destructive war. It is associated with images of large scale battles, like the battle of Verdun or the battle at the Somme, during which tens of thousands of soldiers died within just a few weeks (James, 2003, p. 52). It is much less known that aside from the scenes of the great battles an astonishing calmness often prevailed over long stretches of the front line. And this calmness prevailed although the soldiers in the trenches virtually eyeballed their opponents on the other side. Moreover, as Ashworth demonstrates in his study, these phases of calmness were not merely the expression of comparatively less intensive fighting but the result of a tacit mutual agreement following a kind of "live and let live" principle. Of course this "live and let live"-system was at no time officially tolerated by the military doctrine and open fraternizing was met with severe disciplinary measures.

But what did the "live and let live" system consist of if open arrangements were impossible? Ashworth identifies several forms that the "live and let live" system could take: The exchange of shells and bullets could be limited to certain times of the day. The shooting could be directed to always the same targets, which the enemy soldiers only needed to avoid getting close to if they wanted to stay alive. Finally, it was possible to miss the opposing soldiers on purpose when ordered to shoot at them. This way the soldiers in the trenches could at the same time report the consumption of ammunition to headquarters and signalize their opponents that they did not really intend to hurt them. All this was of course based on mutuality and the conduct could be changed any minute if the other side did not comply. Ashworth has summarized these aspects of the "live and let live" system under the short formula of the "ritualisation of aggression" (Ashworth, 1980, p. 99ff.). The ritualization of aggression between the opponents was completed by the emergence of a proper ethic among the fellow comrades in arms, according to which "disquieters" or "stirrers" that did not honor the tacit agreement of "live and let live" were hated and disdained (Ashworth, 1980, p. 135ff.).

This was just a very brief outline of the most important aspects of the "live and let live" system. In his book Ashworth discusses many more factors, such as the role of different branches of the armed service and the line of command. But it would lead too far to discuss all these details here, although they are by no means unimportant and it is furthermore by no means unimportant that in the game theoretic analysis all of these subtleties must almost by necessity be left unconsidered.

Now that we have seen what the "live and let live" system consists of, how does Ashworth *explain* it? Because the "live and let live" system was widespread one must expect that it has generic causes (in contradistinction to singular historical causes). According to Ashworth's rough estimate it occurred during one third of the front tours of an average division. This also means that it occurred *only* during one third of the front tours. If one wants to explain why it occurred, one must also explain why in most cases it did not occur. In Ashworth's treatment, the following preconditions and causes for the "live and let live" system can be identified:

1. The strategical deadlock. It was virtually impossible to move the front line for either side.

2. The natural desire of most soldiers to survive the war.

3. The impersonal, "bureaucratic structure of aggression" (Ashworth, 1980, p. 76ff.).

4. Empathy with the soldiers on the other side of the front.

5. The "esprit de corps" that can, however, be both either conductive or (in the case of elite troops) impedimental to the emergence of the "live and let live" system.

6. Whether elite troops or non elite troops were fighting on either side. "Live and let live" was much less frequent where elite troops were involved.

7. The branch of service. Infantry soldiers had to face a much greater danger and consequently had a greater interest in "live and let live" than artillery soldiers.

8. The limited means of the military leadership to suppress "live and let live". (Only later did they find an effective way to do so by organizing raids on the enemy trenches.)

9. Initial causes such as Christmas truces, bad weather periods when fighting was impossible, coincidental temporary ceasefire due to similar daily routines on both sides (for example, same meal times).

But why, then, did not the "live and let live" system occur everywhere and all the time? One could of course think of many plausible answers to this question. Because the "live and let live" system did not comply with the objectives and the very purpose of military warfare it is natural to assume that it was in many cases successfully suppressed by the military leadership. But as Ashworth is able to demonstrate from the historical sources it was for a long time almost impossible for the military leaders to efficiently suppress what in their eyes must have been a great nuisance to their military mission. It took them quite a while to find the right means to break the "live and let live" system. (But when they finally succeeded in doing so, their success was lasting.) Furthermore, one might assume that the "live and let live" system was quite error prone as no explicit agreements with the other side could be made. But the most decisive factor among the above listed causes for the emergence or non emergence of the "live and let live" system was – according to Ashworth's empirical study – whether the troops involved were elite troops or "regular" troops.[18] Only when non elite troops were facing each other was there a high chance for the "live and let live" system to emerge and to be sustained.

The means by which the military leadership finally managed to break the "live and let live" system was the ordering of raids into the enemy trenches. Raids could not be faked nor could they be ritualized because either the enemy had casualties or the soldiers of one's own side did not come back. And by stirring up emotions of hatred and revenge the raids deprived the "live and let live" system of its emotional foundation in mutual empathy (Ashworth, 1980, p. 176ff.).

So much for Ashworth's historical description of the "live and let live" system and his explanation of these suprising historical events. What can Axelrod's interpretation on the background of the theory of the "Evolution of Cooperation" add to this explanation?

First and foremost Axelrod argues that the situation of the soldiers in the trench warfare can be interpreted as a repeated Prisoner's Dilemma. In order to do so, Axelrod needs to show that the options that were available to the actors in the historical situation correspond to the possible choices of the players in a repeated two person game and are valued by the soldiers in such a way that the game is a Prisoner's Dilemma. That this is indeed the case is demonstrated by Axelrod quite persuasively: In the historical situation single sided defection would mean to fight and meet so little resistance that victory is possible. Clearly, this would be the preferred alternative on any side of the front. Thus, even without assigning particular preference values, we can safely assume that $T > R, P, S$. But if it was not possible to break through the enemy front line then it was certainly better to "keep quiet" as long as the opponents were willing to "keep quiet" because such an arrangement

---

[18]Among the British troops there was no formal division between elite and non elite, but, as Ashworth points out, military staff as well as the common soldier new fairly well which troop was elite and which was not.

drastically increased the prospects of survival (in Axelrod's formal notation this means that $R > P, S$). Furthermore, mutual abstinence from serious fighting was certainly to be preferred to alternating single sided fighting if that should be considered a viable option at all. Therefore $R > (T + S)/2$ can also be granted. But if the opposing side was not willing to "keep quiet" by ritualizing aggression in the previously described way then it was still better to fight back then to let oneself be overrun $(P > S)$.

In order to apply the theory of the "evolution of cooperation" to the situation of the soldiers in the trenches of World War I, some further points need to be clarified such as whether the "game" played really was a *repeated* Prisoner's dilemma, which requires the identity of the players over a longer period of time. Even though the soldiers at the front were periodically exchanged by fresh troops, the predecessors had to familiarize their successors with the situation at their section of the front. Therefore the successors could pick up the "game" exactly at the point where their predecessors had left it. It is a bit less obvious what the evolutionary transmission mechanism that led to the spreading of the "live and let live" system consists of. Axelrod hints to the fact that the system spread over neighboring sections of the front. But, as has been indicated earlier, one may also assume that the "live and let live" system started independently in many different sections of the front. It does not seem to disturb Axelrod that the way the "live and let live" system was initiated and transmitted bears only very little resemblance to the population dynamical transmission mechanism in his simulation model.

Save for this last point it can be granted that Axelrod's analysis is by and large convincing. But in how far does Axelrod's interpretation go beyond Ashworth's study as far as its explanatory power is concerned? If we consider the whole bundle of conditions that Ashworth discusses as causes of the "live and let live" system (see page 183), it becomes obvious that only one of these conditions is captured by Axelrod's game theoretical interpretation. This condition for the "live and let live" system is the strategic situation of the soldiers in the trenches, which Axelrod describes as a repeated Prisoner's Dilemma. It is important to realize that by doing so Axelrod captures only one of many causes for the "live and let live"-system. Therefore, the evolutionary theory of Axelrod cannot reasonably be regarded as an alternative explanation to the one which is offered by Tony Ashworth in his historical narrative. At best, the theory of reciprocal altruism offers a more precise treatment of one single component of Ashworth's explanation.[19] Whether this is really the case, shall occupy us now.

Is Axelrod at least able to provide a more precise understanding of at least this particular aspect with the help of evolutionary game theory? In order to find out whether such a claim would be warrented it must be examined whether the situation of the soldiers in the trenches can really be described as a repeated Prisoner's Dilemma. Against Axelrod's interpretation the objection has been raised that the front soldiers may have been primarily interested in their own survival after all and that, compared to their survival, being victorious in the battle was much less important to them. Then the soldiers would not really gain any advantage by single sided defection. (The payoff parameter T would be lower or equal the payoff parameter R in Axelrod's notation.) If this interpretation is followed then the problem the soldiers had to solve was a mere coordination problem and not a Prisoner's Dilemma. Independently of how the question is to be answered the objection shows that the assessment of a given situation in terms of game theory is by no means a trivial and unambiguous task. The difficulties become even greater when it comes to estimating concrete values for the different payoff parameters. Axelrod confines himself to establishing the relative proportions of the payoff parameters that are expressed in the two inequalities $T > R > P > S$ and $2R > T + S$, although his model is in fact sensitive to changes in numerical values of the parameters – as has been demonstrated by the simulations in section 4.1.4.

But there exists an even more serious objection to Axelrod's interpretation: The described strategical stalemate was (save for the great battles) more or less the same at all sections of the front line. Nonetheless, the longitudinal analysis showed that the "live and let live" system occurred on average only during roughly one third of the front tours (Ashworth, 1980, p. 171-175). This empirical fact poses a real problem for Axelrod's theory because his theory postulates that in the reiterated Prisoner's Dilemma cooperative strategies will *usually* prevail. However, as the more extensive series of simulations that has been presented earlier (see section 4.1.4) has shown in accordance with earlier criticisms of Axelrod's approach by mathematical game theorists (Binmore, 1998, p. 313ff.), the theoretical foundation for Axelrod's generalizing claim that cooperative strategies like *Tit for Tat* enjoy a high advantage in the repeated Prisoner's Dilemma was lacking. As the results of the simulation series suggest, it is not generally true that cooperative strategies

---

[19]This is a point that Axelrod seems to be aware of as he mentions that some of the insights of Ashworth's study, such as the emergence of an ethics of cooperation, might be used to extend his theory of the evolution of cooperation.

are the best strategies in the reiterated Prisoner's Dilemma. Depending on the particular circumstances, uncooperative strategies like *Hawk* may be much more successful. It might seem tempting to draw the conclusion that Axelrod's computer model was too crude after all and that our more refined simulation series which suggests an only limited evolutionary success of cooperative strategies is in better accordance with the empirical findings of Ashworth. Thus, while Axelrod's theory in its original form failed it only needed to be refined a little bit on its technical side to make it succeed.

Unfortunately, the epistemological situation is not as simple as that. According to Ashworth, the major factor which determined the occurrence of the "live and let live" was whether the troops involved were elite troops or merely regular soldiers. Whenever elite troops were involved, the "live and let live" system was very unlikely to occur. How can this factor (elite soldiers or non elite soldiers) be reflected in our model? It can be done by assuming that for elite troops a different set of payoff parameters holds because elite soldiers value the viable options (fight hard or "live and let live") according to a set of preferences that differs from that of ordinary soldiers. For example, it is not implausible to assume that elite soldiers might consider it dishonorable to avoid fighting just to save one's own life. But while such an assumption might save our theory it remains doubtful whether much is gained in terms of explanatory power. For, instead of reverting to simple standard assumptions about the payoff parameters in a given strategical situation, it would be necessary to conduct an extensive historical inquiry in order find out how different groups of soldiers may valuate one and the same situation. (In fact, without such an inquiry we might not even be aware that there is such an important difference between elite soldiers and non elite soldiers.) But with the historical inquiry at hand, we would not need a game theoretical model any more to tell us what happend. Or, to put it in another way, almost all of the explanatory work would be done by the theories and historical inquiries needed to determine the payoff parameters, while the game theoretical model making use of this work would be little more than a trivial and illustrating addition. Also, once it is accepted as a fact that it depended on the elite status of the troops whether they would fight or attempt to engage into "live and let live" with their enemies, this fact can be explained more simply than by any game theoretical model by the rather obvious assumption that elite soldiers are more likely to follow orders involving great danger than ordinary soldiers. An assumption that has the additional advantage that it is – other than assumptions about payoff values – empirically very easily testable in comparable circumstances.

The more general lesson to be learned from this is that game theoretical models prove to be useful only in situations where we can either proceed from standard assumptions about the relevant payoff parameters or where reliable measurement procedures for the input parameters of the models exist. Apart from the fact that it leaves out too many causally relevant factors, this is the second reason why the theory of the "evolution of cooperation" fails to explain the sort of cooperation that emerged between the opposing soldiers in the trench warfare of World War I. (And with this second reason it is clear that it does not even provide a partial explanation.)

Following an influential argument from Carl Gustav Hempel (Hempel, 1965) it might still be objected that even though the game theoretical model cannot offer more than an *ex post* explanation, it is still of scientific value because it affords a *general* explanation for a course of historical events and thus increases our understanding of historical processes of a particular kind by subsuming them under general laws or principles. Unfortunately this is not the case here. For, as we have seen, the theory of the "evolution of cooperation" provides hardly an explanation for the emergence of the "live and let live"-system in World War I at all. It is not well possible to defend a wrong explanation or a theory that is not an explanation at all with the argument that it affords a generalization. To say this does not mean that historians and social scientists do not need to or should not be interested in general theories. But in the social sciences and especially in history, generalizations that are meaningful and rich in content are typically found on lower levels of abstraction. One of the standard methods for generating and testing general theories in history is the comparison of similar chains of events under different historical circumstances. For example, it might be interesting to compare the situation in the First World War with that in other wars and with the aim of deriving a generalized theory of fraternization, which could then in turn be applied to the "live and let live"-system and other comparable events. But it seems rather hopeless to seek a general theory for the explanation of the "live and let live" system that is still meaningful and rich enough in content on the level of abstraction of the theory of the "evolution of cooperation".

Summing it up, computer simulations of the "evolution of cooperation" hardly add anything to our understanding of the "live and let live" system in the trench warfare of the First World War. The emergence (or the "evolution", if this term is preferred) of "live and let live" is due to an intricate network of interlocking causes that cannot accurately be explained by reference to simulations of the repeated Prisoner's Dilemma game. At best there exists a vague metaphorical resemblance between the situation of the soldiers in the trenches and the repeated Prisoner's Dilemma, but this alone is not sufficient for an explanation and it is hardly sufficient to justify the technical effort of a computer simulation in this particular case.

5.3 Conclusions

The previous survey of empirical studies on the evolution of altruism provided some interesting insights in how and why altruism and cooperation can evolve even under unfavorable conditions. Regarding the epistemological merits of simulation models for the explanation of evolutionary altruism, however, the insights gained from looking at the empirical research are extremely sobering: First of all, it is an undeniable fact that computer simulations on the evolution of altruism have remained largely useless for empirical research. And this does of course also mean that computer simulations of the evolution of altruism hardly provide us with any knowledge about how altruism really evolves. This seems to be especially true for repeated Prisoner's Dilemma simulations of reciprocal altruism because they rely on a setting that plays only a very marginal role in nature (see page 152 for one of the few examples where it does). Secondly, the in-depth discussion of two selected examples where the application of simulation models failed despite the serious attempts of its supporters precisely showed why the simulation models failed. In the biological example the model failed because it relies on payoff parameters that could not be measured, while the model is at the same time sensitive to changes of these parameters. That the fitness relevant payoff is very hard to measure is a general difficulty that evolutionary game theory faces in biology, though it does not always turn out to be as fatal as in this instance.[20] In the sociological example the repeated Prisoner's Dilemma model failed because from the many interlocking causes that brought about cooperation between the enemy front soldiers in World War One, it captured at best one cause that could be described as "the strategical situation" of the front soldier. But then it cannot seriously be maintained that cooperation occurred in the trenches in virtue of the very factors for which it evolves in repeated Prisoner's Dilemma simulations. Apart from that, the very same measurement problems and model stability issues that have already been encountered in the biological example reappear in the sociological example as well.

---

[20]See (Hammerstein, 1998, p. 9ff.) for some reflections on how to remedy this difficulty by means of clever interpretation.

It should not be considered too much of a surprise that the simulation model fared so badly in the sociological example. After all, formal mathematical models can be used in the social sciences only in a few select areas, most notably economics. The reason is that for many explanations that we give in the social sciences, we have to draw on connections for which no formal description exists. One may regret this state of affairs, but it certainly does not get any better by ignoring all factors that cannot be rendered formally. Therefore, in many cases an ordinary historiographical approach may serve the needs of the social scientist much better than a seemingly more refined simulation based approach. Other than that, part of the art of applying formal models in a sociological context certainly consists in picking out the right empirical situations for which a model based approach might indeed be appropriate. How this can possibly be achieved has been hinted at when discussing the internet auction example in section 5.2.1.

All in all, a look into the empirical literature is apt to strengthen some of the skeptical conclusions about computer simulations on the evolution of altruism that have been drawn at the end of the previous chapter (see chapter 4.4), most notably the impression is strengthened that pure model research conveys a distorted picture of how and why altruism evolves. If one really wants to understand how and why altruism evolves then designing models based on "plausible" assumptions alone and uninformed by concrete empirical research is certainly not the way to go. If the simulation based approach to the explanation of the evolution of altruism has thus been a failure then what remains to be clarified is just why it had to fail and what a possible remedy could look like. This is what will occupy us in the next chapter.

Chapter 6

Learning from failure

Ihr Instrumente freilich, spottet mein,
Mit Rad und Kämmen, Walz' und Bügel.
Ich stand am Tor, ihr solltet Schlüssel sein;
Zwar euer Bart ist kraus, doch hebt ihr nicht die Riegel.

Goethe, Faust I

We have so far been looking at several computer simulations that sought to help us to explain reciprocal altruism. We have furthermore looked at a number of empirical example cases that confirmed some of the general ideas suggested by the outcome of the computer simulations but which – at the same time – raised very strong doubts concerning the explanatory power of the computer simulations described. As any theory is only as good as its confirmation and as we certainly want to know, how good a theory of reciprocal altruism based on game theoretical computer simulations *can* be, we need to enter into some general considerations concerning the epistemology or, if preferred, the theory of science of computer simulations. The question here is a question of *can*, because as we have seen previously when looking at the concrete examples, it is a fact that so far explanations of reciprocal altruism based on computer simulations have not been successful.

6.1 Epistemological requirements for computer simulations

As has to be expected for a comparatively new scientific tool like computer simulations, the field of the epistemology of computer simulations is not very far developed. The most important epistemological question concerning any computer simulation is: How do we know that what happens in the simulation represents what happens in reality? (Of course, a simulation does not need to represent exactly what happens empirically, but it should represent what happens empirically well enough, so that we can draw conclusions from the simulation with respect to reality. So, how do we know that this is the case?) In the more technically orientated textbook literature on computer simulations (Gilbert and Troitzsch, 2005) there is little to find that could answer this question. This type of literature centers around how to program a simulation, how to visualize the data and how to debug the program, that is, it tells us how to proceed once we have decided to use the tool of computer simulations, but it does tell us little about whence and where computer simulations are an appropriate tool for investigating a certain scientific question. And astonishingly little thought is usually dedicated to the question what requirements a simulation must meet so that we can say it is a *good* simulation, i.e. a simulation that fulfills its purpose.[1]

A philosophical literature on the epistemology of computer simulations that could fill in the gap which is left open by the technical literature is only beginning to emerge. And often, unfortunately, it amounts to little more than stocktaking of what goes on the field of computer simulations, while only the surface is scratched of the epistemological questions (Hegselmann et al., 1996) concernd. A more recent example, where this is different, is Paul Humphreys' "Extending Ourselves" (Humphreys, 2004), which discusses at length the impact of computer simulations on today's scientific methodology. Regarding agent-based simulations (which is the broader category under which the simulations of the evolution of altruism presented earlier fall) Humphreys' conclusions are somewhat sceptical, as the following quotations may demonstrate:

> One of the more important questions that arise about agent-based modeling is the degree of understanding which is produced by the models. [...]
>
> In fact ... because the goal of many agent-based procedures is to find a set of conditions that is sufficient to reproduce behavior, rather than to isolate conditions which are necessary to achieve that result, a misplaced sense of understanding is always a danger. (Humphreys, 2004, p. 132)

> As we have seen, it has been claimed for agent-based models that one of their primary uses is exploratory, in the sense that it is of interest to show that simple rules can reproduce complex behavior. But this cannot be good advice without imposing extra conditions. [...] Because it is often possible to

---

[1] Troitzsch and Gilbert reserve only three pages for topic of "validation" of computer simulations (Gilbert and Troitzsch, 2005, p. 23-25).

recapture observed structural patterns by using simple models that have nothing to do with the underlying reality, any inference from a successful representation of the observed structure to the underlying mechanisms is fraught with danger and can potentially lock us into a model that is, below the level of data, quite false. (Humphreys, 2004, p. 134)

Actually, as we have seen in the previous chapter (chapter 5), already on "the level of data" the computer simulations of the evolution of altruism hardly represented the "observed structure", let alone on the level of the underlying causal mechanisms. What is important here are the "extra conditions", which according to Humphreys must be imposed so that we do not fall prey to the "misplaced sense of understanding" that computer simulations all too easily convey. In the following I make a proposal concerning the conditions which computer simulations ought to fulfill in order to allow us a real understanding of the simulated phenomena. For this purpose, I first distinguish different types of computer simulations (section 6.1.1). Then I present and discuss a set of criteria for the most important of these types, *explanatory simulations* (section 6.1.2).

6.1.1 Different aims of computer simulations in science

Computer simulations can be employed in science not only for generating explanations but for various different purposes. In order to distinguish different types of computer simulations according to their purpose, we draw on our earlier distinction between a "conceptual level" and an "application level" of the employment of computer simulations (see page 158) and develop it by two further distinctions into a more fine-grained typology of four basic types. The two types that fall under the "conceptual level" are *proof-of-possibility simulations* and *exploratory simulations*. For the application level *predictive simulations* and *explanatory simulations* will be distinguished.[2]

---

[2]The broader distinction between what I have termed a "conceptual level" and an "application level" of simulations is more or less common in the simulation literature, although there is no established terminology. Kliemt, for example, distinguishes between "thin" and "thick" simulations (Kliemt, 1996, p. 15), where thin simulations correspond more or less to what I have termed the "conceptual level" and thick simulation to the "application level" in my terminology. Troitzsch and Gilbert speak of simulations that merely serve the goal of understanding a certain kind of process (Gilbert and Troitzsch, 2005, p. 15ff.) in the cases that I would describe as the "conceptual level". Just as Humphreys, I believe that this kind of "understanding" can be ever so misleading, wherefore I prefer to avoid this terminology. Also the precept – on which I draw in the recipe section (see section 6.3) – to design "conceptual level" simulations as simple as possible and "application level" simulations as accurate (i.e. as complex) as necessary is common knowledge.

The most basic type, *proof-of-possibility simulations*, are computer simulations that are merely used to demonstrate the theoretical possibility of certain assumptions or to disprove the theoretical necessity of certain commonly held beliefs. An example would be computer simulations of the evolution of altruism through group selection, which show that group selection can promote the evolution of altruism in the long run, even if altruism is always selected against within the group (see chapter 4.3.1). Typically, proof-of-possibility simulations are simple, small and not necessarily very "realistic" simulations. Such simulations are quite commonly also referred to as "toy simulations" or "toy models", which is not always meant in a pejorative sense.

Instead of proving theoretical possibilities the scientist already had in mind when constructing a simulation, computer simulations can also be employed to explore the possible consequences or implications of certain assumptions or to search for phenomena which can occur under certain theoretical conditions but which are yet unknown. Simulations that serve this purpose will be called *exploratory simulations*. Typically, this kind of simulation takes the form of large series of simulations, or, as it is sometimes called, "massive" simulations. (It should be understood that the adjective "massive" only refers to the technical complexity and does not say anything about the scientific quality of the simulation or the credibility of its results.) An example for such a "massive" simulation is the simulation series on reciprocal altruism presented in chapter 4.1.4. Just as proof-of-possibility simulations, exploratory simulations are of theoretical nature and do not need to resemble empirical reality. If there exists any resemblance at all, then it is typically vague and consists in the plausibility of the underlying assumptions.

The next class of computer simulations are *predictive simulations*. The purpose of predictive simulations is to generate true predictions of some empirical process. An example might be simulations in meteorology that predict how the weather is going to be in the future. The assumptions that enter into predictive simulations do not need to be in any way realistic. As long as the predictions prove to be reliable, it is permissible to use strongly simplified assumptions about the modeled process or even assumptions which are known to be false. This shows that just because a simulation produces successful predictions it does not necessarily also provide an explanation for the predicted phenomena, even though successful predictions may be one among several indicators for a simulation to be explanatorily valid. As an explanation we would accept a predictive simulation only if the assumptions built into the simulation are consistent with our background knowledge (consisting of the accepted scientific theories) about the modeled process.[3]

The most desired case, however, would be that of an *explanatory simulation*, which is a type of computer simulation that actually allows us to explain the empirical phenomena that are modeled in the simulation. From an explanatory simulation we expect that it does capture the real causes in virtue of which the modeled empirical phenomena happen. In this sense explanatory simulations are epistemologically stronger than predictive simulations. But in another sense they are not, because we do not demand from an explanatory simulation that it generates predictions. Thus a simulation may be explanatory even if it offers only ex-post explanations.[4] Explanatory simulations therefore do not form a subclass of predictive simulations.

Because the simulations of the evolution of altruism largely failed to provide substantial (i.e. not just metaphorical) explanations for the empirical instances of altruism, we will now discuss the criteria that proper explanatory simulations should meet. This will help us to understand the reasons for this failure.

6.1.2 Criteria for "explanatory" simulations

In what sense can a computer simulation be explanatory? And what are the criteria a computer simulation must meet in order to be explanatory?

A computer simulation can be called *explanatory* if it adequately models some empirical situation and if the results of the computer simulation (the *simulation results*) coincide with the outcome of the modeled empirical process (the *empirical results*). If this is the case, we can conclude that the empirical results have been caused by the very factors (or, more precisely, by the empirical correspondents of those factors) that

---

[3]It has to be admitted that this requirement rests on specific epistemological commitments concerning the generality of scope of scientific theories. I assume that if a scientific theory is well confirmed then it tells us something about anything that falls within its scope, even in cases where we have to deal with a configuration that is too complicated to analyze it in terms of the theory. If, in contrast, one follows Nancy Cartwrights "Dappled World" (Cartwright, 1999) and assumes that the validity of scientific theories is always locally restricted to its successful application cases then no conflict between predictive simulations and background theories can arise, because a successful predictive simulation that rests on assumptions that break with the background theories would then merely resemble another limit of the scope of these theories. We would then lose any ground on which we could deny the title of an "explanation" to our simulation.

[4]The motivation for allowing ex-post simulations is founded in the fact that many scientific explanations, especially in the social sciences, only work ex-post. For example, there exists a number of good explanations for the wave of democratization of the former communist states of Eastern Europe in the late 80s and early to mid 90s of the 20th century. But who could have predicted it? It would be unfair to demand from explanations that are based on computer simulations to offer more than can be accomplished by conventional science in the respective field. My criticism of Axelrod-style simulations in the context of social sciences (see chapter 5.2.2) does not rest on the charge that they provide mere ex-post interpretations but that they are far too simplistic.

have brought about the simulation results in the computer simulation.

To take an example, let us say we have a game theoretic computer simulation of the repeated Prisoner's Dilemma where under certain specified conditions the strategy "Tit for Tat" emerges as the clear winner. Now, assume further that we know of an empirical situation that closely resembles the repeated Prisoner's Dilemma with exactly the same conditions as in our simulations. (Probably, the easiest way to bring this about would be by conducting a game theoretic experiment, where the conditions can be closely monitored.) And let us finally assume that also in the empirical situation the "Tit for Tat" strategy emerges as the most successful strategy. Then we are entitled to conclude that "Tit for Tat" was successful in the empirical case, because the situation was a repeated Prisoner's Dilemma with such and such boundary conditions and because – as the computer simulation shows – "Tit for Tat" is a winning strategy in repeated Prisoner's Dilemma situations under the respective conditions.

Now that we have seen how explanations by computer simulations work in principle, let us ask what are the criteria a computer simulation must fulfill in order to deserve the title of an *explanatory simulation*. The criteria should be such as to allow us to check whether the explanation is valid, that is, whether the coincidence of the results is due to the congruence of the operating factors (in the empirical situation and in the computer simulation) or whether it is merely accidental.

As criteria that a computer simulation must meet in order to be an explanatory model of an empirical process, I propose the following:

1. *Adequacy Requirement*: All known[5] causally relevant factors of the modeled empirical process must be represented in the computer simulation.

   (This requirement is roughly equivalent to demanding that the theoretical assumptions built into the simulations should not break with or ignore our background knowledge about the modeled process, because it is only in virtue of this background knowledge that we know about the causally relevant factors of the modeled empirical process.)

   In the case of predictive simulations this first requirement would have to be replaced by the requirement of *predictive success*. A predictive simulation does not need to model the causes of a process

---

[5]The restriction to all *known* causes was suggested by Claus Beisbart to avoid an epistemic impasse when simulations are employed as a tool to find out just what the causally relevant factors of a given empirical process are.

realistically. But if it does not then at least its predictions must come true.

2. *Robustness or Stability Requirement*: The input parameters of the simulation must be measurable with such accuracy that the simulation results are stable within the range of inaccuracy of measurement.[6]

3. *Descriptive Appropriateness or Non-Triviality Requirement*: The results of the computer simulation should reflect at least some important features (that is features the explanation of which is desired) of the results of the modeled empirical process. In particular, the results should not already be deducible without any model or simulation from the empirical description of the process.

If all of these criteria are met, we can say that there exists a *close fit* between model and modeled reality. What I wish to claim is that only if there is a close fit between model and reality are we entitled to say that the model explains anything. Even though these criteria are very straightforward, a little discussion will be helpful for better understanding.

Regarding the first criterion, it should be obvious that if not all causally relevant factors are included, then any congruence of simulation results and empirical results can at best be accidental. Two objections might be raised at this point: 1) If there really is a congruence of simulation results and empirical results, should that not allow us to draw the conclusion that the very factors implemented in the computer simulation are indeed all factors that are causally relevant? 2) If we use computer simulations as a research tool to find out what the causes of a certain empirical phenomenon are, how are we to know beforehand what the causally relevant factors are, and how are we ever to find it out, if drawing reverse conclusions from the compliance of the results to the relevant causes is not allowed?

To these objections the following can be answered: If the simulation is used to generate empirical predictions and if the predictions come true then this can indeed be taken as a strong hint to its capturing all relevant causes of the empirical process in question. With certain reservations we are then entitled to draw reverse conclusions from the compliance of

---

[6]The importance of stability is often emphasized in the simulation literature. Especially so, because there are certain types of systems (chaotic systems) for which stability cannot be achieved in principle. Often, however, stability is merely treated as a kind of internal property of simulations (Gilbert and Troitzsch, 2005, p. 23) and not, as it should be done, as a relational property between simulation and measurement capabilities which bears consequences for the epistemological strength that can be ascribed to a simulation.

the results to the exclusive causal relevance of the incorporated factors or mechanisms. The reservations concern the problem that even if a simulation has predictive success it can still have been based on unrealistic assumptions. Sometimes the predictive success of a simulation can even be increased by sacrificing realism. Therefore, in order to find out whether the factors incorporated in the computer simulation are indeed the causally relevant factors, we should not rely on predictive success alone, but we should consult other sources as well, such as our scientific background knowledge about the process in question. Also, if we already know (for whatever reason) that a certain factor is causally relevant for the outcome of the empirical process under investigation and if this factor is not included in the simulation of this process then even if the simulation predicts correctly, we are bound to conclude that it does so only accidentally.

Furthermore, drawing conclusions from the predictive success of a simulation to its explanatory validity is impermissible in the case of ex-post predictions. For, if we only try hard enough, we are almost sure to find some computer simulation and some set of input parameters that matches a previously fixed set of output data. The task of finding such a simulation amounts to nothing more than finding any arbitrary algorithm that produces a given pattern. But then we will only accidentally have hit on the true causes that were responsible for the results of the empirical process.

Therefore, only if we make sure that at least all factors that are known to be causally relevant are included in the simulation, we can take it as an explanation. And usually we cannot assure this by relying on the conformance of the simulation results and the empirical results alone without any further considerations. Summarizing, we can say: *If the first criterion is not fulfilled, then the computer simulation does not explain.*

The second criterion is even more straightforward. If the model is unstable then we will not be able to check whether the simulation model is adequate. For, if it is not stable within the inevitable inaccuracies of measurement, this means that the model delivers different results within the range of inaccuracy of the measured input parameters. But then we can neither be sure that the model is right, when the model results match the empirical results, nor that it is wrong, when they don't (unless the empirical results are even outside the range of possible simulation results for the range of inaccuracy of the input parameters). Let's for example imagine we had a game theoretic model that tells us whether some actors will cooperate or not cooperate. Now assume, we had some empirical process at hand where we know that the actors cooperate and we would like to know whether they do so for the very reasons the model suggests or, in other words, we would like to know whether our model can explain why they cooperate. If the model is unstable then – due to measurement inaccuracy – we do not know whether the empirical process falls within the range of input parameters for which the model predicts cooperation or not. Then there is no way to tell whether the actors in the empirical process cooperated because of the reasons the model suggests or, quite the contrary, in spite of what the model predicts.

A special case of this problem of model stability and measurement inaccuracies occurs when we can only determine the ordinal relations of greater and smaller of some empirical quantity but not its cardinal value (perhaps, because it does not have a cardinal value by its very nature, which is the case for the quantity of utility in many contexts). In this case the empirical validation of any simulation that crucially depends on the cardinal value of the respective input parameters will be impossible. Briefly put, the morale of the second criterion is: *If condition two is not met, we cannot know whether the computer simulation explains.*

In connection with the first criteria the requirement of model stability (in relation to measurement inaccuracy) gives rise to a kind of dilemma. In many cases an obvious way to make a model more adequate is by including further parameters. Unfortunately, the more parameters are included in the model the harder it becomes to handle. Often, though not necessarily, a model loses stability by including additional parameters. Therefore, in order to assure that the model is adequate (first criterion), we may have to lower the degree of abstraction by including more and more parameters. But then the danger increases that our model will not be sufficiently stable any more to fulfill the second criterion.

There exists no general strategy to avoid this dilemma. In many cases it may not be possible at all. But this should not come as a surprise. It merely reflects the fact that the powers of computer simulations are – as one should certainly expect – limited at some point. With the tool of computer simulations many scientific problems that would be hard to handle with pure mathematics alone come within the reach of a formal treatment. Still, many scientific problems remain outside the realm of what can be described with formal methods, either because of their complexity or because of the nature of the problem. This remains especially true for most areas of the social sciences.

The third criterion requires that the output of the computer simulation should reflect the empirical results with all the details that are regarded as scientifically important and not just – as it sometimes happens – merely a much sparser substructure of them. For example, we may want to use game theoretic models like the Prisoner's Dilemma to study the strategic interaction of states in politics. The game theoretic model will tell us whether the states will cooperate or not, but most probably it will say nothing about the concrete form of cooperation (diplomatic contacts, trade agreements, international contracts etc.) or non cooperation (embargoes, military action, war etc.). Therefore, even if the model or simulation really was predictively accurate, it does at best provide us with a partial explanation, because it does not explain all aspects of the empirical outcome that interest us. In the worst case its explanatory (or, as the case may be, its predictive) power is almost as poor as that of a horoscope. The prediction of a horoscope that tomorrow "something of importance" will happen easily becomes true, because of its vagueness. Similarly, if a game theoretic simulation predicts that the parties of a political conflict will stop cooperating at some stage, but does not tell us whether this implies, say, the outbreak of war or just the breakup of diplomatic relations then it only offers us comparatively unimportant information. We could also say that if the simulation results fail to capture all (or at least the most) important features of the empirical outcome then the computer simulation "misses the point".

Summing it up: Only if a computer simulation closely fits the simulated reality – that is if it adequately models the causal factors involved, if it is stable and if it is descriptively rich enough to "hit the point" – can it claim to be explanatory.

6.2 Reasons for failure

The establishment of criteria for explanatory simulations allows pinpointing the reasons why computer simulations of the evolution of altruism failed to explain the evolution of altruism:

1) For hardly any of the empirical instances of altruism a computer simulation existed which could be called *empirically adequate*. It is very difficult to find an empirical study of the evolution of altruism wherein recourse to a simulation model is taken. In the few instances where this was the case, it ultimately turned out to be a failure (see page 160 and chapter 5.1.3). In the sociological examples the difficulties to capture all causally relevant factors in a computer simulation were even more obvious (see chapter 5.2.2). In neither biology nor sociology, however, do the difficulties seem completely insurmountable in principle. If the right empirical example cases were picked and if the simulation models were built to fit the respective empirical instances of altruism, they might one day indeed contribute to the explanation of the evolution of altruism.

Presumably, one of the main reasons for the explanatory failure of computer simulations consists in a misconception about there being some such thing as an "in principle explanation" by a computer simulation. Robert Axelrod, one of the pioneers of the method, believed that by analyzing how and why cooperation evolves in a computer simulation that is based on sufficiently plausible model assumptions, he could devise an in principle explanation for the evolution of altruism. This explanation, he believed, could then be applied to any empirical instance of cooperation that somehow exposed a pattern of interaction that resembled his winning strategy *Tit for Tat*. It should be obvious by now that the implicit epistemological conception of explanatory computer simulations behind this belief is severely mistaken. Of course, most other authors of simulation models are far more modest about the explanatory claims they derive from their models. Rudolf Schüßler, for example, admits at one point quite frankly that his simulation models, which are similar to Axelrod's, hardly provide any decisive argument in the debate about sociological normativism to which they are related (Schüßler, 1990, p. 91).[7] But then he leaves the reader with the question what his simulations are good for, if they cannot prove any point at all.

2) Just as the requirement of empirical adequacy, the second requirement, stability, was hardly anywhere fulfilled. It should be understood that stability is a relational property between the model and its empirical application case. Except for the special case of chaotic processes, stability issues can therefore be resolved either by redesigning the model so that it reacts less sensitively to changes in parameter values or by devising more precise measurement procedures. Regarding the latter, however, it seems that in biology the problem of measuring the payoff parameters for game theoretical models poses an extremely obstinate problem (see page 160). In the social sciences this problem can to some degree be remedied if the payoff is understood in monetary terms. This is especially true for experimental economics, where the experimenter simply can pay the participants a certain amount of money depending

---

[7]The passage from Schüßler's book reads: "Game theoretical arguments can usually explain little empirically, but they can help to correct unfounded judgements, point out possibilities, and reduce fears of the ever looming decline of values und the stability of modern societies. How much or little that is, is a question of perspective and aptitude to make do with the art of the possible (Kunst des Möglichen)". It seems that for Schüßler game theoretical arguments do more to serve a therapeutical purpose or one of political propaganda for that matter, than a scientific one. But then it would be more logical to conclude that game theory may just not be the right tool to tackle the sort of questions that Schüßler deals with and that one should rather give other methods a try instead of confining oneself to the "art of the possible" within the narrow limits of game theoretical arguments.

on the outcome of the games played. However, as far as evolutionary models are concerned, there would still remain the problem of linking the monetary payoff to the replicator dynamics.

In some cases a model seems to be appropriate even if the parameters cannot be measured and just on behalf of the fact that the empirical process exposes a strong similarity to the modeled process on the phenomenological level. For example, grooming behavior in impala (see page 152) seems to resemble very closely the kind of interaction that takes place in the repeated Prisoner's Dilemma. Yet, because the model is sensitive to variations of the numerical values of the payoff parameters and because we cannot measure the parameter values, we cannot strictly check the validity of the model. Therefore, the model can at best be granted the epistemological status of a good metaphor in such a case.

The problem of model instability due to the use of immeasurable input parameters in the simulation models suggests that one should first consider what kinds of parameters can be measured in a given empirical situation and then try to construct the simulations around the measurable quantities. This principle could be called the *build to order principle*, because it means that the models should be build according to the restrictions and demands of empirical research just as a customer configurable product should be built according to the order of the customer. Of course, there exists a possibility of conflict between this principle and the empirical adequacy requirement in the case where certain factors which are known to be causally relevant depend on quantities which are not measurable. But then we should also consider that the underlying theory which makes use of immeasurable (hidden) factors may not be a very suitable one. (Example: Game theory which relies on payoff parameters when applied in situations where the concept of utility appears questionable.)

3) While the first requirement, empirical adequacy, is related to the input parameters of simulation models, the third criterion, *descriptive appropriateness or non triviality*, is related to the output parameters. In the case of repeated game models of the evolution of altruism the output is some kind of altruistic or non altruistic strategy. This is just what the scientist asks for when investigating altruistic behavior so that it can be granted that at least the third criteria is fulfilled for repeated game simulations of the evolution of altruism.

There are, of course, borderline cases, where even this might be disputed. In the case of the "live and let live"-system in World War One, the output of the model certainly does not capture all the nuances of the strategies that the soldiers employed to keep alive the "live and let live"-system. Most notably it does not capture the means of signaling and clandestine communication that the soldiers invented as part of their strategy. Still, as the information whether the front soldier's actions will converge to a cooperative or non cooperative equilibrium is far from trivial, it is not the non-triviality requirement because of which the simulation largely fails to explain the "live and let live"-system, but the fact that it misses many of the causes that were decisive for the evolution of this system (see chapter 5.2.2).

Summing it up, the reason why the computer simulations of the evolution of altruism failed to explain the evolution of altruism in reality, can now precisely be stated as the result of the violation of – in almost all cases – the stability criteria and additionally – in many cases – the empirical adequacy criteria.

6.3 How to do it better

If the common brand of computer simulations of the evolution of cooperation or altruism has been largely a failure, the question naturally arises how such computer simulations can possibly be done better. Turning from diagnosis to therapy, I am therefore going to to make a few proposals on what precautions must be taken when devising computer simulations so that they do not remain mere toys but become useful and valuable tools of science. For the sake of simplicity, these proposals will be cast in the form of four simple recipes, each of which covers one of the above distinguished types of simulations. Doing so, my aim is not so much to give technical advice on how to design and program computer simulations, but to give recommendations that may help to get the epistemological issues right, so that in the end the computer simulations really yield some substantial scientific results and do not remain mere toys.

6.3.1 Recipe 1: Proof-of-possibility simulations

The object of a proof-of-possibility simulation is to demonstrate theoretical possibilities. In order to assure that the proof of a theoretical possibility via a computer simulation is scientifically valuable the following steps should be taken:

1. *Does the proof of the theoretical possibility in question really contribute to answering the scientific question by which it was motivated? If not, a computer simulation may not be the tool of choice.*

Often, what is needed to be known in order to decide a certain question are not theoretical possibilities but real possibilities. But then the proof of a mere theoretical possibility bears no significance at all for the original question.

Examples of the violation of this principle:

(a) Rudolf Schüßler demonstrated with the help of a computer simulation that cooperation can evolve on "anonymous markets" without norms or enforced repetition of interaction as in the common reiterated games models (see appendix 8.5). This was meant as a contribution to the discussion about sociological normativism, i.e. the position that social order (cooperation) crucially depends on the norms of the society and the social bonds between its members. Since sociological normativists are not at all forced to deny that there exists a theoretical possibility of cooperation without norms in some arbitrary game theoretical setting, Schüßler's demonstration remains without much relevance for the original question.

(b) Michael Taylor somewhat famously demonstrated the theoretical possibility of an anarchic political order by game theoretical reasoning. Since among the many historical precedents of anarchy there exists hardly a single one where the state of anarchy was a state of order, his possibility-proof remains extremely question-begging (Taylor, 1997).[8]

(c) Somewhat similar to Taylor, Brian Skyrms employs computer simulations of the stag-hunt-game allegedly to investigate the evolution of political order (Skyrms, 2004). Again, as these abstract game theoretical models bear hardly any resemblance to any historical instances of the genesis of political order, they remain very question-begging. In contrast, the just-so-stories of 17th century social contract theorists like Thomas Hobbes draw their plausibility from the historical and political experiences they are related to, which makes them far more convincing than any of the game theoretical models.

2. *Can the same results non-trivially be derived from the background theories, anyway? If yes, there is not really a need to build a computer simulation.*

---

[8]The only examples that come close to Taylor's vision concern highly decentralized federal state systems which, however, are not anarchic in the sense of a more or less equal distribution of power on the level of individuals (or at least small families) or the non existence of any centers of power whatsoever.

Of course a computer simulation can in this case still serve as an illustration. Also, there may be cases, where it is not obvious how a result could be derived from the theory, so that a computer simulation may be a faster way to obtain the result.

3. *Design the simulation as simple as possible.*

   As for proof-of-possibility simulations only extremely weak empirical adequacy requirements ("plausibility") must be fulfilled, the simulation does not need to be overly complex. It should only demonstrate the possibility in question in the simplemost way and not more.

4. *Massive simulations should be avoided when only a possibility proof is needed.*

   Massive simulations may be useful to search for unknown theoretical possibilities (see recipe 2). But to merely demonstrate a theoretical possibility, running a whole series of simulation is superfluous.

5. *Don't tell stories and avoid jumping to conclusions by drawing empirical analogies.*

   If a computer simulation proves a certain theoretical possibility, say, for example, the possibility that *Tit for Tat* can be evolutionary successful in the repeated two person Prisoner's Dilemma, then it proves just that, nothing more and nothing less. It should not be pretended that the computer simulation demonstrates how Palestinians and Israelis can live in peace together or the like. To relate proven theoretical possibilities to empirical questions in a meaningful way is a matter of careful and cautious interpretation.

6.3.2 Recipe 2: Exploratory simulations

The object of exploratory simulations is to detect new theoretical phenomena or possibilities within a certain artificial setting. The epistemological and pragmatic questions involved are very similar to those involved in proof-of-possibility simulations.

1. *Is it to be expected that any theoretical phenomena will be discovered that are of scientific relevance? If not, simulations might be beside the point.*

   This is very much the same point as in the first recipe. The rationale behind this precept is that one should have some strategic goal in mind regarding what shall be achieved with the simulation. Merely toying with computer simulations is just not sufficient. It might be objected that playful behavior should have its place in science and that some of the most brilliant discoveries of science have been found by accident. But then, one can hardly base a research strategy on the hope for accidental discoveries.

2. *Use "massive" simulations and "Monte-Carlo" simulations for exploring.*

Unlike the case of merely demonstrating a theoretical possibility, increased complexity of the simulation may pay in the case of exploratory simulations. If one has a certain idea in mind what kind of phenomena could appear, one might also employ systematic search algorithms instead of random searching ("Monte-Carlo simulation") or even evolutionary algorithms to look for the presumed phenomena.

3. *If new phenomena have been discovered, try to isolate them and demonstrate them in a simpler setting.*

In order to understand the phenomenon, it needs to be isolated. For example, the simulation series on reciprocal altruism presented earlier (chapter 4.1.4) uncovered two "surprising" phenomena: A strong success of the strategy *Hawk*, and a more than marginal success of the strategy *Dove*. Both phenomena could then be explained by isolating them (see pages 104 and 109). In order to demonstate that *Dove* can be more successful than *Tit For Tat* even in the presence of exploiting strategies, the phenomenon was isolated in a single simpler proof-of-possibility simulation (see figure 4.16).

4. *Don't tell stories and avoid jumping to conclusions by drawing empirical analogies.*

"Massive simulation" or "Monte-Carlo simulation" sound awfully impressive, but as long as they are not grounded empirically, they remain completely theoretical and, as has been shown at length in chapter 5, there is a certain danger that the thereby obtained results may ultimately turn out to be highly irrelevant for empirical science.

6.3.3 Recipe 3: Predictive simulations

Predictive simulations are simulations that are meant to predict empirical(!) phenomena of a certain class. Predictive simulations do not need to be realistic, as long as the predictions are successful. Because they are intended for empirical application, building predictive simulations is a much more demanding process.

1. *Clearly determine the empirical process(es) which the simulation is supposed to simulate and give an empirical specification of the input and output parameters.*

   This implies that the input parameters must be measurable (or at least determinable) quantities and not hidden factors. For example, in many empirical situations, the utility payoff assumed in game theoretical models is a hidden quantity. Often it is not even clear whether this quantity has a direct empirical counterpart at all. To avoid stability issues, the simulation should therefore be constructed around empirically interpretable and measurable input parameters that is, it should be "built to order" (see above).

2. *Assure that the stability and descriptive appropriateness requirement are met.*

   The simulation model must deliver stable results within the measurement inaccuracies of the input parameters (stability) and its output must be informative within the measurement inaccuracies of the output parameters.

3. *Calibration of the simulation:*

   In order to calibrate the simulation properly, proceed by the following steps:

   (a) Pick an empirical sample case, measure the input parameters, let the simulation generate a prediction and compare it with the empirical data.

   (b) If the simulation predicted the data correctly, it is calibrated and the calibration process is finished.

   (c) If not, revamp the simulation so that it fits (i.e. correctly predicts) the sample case. Pick a new sample case and proceed with step one. Repeat, until the simulation fits a sample case right away. When revamping, make sure that the simulation continues to fit all previous sample cases.

Calibration can also take place ex post, as long as there are enough sample cases and the sample cases are not "used up" before calibrating is finished.

4. *Only when a simulation has been calibrated properly, which is testified by its having made at least one successful prediction, can we say that it simulates the process.*

It is a mistake to assume that merely by revamping and tweaking a computer simulation until it fits the data of some empirical process, we get a simulation of that process. At best what we obtain is an arbitrary (and probably unnecessary complicated) algorithm to produce a certain pattern of output data. But if the simulation predicts correctly then it would be a "miracle", had it not hit upon some underlying causal structure of the simulated empirical process.

The requirement of proper calibration may turn out to be frustrating, because in many cases we may – following the above procedure – fail to reach a calibrated simulation. But then this just means that devising a proper computer simulation is a much more demanding process than it is often thought to be. Merely fitting a simulation ex-post on some set of data is simply not enough. *Only a calibrated simulation simulates.*

6.3.4 Recipe 4: Explanatory simulations

Differently from purely predictive simulations, we demand from an explanatory simulation that it models the real causes of the simulated process. While it is desirable that an explanatory simulation should also be predictive, this is not a requirement. But if it is not predictive, its empirical adequacy must be secured by other means. To devise a truly explanatory simulation, I recommend the following steps.

1. *Check whether really all causally relevant factors of the simulated process can be rendered in a formal simulation model. If the simulation models only a substructure of the process then it must be assured that this substructure can be causally isolated.*

Often it is only a substructure of a more complicated process that can be rendered in formal terms. For example, the strategic component of the diplomatic, economic, or – as the case may be – military interaction of nation states can in many cases be rendered in game theoretical terms. However, as the outcome of the respective interaction processes is also determined by other factors (psychological, ideological, cultural factors etc.) that cannot be rendered in formal terms, constructing too elaborate game theoretical models is probably not worth the effort.

2. *Clearly determine the empirical process(es) which the simulation is supposed to simulate and give an empirical specification of the input and output parameters.*

Same as above.

3. *Assure that the stability and non triviality requirement are met.*

Again, same as above.

4. *Finally, check whether the simulation results really match the empirical data.*

If changes in the simulation are necessary to make it match the data, the question should be clarified whether these changes are consistent with the background knowledge (or, respectively, the known causal factors) about the simulated process.

6.4 Closing Words

The general morale of this chapter can be summarized as follows: Computer simulations are not an end in themselves but a scientific tool the use of which ought to depend on the scientific purpose. This means that computer simulations should be designed in view of the purpose that they are to serve and in such a way that in the end we can check whether the simulations were an appropriate means to their designated end. There may be cases where this is impossible to achieve. But then it is also doubtful whether employing computer simulations in these cases is worthwhile. The most important purpose that computer simulations can serve is that of finding scientific explanations for phenomena that appear in the real world. In order to assess whether computer simulations will serve the purpose of providing an explanation for some empirical phenomenon, I have proposed the three criteria of *empirical adequacy, robustness* and *non-triviality*. Having analyzed with the help of these criteria the reasons why computer simulations of the evolution of altruism largely fail to provide an explanation for why altruism evolves in nature and society, it is difficult to avoid the conclusion that the tool of computer simulations is only of limited use in this context.

However, the value of a scientific tool should not only be judged by its present usefulness, but also by its future potential. If the epistemological justification requirements are raised too high, there is a certain danger of discouraging a new approach with good prospects or rejecting a promising new scientific tool just because it does not live up to all expectations in its premature stages. Regarding this aspect, the tool of computer simulations may still become useful for the explanation of phenomena as empirical research progresses and as new experiments and measurement techniques are developed. But in order to ever become a useful tool of science it is important to have an idea of the direction into which the development of computer simulations must go. The wrong direction would certainly be to continue, as it has been done before, by basing computer simulations on plausible assumptions or on existing computer simulations through adding or changing a few parameters. Such aimless simulating just leads astray from the "real" questions of the evolution of altruism and gives a false impression of knowledge about empirical processes that in reality we do not possess. In the fashion that computer simulations have been used to study the evolution of altruism until now, they have mostly been more of a toy than a useful scientific tool.

Chapter 7

Summary and final reflections

The object of this book was to examine a certain type of explanations for altruism, namely evolutionary explanations of altruism based on computer simulations of the evolution of altruism. It set out with the "riddle" of how altruism can evolve and subsist in a world that is supposedly ruled by the "survival of the fittest" in nature and by the laws of economics and power politics in culture (chapter 2). That various forms of altruism and cooperation exist both in nature and in human society is a fact that cannot be denied so that the question is not if it can exist but why it does exist. One set of possible explanations – and as far as nature is concerned, the only set of possible explanations – consists of evolutionary explanations. Darwin's theory of evolution is *prima facie* only a theory of the evolution of species in nature. In order to transfer it to cultural phenomena, a more abstract, generalized theory of evolution must be devised (chapter 3). This generalized theory of evolution treats any directed development process the course of which is determined by the three "Darwinian modules" reproduction, variation and selection as an evolutionary process. The evolution of species in nature is then just a particular instance of an evolutionary process that is concerned with the evolution of biological organisms and which is characterized by the addition of the laws of genetics to the three "Darwinian modules" that explain the evolution of species. As far as cultural evolution is concerned, there exist different and partly competing brands of evolutionary theories. One brand of evolutionary theories of culture (sociobiology, evolutionary psychology) treats the evolution of culture very much as just another instance of genetic evolution (chapter 3.3.1, page 35ff.). This is not as implausible as it might appear at first sight. For, given that many of the psychological traits of humans are inborn, the explanation for their existence can only be one on the basis of the genetic evolution of humans. That human altruism is to some extent genetically determined appears highly plausible. Yet, certainly not all aspects of human behavior and conduct can be explained on a genetic basis. This is where genuine theories of cultural evolution come into play (chapter 3.3.2, page 40ff.). According to these theories, the evolution of culture constitutes an evolutionary process in its own right that runs largely independently from the process of genetic evolution (though there may have been instances of gene-cultural co-evolution in human history). Altruism, if understood within this framework, does emerge from evolutionary selection processes quite similar to those that take place in genetic evolution, only that it is not altruistic genes that are selected but altruistic social norms. And selection does not take place by the extinction of "unfit" organisms, but by people choosing to adhere to norms that they believe or experience to be advantageous.

When examining the theory of cultural evolution it became apparent, however, that despite the "imperialistic" aspirations of some of its proponents it is at its present stage hardly able to deliver a comprehensive framework for the explanation of human culture that could replace all other rivalling approaches (chapter 3.3.2, page 47ff.). (Unlike biology where the theory of evolution provides the one and only uncontested theoretical framework, there exist many rivalling paradigms that claim to explain the evolution of culture in the social sciences.) Therefore, while certainly some instances of culturally evolved altruism can be explained within the framework of this theory, we should not *a priori* assume that all instances of human altruism must be explainable in this way. The largely unjustified "imperialistic" claims of this approach are particularly regrettable, because they are apt to discredit a fresh approach to cultural phenomena that could otherwise still prove very fertile in many respects.

Given that we have decided to look for evolutionary explanations of altruism, there are theoretical as well as empirical questions that have to be solved. The theoretical question is how the evolution of altruism can be conceived within an evolutionary framework. This theoretical question can be dealt with by formal modeling, of which computer simulations form a special kind. Although the distinction is only introduced later, both conceptual simulation models (chapter 4.1.1 and 4.3.1) as well as exploratory models (chapter 4.1.4) of the evolution of altruism have been presented in this book. The empirical question is, how we can identify instances of evolutionary altruism in nature.

Already when merely examining the computer simulations and before looking at the empirical examples, it became apparent that the use of computer simulations for the understanding of the evolution of altruism faces certain limitations which strongly limit its value as a research tool. While it is possible with the help of simulations to get some general understanding of how altruism could possibly evolve, it is hardly possible to move beyond that point, even with much more refined simulations. There are innumerable plausible ways in which the evolution of altruism can be cast into a computer simulation and at the same time there exist hardly any generalizable conclusions from computer simulations of the evolution of altruism that remain true across all the different simulation scenarios (chapter 4.1.5 and 4.1.6). But then analyzing the artificially generated data from computer simulations is certainly not a feasible way to learn more about the evolution of altruism. The principal misunderstanding that is involved here can very nicely be illustrated by an example which Paul Humphreys has given:

> ... when simulated data rather than real data are fed into the simulation, the prospects for informing us about the world are minimal. To take a simple example, consider a simulation of tossing a coin. Here the independence of the tosses and the equal probabilities of the outcomes are built into the output of the pseudo-random number generator, and so it would be pointless to use the such results as a test of whether the binomial distribution accurately modeled real coin tosses. (Humphreys, 2004, p. 134/135)

If, thus, the artificially generated data from computer simulations alone can at best inspire us to generate hypotheses about the evolution of altruism, we do of course need empirical research to check which of these are true and which are not (chapter 5). Unfortunately, this is where the real trouble starts. For, even a brief look at the empirical research on altruism shows that hardly any of the scenarios that have been examined in the simulation models can be linked to any of the empirical instances of the evolution of altruism in a more than extremely superficial way. This is particularly true for the ever so popular models of the reiterated Prisoner's Dilemma, for which almost nowhere there exits an exact counterpart in nature (or society, for that matter). Now, who is to blame for that? Is it the fault of the empirical researchers and experimenters who just did not pay enough attention to devising experiments that match the simulation models, or is the fault the theoreticians' who do not take into account the restrictions in terms of measurability and observability that are inevitably set to empirical research. In my opinion the fault clearly lies with the theoreticians, because the restrictions that the experimenters face when, for example, trying to measure payoff parameters are much harder to overcome than it is for the computer programmer to redesign a simulation program.

Therefore, the theoreticians must take the restrictions and conditions of empirical research into account in order to design models that can be tested empirically.

(As a side note it can be mentioned that the fact that the investigation of the evolution of altruism does therefore strongly depend on the conditions of empirical research in the fields where altruism appears, has consequences for the division of labor in science. The evolution of altruism is obviously not the kind of problem that can be investigated primarily by theoretical reasoning as it can take place in the philosopher's armchair. Because it strongly depends on a substantial background knowledge in the respective empirical sciences and – as the case may be – on the access to the means for experimentation (even the relatively simple experiments of behavioral economics are costly in terms of instruments, i.e. computer networks, and money), the scientific investigation of the evolution of altruism is not so much a job a typical academic philosopher can contribute to, but more one for the special scientists in the respective fields of the social sciences and biology. It is quite regrettable that analyical philosophy in particular while being so deliberately forgetful of the philosophical heritage does often only offer second rate imitations of the special sciences as compensation.)

If the computer simulations of the evolution of altruism have proved to be a failure in the sense that it has been impossible to validate their results by empirical research beyond what can at best be called weak analogies, the question arises what can be learned from this failure or how it could be done better. It should be clear by now that the problem does not consist in getting the technical side of computer simulations right, but that it is about understanding the epistemological conditions. Traditionally (at least in the branch of simulations of the evolution of cooperation or altruism), the approach has often been very naive: Start with a few plausible assumptions about the subject matter, build your simulation and eventually revamp the simulation so that it produces some "interesting" results, confirms your envisaged hypothesis or fits some set of empirical data. But even, if the last step, fitting the simulation to data, is taken (which has not been the case for most models and simulations of the evolution of cooperation) this may not be sufficient. As for that matter, before we can earnestly say that a simulation simulates some given empirical process it must at least have produced one proper prediction, a requirement that has been incorporated into the rules for calibrating simulations in the recipe for predictive simulations (chapter 6.3.3). If a simulation is to explain the process it simulates, the requirements are even higher: It must be empirically adequate, robust and non trivial (chapter 6.1.2). If this seems to raise the bar for proper computer simulations quite high then it merely reflects of how poor quality (epistemologically considered) many computer simulations are. Of course it might be objected that the criteria are too strict. As to this objection, I can only refer to the reasons laid down in chapter 6.1.2. As such they are open to future debate.

Chapter 8

Appendices

8.1 Strategies for the reiterated Prisoner's Dilemma

In the following subsections all strategies that occur in the reiterated two person Prisoner's Dilemma simulations in chapter 4 will be described. In subsection 8.1.1 all of the strategies that were used in the first simple model of reciprocal altruism (see chapter 4.1.1) will be described. The following subsections 8.1.2 and 8.1.3 explain the strategies that were used in the simulation series of chapter 4.1.4. Finally, subsection 8.1.4 describes the family of *Signaling Cheater*-strategies plus the strategy *Signaling Cheater*, a member of which was used in the group selection scenario in chapter 4.3.1. The verbal description of the strategies is supplemented by their implementation in the **Python** programing language. For the better understanding of the program code, it should be kept in mind that a return value of one signifies a cooperative move, while a return value of zero translates into a defective move in the game.

8.1.1 Ordinary strategies

Following is a description of the strategies that were used for the "simple model" of chapter 4.1.1.

Tit for Tat The strategy *Tit for Tat* starts with a cooperative move in the first round. In the subsequent rounds *Tit for Tat* cooperates if the other player cooperated in the previous rounds. If the other player defected in the previous round, *Tit for Tat* punishes the defector by defecting itself.

```
class TitForTat(Strategy):
    def firstMove(self):
        return 1          # cooperate in the first round
    def nextMove(self, myMoves, opMoves):
        return opMoves[-1]  # reciprocate opponent's last move
```

Grim   The strategy *Grim* starts with a cooperative move and continues to cooperate unless the other player defects. Once the other player has failed to reciprocate cooperation *Grim* defects unanimously throughout the remainder of the game.

```
class Grim(Strategy):
    def firstMove(self):
        self.punish = False
        return 1
    def nextMove(self, myMoves, opMoves):
        if self.punish:  return 0
        elif opMoves[-1] == 1:  return 1
        else:
            self.punish = True
            return 0
```

Dove   The strategy *Dove* always cooperates, no matter what the other player does.

```
class Dove(Strategy):
    def firstMove(self):
        return 1
    def nextMove(self, myMoves, opMoves):
        return 1
```

Hawk   The strategy *Hawk* never cooperates.

```
class Hawk(Strategy):
    def firstMove(self):
        return 0
    def nextMove(self, myMoves, opMoves):
        return 0
```

Random   The strategy *Random* cooperates or defects at random with a 50% chance.

```
class Random(Strategy):
    def firstMove(self):
        return random.randint(0,1)
    def nextMove(self, myMoves, opMoves):
        return random.randint(0,1)
```

Tester   The strategy *Tester* starts off with two defections. If the opponent does not answer these defections with punishment, *Tester* classifies the opponent as an exploitable strategy and defects every second round during the remainder of the match. Otherwise *Tester* tries to appease the other player with two cooperative moves in round three and four and then switches to the fairly reliable strategy *Tit for Tat* for the remainder of the reiterated game.

```
class Tester(Strategy):
    def firstMove(self):
        self.state = "Test"
        return 0
    def nextMove(self, myMoves, opMoves):
        if self.state == "Test":
            self.state = "Evaluate"
            return 0
        elif self.state == "Evaluate":
            if opMoves[-1] == 0:
                self.state = "Consolation"
```

```
        return 1
    else:
        self.state = "Dove"
        return 0
elif self.state == "Consolation":
    self.state = "TitForTat"
    return 1
elif self.state == "Dove":
    self.state = "Hawk"
    return 1
elif self.state == "Hawk":
    self.state = "Dove"
    return 0
elif self.state == "TitForTat":
    return opMoves[-1]
else:
    raise AssertionError, \
        "Tester: state %s is not a valid state!"%self.state
```

Pavlov Named after the famous Russian physiologist who discovered the "conditional reflex", the strategy *Pavlov* plays "win stay, lose shift", starting with a defection. Other than for example *Tit for Tat* it will continue with defecting, if the opponent fails to punish defections.

```
def invertMove(move):
    """--> inverted move. (0 becomes1 and 1 becomes 0)"""
    if move == 0:  return 1
    else:  return 0
class Pavlov(Strategy):
    def firstMove(self):
        self.condition = 0
        return self.condition
    def nextMove(self, myMoves, opMoves):
        if opMoves[-1] == 0:
            self.condition = invertMove(self.condition)
        return self.condition
```

Tranquilizer The strategy *Tranquilizer* is a refinenement of the strategy "Tit for two tats" which usually cooperates and only punishes the opponent with a defection if the opponent has defected during the two previous rounds. But in contrast to "Tit for two tats", *Tranquillizer* also defects unmotivated with a random probability that increases during the course of the repeated game. (This reflects the consideration that good relations with the other player become less important the shorter the shadow of the future is.) The random defection probability is zero in the beginning and is increased by 1% before each round, up to a limit of 50%.

```
class Tranquilizer(Strategy):
    def firstMove(self):
        self.evilFactor = 0.0
        return 1
    def nextMove(self, myMoves, opMoves):
        if self.evilFactor < 0.5:  self.evilFactor += 0.01
        if opMoves[-2:] == [0,0]:
            return 0
        else:
            if random.random() < self.evilFactor: return 0
            else:  return 1
```

Joss   The strategy *Joss* basically plays "Tit for tat", but it defects unmotivated (i.e. in cases where it does not defect to punish the opponent for a defection in the previous round) with a random probability of 10%.

```
class Joss(Strategy):
    def firstMove(self):
        return 1
    def nextMove(self, myMoves, opMoves):
        if opMoves[-1] == 0:  return 0
        else:
            if random.random() < 0.1:  return 0
            else:  return 1
```

8.1.2 Parameterized *Tit for Tat*-strategies

The *Parameterized Tit for Tat*-strategies are derived from *Tit for Tat*
by adding the two parameters *good rate* and *evil rate* to modify the
behavior of *Tit for Tat*. The *good rate* is a probability with which the
Parametrized Tit for Tat makes a cooperative move when the ordinary
Tit for Tat would not. And, conversely, the *evil rate* defines a probability
with which the parametrized strategy defects when normally *Tit for Tat*
would cooperate. If both the *good rate* and the *evil rate* are zero then
the *Parametrized Tit for Tat*-strategy is the same as the ordinary *Tit
for Tat*. If the *good rate* is 1 and the evil rate is 0 then it is the same as
Dove. If, conversely, the *evil rate* is 1 and the *good rate* is 0 then then
strategy played is the same as *Hawk*. If both rates are 0.5 it is the same
as the *Random*-strategy.

The implementation of the *Parameterized Tit for Tat*-strategies below takes account of these connections by appending appropriate suffixes
to the name of the strategy in these special cases. The names of the
Paramterized Tit for Tat-strategies consist of the "family name", which
is "P_TFT" followed by the goodrate and the evil rate and possibly by
a suffix to indicate a meaningful speacial case. Thus "P_TFT 0.2 0.4" is
the name of the *Parameterized Tit for Tat*-strategy with a *good rate* o
f 20% and an *evil rate* of 40%, while "P_TFT 0.5 0.5 (Random)" names
the *Parameterized Tit for Tat* strategy with both a *good-* and *evil rate*
of 50%, which is in effect the *Random*-strategy.

```
class ParameterizedTFT(Strategy):
    def __repr__(self):
        return self.__class__.__name__ + "(" + repr(self.goodrate) + \
               ", " + repr(self.evilrate) + ")"
    def __init__(self, goodrate=0.2, evilrate=0.05):
        assert goodrate >= 0.0 and goodrate <= 1.0, "goodrate must be >= 0 and
<= 1!"
        assert evilrate >= 0.0 and evilrate <= 1.0, "evilrate must be >= 0 and
<= 1!"
        Strategy.__init__(self)
        self.randomizing = True
        self.goodrate = goodrate
        self.evilrate = evilrate
        self.name = "P_TFT %1.2f %1.2f" % (self.goodrate,self.evilrate)
        if self.goodrate == 1.0 and self.evilrate == 0.0:
            self.name += " (Dove)"
        elif self.evilrate == 1.0 and self.goodrate == 0.0:
            self.name += " (Hawk)"
        elif self.goodrate == 0.0 and self.evilrate == 0.0:
            self.name += " (TitForTat)"
        elif self.goodrate == 0.5 and self.evilrate == 0.5:
            self.name += " (Random)"
        elif self.goodrate == 1.0 and self.evilrate == 1.0:
            self.name += " (Inverted)"
    def firstMove(self):
        if random.random() < self.evilrate:  return 0
        else:  return 1
    def nextMove(self, myMoves, opMoves):
        if opMoves[-1] == 0:
            if random.random() < self.goodrate:  return 1
            else:  return 0
```

```
else:
    if random.random() < self.evilrate:  return 0
    else:  return 1
```

8.1.3   Two state automata and their implementation

One way of representing strategies in the reiterated Prisoner's Dilemma is by using finite automata. An automaton is here understood as a machine that can take one of several different states. The state of the machine determines what move a player (whose strategy is represented by the machine) makes in each round of the reiterated Prisoner's Dilemma. Depending on the opponent's move the machine then changes its state for the next round. Theoretically, any deterministic strategy in the reiterated Prisoner's Dilemma can be represented by an automaton, if we only allow the automaton to be complex enough. In this book, only *two state automata* are used in order to represent strategies of a limited complexity. Where more complex strategies are used in the simulations, the usual algorithmic representation is used instead of automata.

Two state automata are always in one of two different states, which in the following will be called state D and state H. Each state is defined by the move the player makes in this state and the transition rules which tell us to which target state the automaton switches depending on the opponent's move. Because there are only two possible moves and exactly two states, we can by convenience assume that state D is the state in which the automaton makes a cooperative move and state H is the state in which the automaton makes a defective move.[1] For each state there are two transition rules, one which tells us into which state the automaton switches when the opponent has played dove and one which tells us into which state the automaton switches when the opponent plays hawk. Finally, we need to decide which state the automaton starts with. All in all an automaton is thus defined by five different parameters which can conveniently be represented by a five character string of Ds and Hs as shown in figure 8.1:

Accordingly, two state automata can be implemented by a simple table look-up algorithm, as can be seen in the following abbreviated code snippet:

---

[1] This may seem awkward at first, because logically the state itself (which is defined by both the move *and* the transition rules) and the move a players makes when in a specific state are quite different things. How can it then be identified by the move alone? To understand that this is possible, it should be observed that if both states result in the same move (either cooperative or defective) then the transition rules do not matter any more, because the automaton always makes the same move anyway. But if the automaton makes different moves in each state then there exists only one set of transition rules for each of the two possible moves and the state can perfectly be identified by the respective move alone.

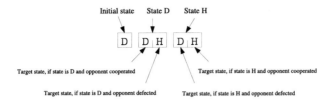

Figure 8.1: Coding players in the repeated Prisoner's Dilemma as two state automata. The example shows the string representation for the automaton that plays *Tit for Tat*.

```
class TwoStateAutomaton(Strategy):

    def __init__(self, programString="DDHDH"):
        Strategy.__init__(self)
        self.name = "AM: " + programString

        dic = { 'D':1, 'H':0 }
        self.initialState = dic[programString[0]]
        self.state = self.initialState
        self.progString = programString
        self.prog = [ [dic[programString[4]], dic[programString[3]]], \
                      [dic[programString[2]], dic[programString[1]]] ]

    def firstMove(self):
        self.state = self.initialState
        return self.state

    def nextMove(self, myMoves, opMoves):
        self.state = self.prog[self.state][opMoves[-1]]
        return self.state
```

The string representation allows for 32 (2^5) different encodings, but in fact there exist only 26 different automata, because the automata that represent the strategies *Dove* and *Hawk* can be encoded in four different ways (since there are four (2^2) different codings for the state that is never reached). By convenience we will pick the string representation "DDDDD" for the strategy *Dove* and "HHHHH" for the strategy *Hawk*. Table 8.2 shows all possible two state automata. Some of them have been given names either to indicate which algorithmic strategy they represent or just fancy names that where partly taken from (Binmore, 1998, p. 296) (who in turn borrowed them from "Alice in Wonderland").

1.	DDDDD (Dove)	14.	HDDDD
2.	DDHDD (Tweedledee)	15.	HDDDH
3.	DDHDH (Tit for Tat)	16.	HDDHD (Tweetypie)
4.	DDHHD (Tweedledum)	17.	HDHDD (Simpleton)
5.	DDHHH (Grim)	18.	HDHDH
6.	DHDDD	19.	HDHHD (Pavlov)
7.	DHDDH	20.	HHDDD
8.	DHDHD	21.	HHDDH
9.	DHDHH	22.	HHDHD (Inverted TFT)
10.	DHHDD	23.	HHHDD
11.	DHHDH	24.	HHHDH
12.	DHHHD	25.	HHHHD
13.	DHHHH	26.	HHHHH

Figure 8.2: List of all possible two state automata. The additional names are mostly taken from (Binmore, 1998, p. 296).

8.1.4 The family of *Signaling Cheater* strategies

A *Singalling Cheater*-strategy is a strategy that plays a predefined sequence of cooperative and defective moves in the first n rounds of the repeated Prisoner's Dilemma. If the opponent player starts with exactly the same sequence of moves, *Signaling Cheater* assumes that it has met another *Signaling Cheater* and cooperates unconditionally for the remaining rounds of the repeated game. Otherwise *Signaling Cheater* defects for the rest of the game. Thus, *Signaling Cheater* is a strategy that is designed to cooperate only with its own kind (that is other *Signaling Cheaters* that use the same starting sequence as a signal) and not to cooperate with any other strategy. The `Python` implementation of *Signaling Cheater* follows below:

```
class SignalingCheater(Strategy):
    def __repr__(self):
        return self.__class__.__name__+"("+repr(self.signal)+")"
    def __init__(self, signal=(0,1,1)):
        Strategy.__init__(self)
        self.signal = signal
        for i in self.signal: self.name += str(i)
    def firstMove(self):
        self.pos = 0
        return self.signal[self.pos]
    def nextMove(self, myMoves, opMoves):
        self.pos += 1
        if self.pos < len(self.signal):
            return self.signal[self.pos]
        else:
            if tuple(opMoves[:len(self.signal)]) == self.signal:
                return 1
            else: return 0
```

8.2 Implementation details of the population dynamics

The population dynamical processes at the base of the simulations in this book are modeled in a very common and straight forward way: At the center of most simulations is the evolutionary success of certain strategies in games such as the repeated Prisoner's Dilemma game. We assume a population of players where each player plays one of the strategies. (If this seems to abstract, it may help to think of the strategies as species and of the players as individuals belonging to the one or the other species, or to think of the strategies as mutually exclusive social norms and the players as people that chose which norm they adhere to.) The players that play a certain strategy thus constitute the population share of this strategy. For the sake of simplicity an infinitely large population of players is assumed. The size of the population share of a strategy is expressed as a fraction of 1. In the beginning the shares are usually divided equal among all strategies. The evolutionary process is modeled as a sequence of non overlapping generational cycles. During each generation the fitness of every strategy is determined by the average score in the tournament, where the score of each match is weighted with the population share of the opponent. Thus the fitness is determined by:

$$F_i = \sum_{k=1}^{n} S_{ik} P_k \tag{8.1}$$

F_i the Fitness of the i-th strategy
S_{ik} the score of the i-th strategy when playing against the k-th strategy
P_k the population share of k-th strategy
n the total number of strategies in the simulation
i, k indices of the strategies

In the simulation program the calculation of the fitness is performed by one of the different Fitness functions in module Dynamics.py of package PopulationDynamics. The simplemost of these is the function Dynamics._QuickFitness2. If calculates the fitness values of a population of strategies based on a two player game. The function _QuickFitness2 is called with the tuple of population shares and the payoff matrix as parameters. The payoff matrix contains the payoff of the matches of each strategy against every other strategy. The function returns the list of fitness values of the strategies.[2]

```
 1: def _QuickFitness2(population, payoff):
 2:     n = population
 3:     L = len(n)
 4:     p = []
 5:     for i in xrange(L):
 6:         s = 0.0
 7:         for k in xrange(L):
 8:             s += payoff[i,k]*n[k]
 9:         p.append(s)
10:     return p
```

The fitness F_i of equation 8.1 is calculated in the `for` loop in lines 7 and 8. The outer `for` loop (lines 5 to 9) calculates the fitness for each strategy and appends it to the list of fitness values. (The assignment in line 2 is done just for convenience to avoid to many long variable names in line 8.)

One of the parameters that is varied in the simulation series' (see 4.1.4) is the parameter e for the correlation of players of the same strategy. If e is nonzero then players with the same strategy interact more often than with purely random matching. In order to integrate correlation into the model the original fitness equation (8.1) must be slightly changed.[3]

$$F_i = \sum_{\substack{k=1 \\ k \neq i}}^{n} S_{ik}(1-e)P_k + S_{ii}(P_i + e(1-P_i)) \qquad (8.2)$$

F_i the Fitness of the i-th strategy
S_{ik} the score of the i-th strategy when playing against the k-th strat
P_k the population share of k-th strategy
n the total number of strategies in the simulation
i, k indices of the strategies
e the correlation factor, ranging from 0 to 1

It should be observed that if the correlation $e = 0$ then equation (8.2 resolves to the simpler equation (8.1). But if the correlation $e = 1$ (perfect correlation) then $F_i = S_{ii}$, which is exactly what we would expect: When the correlation is perfect, players of one strategy never interact with players of any other strategy and their fitness depends entirely on how the strategy scores against itself. The implementation of the fitness functions that includes correlation looks accordingly:

---

[2]This and the following code snippets are taken from module `PopulationDynamics.Dynamics`. For the sake of brevity and better readability the error checking code has been left out here.

[3]This very simple model of correlation was taken from (Skyrms, 1996, p. 113, note 30).

```
1: def _Fitness2(population, payoff, e):
2:     n = population
3:     L = len(n)
4:     p = []
5:     for i in xrange(L):
6:         s = 0.0
7:         for k in xrange(L):
8:             if i == k:
9:                 s += payoff[i,k]*(n[i]+e*(1.0-n[i]))
10:             else:
11:                 s += payoff[i,k]*(n[k]-e*n[k])
12:         p.append(s)
13:     return p
```

The population shares of the next generation are then determined simply by multiplying the population share of each strategy with its fitness. Since we calculate with population shares and not with absolute population sizes the fitness values always express relative fitness. (It makes no difference if strategy A has a fitness of 1 and strategy B has a fitness of 2 or if A has fitness 50 and B fitness 100.) For convenience, the population shares are normalized (by dividing them through the sum of the not normalized population shares) so that they nicely add up to 1:

$$P_i^{g+1} = \frac{P_i^g F_i^g}{\sum_{k=1}^{n} P_k^g F_k^g} \tag{8.3}$$

P_i^g the population share of strategy i in generation g
F_i^g the fitness of the i-th strategy in generation g
g the number of the current generation
i, k indices of the strategies

The program code that performs these calculations looks as follows:

```
1: def _QuickReplicator(population, fitness):
2:     n = list(population)
3:     L = len(population)
4:     f = fitness(population)
5:     for i in xrange(L): n[i] *= f[i]
6:     N = sum(n)
7:     for i in xrange(L): n[i] /= N
8:     return tuple(n)
```

The function Dynamics._QuickReplicator of package Population-Dynamics takes the tuple of population shares and a fitness function as parameters and returns the tuple of population shares of the next generation. The fitness function is called in line 4. It is expected to return a list with the fitness values of the strategies. (As it takes only one parameter the above fitness function, which takes two parameters, cannot be called directly from the replicator function, but must be called indirectly through a dynamically created function that includes the payoff matrix as a constant parameter. There are technical reasons for using this construction instead of passing through the payoff matrix from the caller of the replicator function to the fitness function.) The actual calculation of the next generation's population shares P_i^{g+1} of equation 8.3 are carried out in lines 5 to 8.

Just as in the case of the fitness equation (8.1) and the related program code there exists an extended version of the population equation (8.3) for the case when the background noise $b > 0$:

$$P_i^{g+1} = \frac{P_i^g F_i^g (1 - bR_i^g)}{\sum_{k=1}^{n} P_k^g F_k^g (1 - bR_k^g)} \tag{8.4}$$

P_i^g the population share of strategy i in generation g
F_i the fitness of the i-th strategy in generation g
g the number of the current generation
i, k indices of the strategies
b evolutionary background noise $0 \leq b \leq 1$
R_i^g a random number $0 \leq R_i^g < 1$

The implementation in **Python** code is likewise:

```
1: def _Replicator(population, fitness, noise):
2:     n = list(population)
3:     L = len(population)
4:     f = fitness
5:     for i in xrange(L):  n[i] *= f[i]- random.uniform(0,f[i]*noise)
6:     N = sum(n)
7:     for i in xrange(L): n[i] /= N
8:     return tuple(n)
```

A few things need to be noted about the model as well as its implementation. When using infinite populations this is of course an idealization. It makes it easier to calculate with population shares and, as the model is purely conceptual and we do not have any particular empirical application of the model in mind, any fixed finite population size would be arbitrary anyway. However, the use of infinite populations for modeling processes that take place in finite populations slightly distorts the evolutionary process in two ways: 1) Even the slightest variations in fitness lead to variations in population shares. In real life, or in nature for that matter, it is conceivable that very small fitness differences are not strong enough to transform into a different number of offspring[4] and 2) and more importantly, as long as the fitness value remains above zero, a species (or strategy respectively) can never die out. Its population share could be arbitrarily small, yet there is still a possibility that it will eventually recover, even though in "real life" it would never be

---

[4]It is important here that the fitness and the number of offspring are not the same by definition. For a short discussion of this point see page 32.

given a second chance. Of course, both of these distortions can, if necessary, easily be remedied by 1) mapping the fitness onto a discrete set of numbers before calculating the population shares of the next generation and 2) defining a threshold population share below which a species (or strategy in our case) will be eliminated from the population, but it is important to keep these points in mind.

They way in which the fitness is derived from the payoffs in the (Prisoner's Dilemma) game also introduces certain peculiarities. Because the weighted average payoff is used as fitness value, negative payoffs are impermissible. This may seem awkward given that negative payoffs are usually perfectly legitimate in game theory and might even be given a reasonable interpretation, for example, to indicate a loss of money in an economical context. But if we think of fitness in an evolutionary context, it makes perfectly good sense to exclude negative payoffs, because the reproduction rate cannot conceivably fall below zero. A reproduction rate of zero already means – depending on the context – the extinction of a species, the vanishing of a gene or the disappearance of a social norm. What worse could happen in evolution than extinction?

The simulation models described in sections 4.1.1 and 4.1.4 do even make it impossible that the fitness value will be exactly zero, because even though some strategies may be left with a payoff of zero in the repeated Prisoner's Dilemma match against another strategy (as, for example, *Dove* against *Hawk*) the average payoff of a strategy in the tournament can never be zero, because no strategy gets a zero payoff in the match against itself. This simplifies calculations greatly, because no provisions for the special case of a zero fitness need to be made. Otherwise, care would have to be taken to avoid divisions by zero and the like.

8.3 Comprehensive results of the simualtion series

The following tables and figures list all of aggregated data of the simulation series described in chapter 4.1.4. First (section 8.3.1) the overall results of the big series are given, both as tables and then in a graphical form. The stratgey set of *Two State Automata* (section 8.1.3 above) and the set of *Parameterized Tit for Tats* (section 8.1.2) are always considered separately. In the tables the the average final population shares of the evolutionary simulations is displayed. (The simulations in the series were stopped either when no changes in the composition of the population occured any more or when the 25,600th generation had been reached.) The strategies are always ranked after their average final population share in the whole series. The graphical representation depicts in three columns the tournament ranking (in lexical order that is, if a strategy has been the the winner of the tournament two times over the whole series it is always better than a strategy that has won the tournament only once, no matter how often it was placed second), the evolutionary ranking (by the average final population share) and a more illustrative representation of the evolutionary ranking. On the graphical representation, the strategies are represented by colored bars, which represent their degree of altruism. A green color means that the strategy is fully (e.g. *Dove*) or to some degree (e.g. *Tweedledee*) genuinely altruistic. A blue color means that it is either reciprocal (e.g. *Tit for Tat*, *Grim*) or cannot be classified (e.g. *Inverted*). Red means that the strategy is a cheater or (primarily) non altruistic (e.g. *Hawk*). (See page 99 for detailed description of the color scheme and its motivation.)

In order to determine the influence of single parameters on the simulation, the aggregated results for every parameter held constant at each of its values (see page 89) was calculated as well. This helps to find out about the influence of single parameters on the simulation, though possible joint effects of several parameters still remain opaque. For each parameter and strategy set, a table is presented that shows how the average final population share of each strategy changes for different values of the parameter. There is also a graphical representation of the tournament rankings and evolutionary outcomes for each parameter value and strategy set.

8.3.1 "Big series" overall results

	Average Final Population Share
Strategy	overall results
AM: HHHHH (HAWK)	34.61 %
AM: DDHHH (GRIM)	17.28 %
AM: DDHDH (TIT FOR TAT)	10.22 %
AM: HDHHD (PAVLOV)	10.01 %
AM: DDDDD (DOVE)	9.27 %
AM: DDHHD (TWEEDLEDUM)	7.12 %
AM: DDHDD (TWEEDLEDEE)	2.91 %
AM: HDHDH (TAT FOR TIT)	1.73 %
AM: DHHHH	1.56 %
AM: DHHDH	1.39 %
AM: HDHDD (SIMPLETON)	1.28 %
AM: HHHDH	1.09 %
AM: HHHHD	0.52 %
AM: DHHDD	0.39 %
AM: HHHDD	0.36 %
AM: DHHHD	0.13 %
AM: DHDHH	0.10 %
AM: HDDHD (TWEETYPIE)	0.00 %
AM: HHDHD (INVERTED)	0.00 %
AM: DHDHD	0.00 %
AM: HDDDD	0.00 %
AM: HHDDD	0.00 %
AM: DHDDD	0.00 %
AM: HDDDH	0.00 %
AM: HHDDH	0.00 %
AM: DHDDH	0.00 %

	Average Final Population Share
Strategy	overall results
P_TFT 0.00 0.00 (TitForTat)	38.54 %
P_TFT 0.00 1.00 (Hawk)	28.50 %
P_TFT 0.20 0.00	8.98 %
P_TFT 1.00 0.00 (Dove)	8.30 %
P_TFT 0.40 0.00	8.27 %
P_TFT 0.80 0.00	2.16 %
P_TFT 1.00 1.00 (Inverted)	1.55 %
P_TFT 0.00 0.80	1.06 %
P_TFT 0.20 0.40	0.93 %
P_TFT 0.60 0.00	0.51 %
P_TFT 0.40 0.20	0.46 %
P_TFT 0.60 1.00	0.38 %
P_TFT 0.40 0.40	0.23 %
P_TFT 0.60 0.20	0.12 %
P_TFT 0.80 1.00	0.01 %
P_TFT 0.40 1.00	0.00 %
P_TFT 0.20 1.00	0.00 %
P_TFT 0.00 0.60	0.00 %
P_TFT 0.80 0.20	0.00 %
P_TFT 1.00 0.20	0.00 %
P_TFT 0.80 0.40	0.00 %
P_TFT 0.20 0.20	0.00 %
P_TFT 0.60 0.40	0.00 %
P_TFT 1.00 0.40	0.00 %
P_TFT 0.00 0.40	0.00 %
P_TFT 0.80 0.60	0.00 %
P_TFT 1.00 0.60	0.00 %
P_TFT 0.00 0.20	0.00 %
P_TFT 0.60 0.60	0.00 %
P_TFT 0.40 0.60	0.00 %
P_TFT 0.20 0.60	0.00 %
P_TFT 0.80 0.80	0.00 %
P_TFT 0.20 0.80	0.00 %
P_TFT 0.60 0.80	0.00 %
P_TFT 0.40 0.80	0.00 %
P_TFT 1.00 0.80	0.00 %

233

Results for strategy set: "Automata"

Tournament Ranking · Evolutionary Ranking · Average Final Population

Figure 8.3: The aggregated results of all simulations of the "big series" using *Automata* strategies.

234

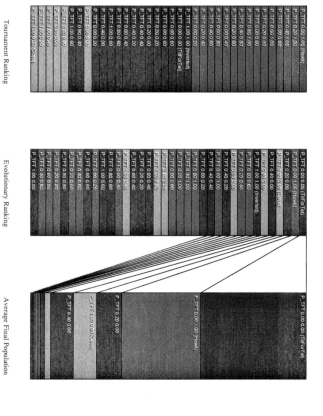

Figure 8.4: The aggregated results of all simulations of the "big series" using *Parameterized Tit for Tat* strategies.

8.3.2 The influence of correlation

The correlation factor describes the probability by which players are more likely to meet opponents with the same strategy than opponents with a different strategy. A correlation of 0% means that the players are randomly matched, while with a correlation of 100% players do exclusively play against players of the same strategy.

Automata

Strategy	overall	c = 0.0	c = 0.1	c = 0.2
	Average Final Population Share			
AM: HHHHH (HAWK)	34.61 %	44.30 %	33.71 %	25.81 %
AM: DDHHH (GRIM)	17.28 %	21.73 %	16.27 %	13.85 %
AM: DDHDH (TIT FOR TAT)	10.22 %	9.51 %	13.47 %	7.69 %
AM: HDHHD (PAVLOV)	10.01 %	2.08 %	4.83 %	23.11 %
AM: DDDDD (DOVE)	9.27 %	8.04 %	11.29 %	8.48 %
AM: DDHHD (TWEEDLEDUM)	7.12 %	2.58 %	4.95 %	13.82 %
AM: DDHDD (TWEEDLEDEE)	2.91 %	2.70 %	4.40 %	1.63 %
AM: HDHDH (TAT FOR TIT)	1.73 %	0.00 %	1.88 %	3.32 %
AM: DHHHH	1.56 %	4.69 %	0.00 %	0.00 %
AM: DHHDH	1.39 %	0.53 %	2.62 %	1.02 %
AM: HDHDD (SIMPLETON)	1.28 %	0.62 %	2.57 %	0.66 %
AM: HHHDH	1.09 %	0.56 %	2.11 %	0.61 %
AM: HHHHD	0.52 %	0.78 %	0.79 %	0.00 %
AM: DHHDD	0.39 %	0.86 %	0.32 %	0.00 %
AM: HHHDD	0.36 %	0.70 %	0.39 %	0.00 %
AM: DHHHD	0.13 %	0.00 %	0.40 %	0.00 %
AM: DHDHH	0.10 %	0.29 %	0.00 %	0.00 %
AM: HDDHD (TWEETYPIE)	0.00 %	0.00 %	0.00 %	0.00 %
AM: HHDHD (INVERTED)	0.00 %	0.00 %	0.00 %	0.00 %
AM: DHDHD	0.00 %	0.00 %	0.00 %	0.00 %
AM: HDDDD	0.00 %	0.00 %	0.00 %	0.00 %
AM: HHDDD	0.00 %	0.00 %	0.00 %	0.00 %
AM: DHDDD	0.00 %	0.00 %	0.00 %	0.00 %
AM: HDDDH	0.00 %	0.00 %	0.00 %	0.00 %
AM: HHDDH	0.00 %	0.00 %	0.00 %	0.00 %
AM: DHDDH	0.00 %	0.00 %	0.00 %	0.00 %

236

Results for strategy set: "Automata"

Tournament Ranking   Evolutionary Ranking   Average Final Population

Figure 8.5: The aggregated results of those simulations of the "big series" for which the correlation value was 0%.

237

Results for strategy set: "Automata"

Figure 8.6: The aggregated results of those simulations of the "big series" for which the correlation value was 10%.

238

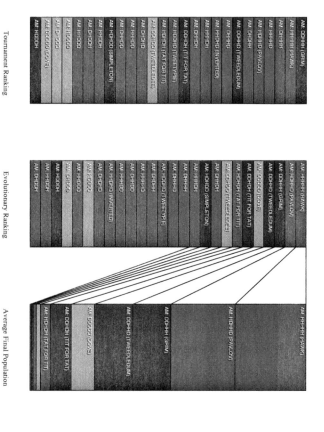

Figure 8.7: The aggregated results of those simulations of the "big series" for which the correlation value was 20%.

Parameterized Tit for Tats

	Average Final Population Share			
Strategy	overall	c = 0.0	c = 0.1	c = 0.2
P_TFT 0.00 0.00 (TitForTat)	38.54 %	32.71 %	42.20 %	40.72 %
P_TFT 0.00 1.00 (Hawk)	28.50 %	54.45 %	25.76 %	5.29 %
P_TFT 0.20 0.00	8.98 %	0.87 %	6.84 %	19.22 %
P_TFT 1.00 0.00 (Dove)	8.30 %	1.27 %	7.15 %	16.49 %
P_TFT 0.40 0.00	8.27 %	4.14 %	9.60 %	11.06 %
P_TFT 0.80 0.00	2.16 %	0.70 %	2.11 %	3.68 %
P_TFT 1.00 1.00 (Inverted)	1.55 %	1.24 %	1.54 %	1.88 %
P_TFT 0.00 0.80	1.06 %	1.80 %	1.37 %	0.00 %
P_TFT 0.20 0.40	0.93 %	2.78 %	0.00 %	0.00 %
P_TFT 0.60 0.00	0.51 %	0.05 %	0.78 %	0.70 %
P_TFT 0.40 0.20	0.46 %	0.00 %	1.39 %	0.00 %
P_TFT 0.60 1.00	0.38 %	0.00 %	0.37 %	0.78 %
P_TFT 0.40 0.40	0.23 %	0.00 %	0.69 %	0.00 %
P_TFT 0.60 0.20	0.12 %	0.00 %	0.19 %	0.17 %
P_TFT 0.80 1.00	0.01 %	0.00 %	0.02 %	0.01 %
P_TFT 0.40 1.00	0.00 %	0.00 %	0.00 %	0.00 %
P_TFT 0.20 1.00	0.00 %	0.00 %	0.00 %	0.00 %
P_TFT 0.00 0.60	0.00 %	0.00 %	0.00 %	0.00 %
P_TFT 0.80 0.20	0.00 %	0.00 %	0.00 %	0.00 %
P_TFT 1.00 0.20	0.00 %	0.00 %	0.00 %	0.00 %
P_TFT 0.80 0.40	0.00 %	0.00 %	0.00 %	0.00 %
P_TFT 0.20 0.20	0.00 %	0.00 %	0.00 %	0.00 %
P_TFT 0.60 0.40	0.00 %	0.00 %	0.00 %	0.00 %
P_TFT 1.00 0.40	0.00 %	0.00 %	0.00 %	0.00 %
P_TFT 0.00 0.40	0.00 %	0.00 %	0.00 %	0.00 %
P_TFT 0.80 0.60	0.00 %	0.00 %	0.00 %	0.00 %
P_TFT 1.00 0.60	0.00 %	0.00 %	0.00 %	0.00 %
P_TFT 0.00 0.20	0.00 %	0.00 %	0.00 %	0.00 %
P_TFT 0.60 0.60	0.00 %	0.00 %	0.00 %	0.00 %
P_TFT 0.40 0.60	0.00 %	0.00 %	0.00 %	0.00 %
P_TFT 0.20 0.60	0.00 %	0.00 %	0.00 %	0.00 %
P_TFT 0.80 0.80	0.00 %	0.00 %	0.00 %	0.00 %
P_TFT 0.20 0.80	0.00 %	0.00 %	0.00 %	0.00 %
P_TFT 0.60 0.80	0.00 %	0.00 %	0.00 %	0.00 %
P_TFT 0.40 0.80	0.00 %	0.00 %	0.00 %	0.00 %
P_TFT 1.00 0.80	0.00 %	0.00 %	0.00 %	0.00 %

240

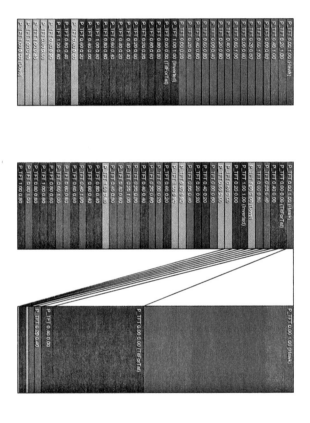

Figure 8.8: The aggregated results of those simulations of the "big series" for which the correlation value was 0%.

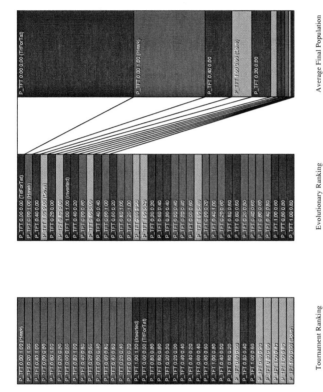

Figure 8.9: The aggregated results of those simulations of the "big series" for which the correlation value was 10%.

242

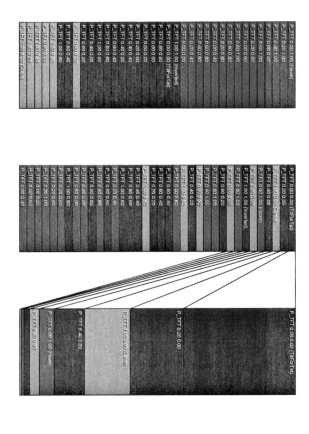

Figure 8.10: The aggregated results of those simulations of the "big series" for which the correlation value was 20%.

8.3.3 The influence of game noise

The game noise parameter specifies a probability with which the intended move of a player is randomly turned into its opposite.

Automata

Strategy	Average Final Population Share			
	overall	g = 0.0	g = 0.05	g = 0.1
AM: HHHHH (HAWK)	34.61 %	7.45 %	36.38 %	59.99 %
AM: DDHHH (GRIM)	17.28 %	38.23 %	10.42 %	3.19 %
AM: DDHDH (TIT FOR TAT)	10.22 %	15.82 %	7.78 %	7.07 %
AM: HDHHD (PAVLOV)	10.01 %	5.03 %	16.48 %	8.51 %
AM: DDDDD (DOVE)	9.27 %	22.58 %	3.67 %	1.56 %
AM: DDHHD (TWEEDLEDUM)	7.12 %	7.08 %	9.13 %	5.14 %
AM: DDHDD (TWEEDLEDEE)	2.91 %	3.81 %	4.66 %	0.26 %
AM: HDHDH (TAT FOR TIT)	1.73 %	0.00 %	2.57 %	2.64 %
AM: DHHHH	1.56 %	0.00 %	0.74 %	3.95 %
AM: DHHDH	1.39 %	0.00 %	1.72 %	2.45 %
AM: HDHDD (SIMPLETON)	1.28 %	0.00 %	0.93 %	2.92 %
AM: HHHDH	1.09 %	0.00 %	2.02 %	1.26 %
AM: HHHHD	0.52 %	0.00 %	1.46 %	0.12 %
AM: DHHDD	0.39 %	0.00 %	1.01 %	0.17 %
AM: HHHDD	0.36 %	0.00 %	0.86 %	0.23 %
AM: DHHHD	0.13 %	0.00 %	0.16 %	0.24 %
AM: DHDHH	0.10 %	0.00 %	0.00 %	0.29 %
AM: HDDHD (TWEETYPIE)	0.00 %	0.00 %	0.00 %	0.00 %
AM: HHDHD (INVERTED)	0.00 %	0.00 %	0.00 %	0.00 %
AM: DHDHD	0.00 %	0.00 %	0.00 %	0.00 %
AM: HDDDD	0.00 %	0.00 %	0.00 %	0.00 %
AM: HHDDD	0.00 %	0.00 %	0.00 %	0.00 %
AM: DHDDD	0.00 %	0.00 %	0.00 %	0.00 %
AM: HDDDH	0.00 %	0.00 %	0.00 %	0.00 %
AM: HHDDH	0.00 %	0.00 %	0.00 %	0.00 %
AM: DHDDH	0.00 %	0.00 %	0.00 %	0.00 %

Results for strategy set: "Automata"

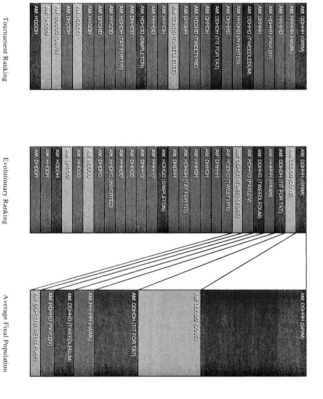

Figure 8.11: The aggregated results of those simulations of the "big series" for which the game noise was 0%.

Figure 8.12: The aggregated results of those simulations of the "big series" for which the game noise was 5%.

246

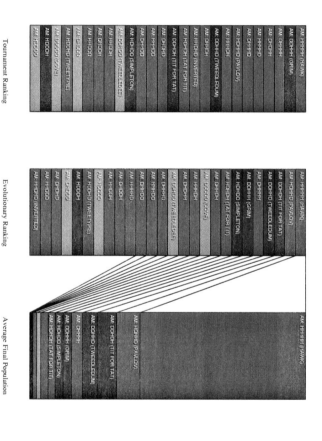

Results for strategy set: "Automata"

| Tournament Ranking | Evolutionary Ranking | Average Final Population |

Figure 8.13: The aggregated results of those simulations of the "big series" for which the game noise was 10%.

Parameterized Tit for Tats

Strategy	Average Final Population Share			
	overall	g = 0.0	g = 0.05	g = 0.1
P_TFT 0.00 0.00 (TitForTat)	38.54 %	82.41 %	18.98 %	14.24 %
P_TFT 0.00 1.00 (Hawk)	28.50 %	0.00 %	27.39 %	58.11 %
P_TFT 0.20 0.00	8.98 %	6.84 %	8.60 %	11.48 %
P_TFT 1.00 0.00 (Dove)	8.30 %	6.56 %	11.80 %	6.56 %
P_TFT 0.40 0.00	8.27 %	2.60 %	18.94 %	3.25 %
P_TFT 0.80 0.00	2.16 %	0.93 %	4.17 %	1.39 %
P_TFT 1.00 1.00 (Inverted)	1.55 %	0.00 %	3.00 %	1.66 %
P_TFT 0.00 0.80	1.06 %	0.00 %	3.17 %	0.00 %
P_TFT 0.20 0.40	0.93 %	0.00 %	2.78 %	0.00 %
P_TFT 0.60 0.00	0.51 %	0.65 %	0.00 %	0.87 %
P_TFT 0.40 0.20	0.46 %	0.00 %	0.00 %	1.39 %
P_TFT 0.60 1.00	0.38 %	0.00 %	0.13 %	1.02 %
P_TFT 0.40 0.40	0.23 %	0.00 %	0.69 %	0.00 %
P_TFT 0.60 0.20	0.12 %	0.00 %	0.36 %	0.00 %
P_TFT 0.80 1.00	0.01 %	0.00 %	0.00 %	0.03 %
P_TFT 0.40 1.00	0.00 %	0.00 %	0.00 %	0.00 %
P_TFT 0.20 1.00	0.00 %	0.00 %	0.00 %	0.00 %
P_TFT 0.00 0.60	0.00 %	0.00 %	0.00 %	0.00 %
P_TFT 0.80 0.20	0.00 %	0.00 %	0.00 %	0.00 %
P_TFT 1.00 0.20	0.00 %	0.00 %	0.00 %	0.00 %
P_TFT 0.80 0.40	0.00 %	0.00 %	0.00 %	0.00 %
P_TFT 0.20 0.20	0.00 %	0.00 %	0.00 %	0.00 %
P_TFT 0.60 0.40	0.00 %	0.00 %	0.00 %	0.00 %
P_TFT 1.00 0.40	0.00 %	0.00 %	0.00 %	0.00 %
P_TFT 0.00 0.40	0.00 %	0.00 %	0.00 %	0.00 %
P_TFT 0.80 0.60	0.00 %	0.00 %	0.00 %	0.00 %
P_TFT 1.00 0.60	0.00 %	0.00 %	0.00 %	0.00 %
P_TFT 0.00 0.20	0.00 %	0.00 %	0.00 %	0.00 %
P_TFT 0.60 0.60	0.00 %	0.00 %	0.00 %	0.00 %
P_TFT 0.40 0.60	0.00 %	0.00 %	0.00 %	0.00 %
P_TFT 0.20 0.60	0.00 %	0.00 %	0.00 %	0.00 %
P_TFT 0.80 0.80	0.00 %	0.00 %	0.00 %	0.00 %
P_TFT 0.20 0.80	0.00 %	0.00 %	0.00 %	0.00 %
P_TFT 0.60 0.80	0.00 %	0.00 %	0.00 %	0.00 %
P_TFT 0.40 0.80	0.00 %	0.00 %	0.00 %	0.00 %
P_TFT 1.00 0.80	0.00 %	0.00 %	0.00 %	0.00 %

248

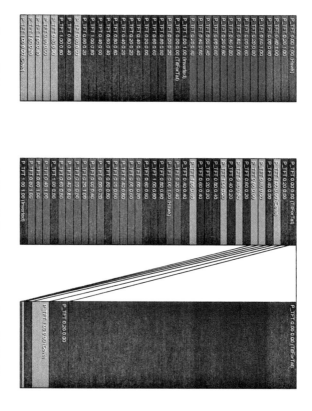

Figure 8.14: The aggregated results of those simulations of the "big series" for which the game noise was 0%.

249

Results for strategy set: "TFTs"

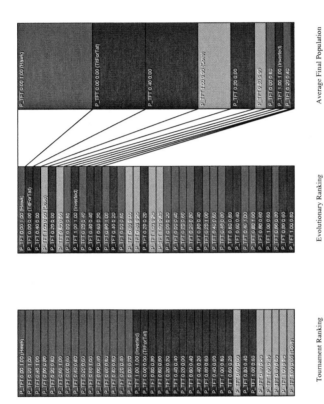

Tournament Ranking   Evolutionary Ranking   Average Final Population

Figure 8.15: The aggregated results of those simulations of the "big series" for which the game noise was 5%.

Results for strategy set: "TFTs"

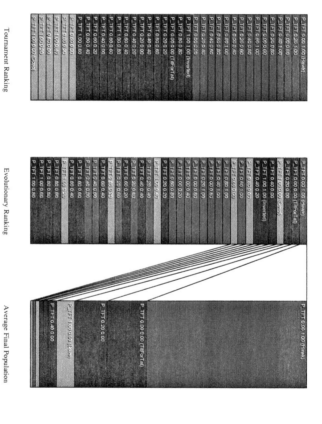

Tournament Ranking   Evolutionary Ranking   Average Final Population

Figure 8.16: The aggregated results of those simulations of the "big series" for which the game noise was 10%.

8.3.4 The influence of evolutionary noise

Evolutionary noise is here understood as a random distortion of a certain percentage that will decrease or increase the fitness value of each strategy in the population dynamics.

Automata

Strategy	Average Final Population Share				
	overall	n = 0.0	n = 0.05	n = 0.1	n = 0.15
AM: HHHHH (HAWK)	34.61 %	32.80 %	33.92 %	35.58 %	36.13 %
AM: DDHHH (GRIM)	17.28 %	20.28 %	16.40 %	16.29 %	16.16 %
AM: DDHDH (TIT FOR TAT)	10.22 %	9.69 %	10.59 %	9.77 %	10.84 %
AM: HDHHD (PAVLOV)	10.01 %	10.84 %	10.56 %	9.01 %	9.61 %
AM: DDDDD (DOVE)	9.27 %	9.19 %	9.98 %	9.85 %	8.07 %
AM: DDHHD (TWEEDLEDUM)	7.12 %	6.45 %	6.22 %	10.10 %	5.69 %
AM: DDHDD (TWEEDLEDEE)	2.91 %	2.70 %	3.61 %	2.45 %	2.89 %
AM: HDHDH (TAT FOR TIT)	1.73 %	1.25 %	1.14 %	1.56 %	3.00 %
AM: DHHHH	1.56 %	1.47 %	2.10 %	1.08 %	1.61 %
AM: DHHDH	1.39 %	1.34 %	1.24 %	1.26 %	1.72 %
AM: HDHDD (SIMPLETON)	1.28 %	1.30 %	1.37 %	1.00 %	1.46 %
AM: HHHDH	1.09 %	1.37 %	0.93 %	0.69 %	1.39 %
AM: HHHHD	0.52 %	0.07 %	0.99 %	0.05 %	0.99 %
AM: DHHDD	0.39 %	0.57 %	0.32 %	0.44 %	0.24 %
AM: HHHDD	0.36 %	0.41 %	0.25 %	0.63 %	0.17 %
AM: DHHHD	0.13 %	0.20 %	0.13 %	0.18 %	0.02 %
AM: DHDHH	0.10 %	0.06 %	0.24 %	0.07 %	0.01 %
AM: HDDHD (TWEETYPIE)	0.00 %	0.00 %	0.00 %	0.00 %	0.00 %
AM: HHDHD (INVERTED)	0.00 %	0.00 %	0.00 %	0.00 %	0.00 %
AM: DHDHD	0.00 %	0.00 %	0.00 %	0.00 %	0.00 %
AM: HDDDD	0.00 %	0.00 %	0.00 %	0.00 %	0.00 %
AM: HHDDD	0.00 %	0.00 %	0.00 %	0.00 %	0.00 %
AM: DHDDD	0.00 %	0.00 %	0.00 %	0.00 %	0.00 %
AM: HDDDH	0.00 %	0.00 %	0.00 %	0.00 %	0.00 %
AM: HHDDH	0.00 %	0.00 %	0.00 %	0.00 %	0.00 %
AM: DHDDH	0.00 %	0.00 %	0.00 %	0.00 %	0.00 %

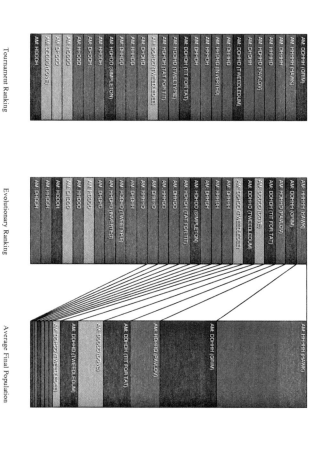

Figure 8.17: The aggregated results of those simulations of the "big series" for which the evolutionary noise was 0%.

Figure 8.18: The aggregated results of those simulations of the "big series" for which the evolutionary noise was 5%.

254

Figure 8.19: The aggregated results of those simulations of the "big series" for which the evolutionary noise was 10%.

Figure 8.20: The aggregated results of those simulations of the "big series" for which the evolutionary noise was 15%.

Parameterized Tit for Tats

Strategy	Average Final Population Share				
	overall	n = 0.0	n = 0.05	n = 0.1	n = 0.15
P_TFT 0.00 0.00 (TitForTat)	38.54 %	41.98 %	38.40 %	35.63 %	38.17 %
P_TFT 0.00 1.00 (Hawk)	28.50 %	26.85 %	28.63 %	29.38 %	29.14 %
P_TFT 0.20 0.00	8.98 %	9.04 %	10.12 %	7.12 %	9.62 %
P_TFT 1.00 0.00 (Dove)	8.30 %	6.09 %	7.59 %	11.21 %	8.31 %
P_TFT 0.40 0.00	8.27 %	8.30 %	7.71 %	7.79 %	9.26 %
P_TFT 0.80 0.00	2.16 %	1.94 %	1.96 %	2.78 %	1.97 %
P_TFT 1.00 1.00 (Inverted)	1.55 %	1.82 %	1.57 %	2.17 %	0.66 %
P_TFT 0.00 0.80	1.06 %	1.02 %	1.03 %	1.27 %	0.91 %
P_TFT 0.20 0.40	0.93 %	0.93 %	0.93 %	0.93 %	0.93 %
P_TFT 0.60 0.00	0.51 %	0.41 %	0.67 %	0.28 %	0.68 %
P_TFT 0.40 0.20	0.46 %	0.00 %	0.93 %	0.93 %	0.00 %
P_TFT 0.60 1.00	0.38 %	0.48 %	0.26 %	0.42 %	0.37 %
P_TFT 0.40 0.40	0.23 %	0.93 %	0.00 %	0.00 %	0.00 %
P_TFT 0.60 0.20	0.12 %	0.19 %	0.21 %	0.08 %	0.00 %
P_TFT 0.80 1.00	0.01 %	0.02 %	0.01 %	0.01 %	0.00 %
P_TFT 0.40 1.00	0.00 %	0.00 %	0.00 %	0.00 %	0.00 %
P_TFT 0.20 1.00	0.00 %	0.00 %	0.00 %	0.00 %	0.00 %
P_TFT 0.00 0.60	0.00 %	0.00 %	0.00 %	0.00 %	0.00 %
P_TFT 0.80 0.20	0.00 %	0.00 %	0.00 %	0.00 %	0.00 %
P_TFT 1.00 0.20	0.00 %	0.00 %	0.00 %	0.00 %	0.00 %
P_TFT 0.80 0.40	0.00 %	0.00 %	0.00 %	0.00 %	0.00 %
P_TFT 0.20 0.20	0.00 %	0.00 %	0.00 %	0.00 %	0.00 %
P_TFT 0.60 0.40	0.00 %	0.00 %	0.00 %	0.00 %	0.00 %
P_TFT 1.00 0.40	0.00 %	0.00 %	0.00 %	0.00 %	0.00 %
P_TFT 0.00 0.40	0.00 %	0.00 %	0.00 %	0.00 %	0.00 %
P_TFT 0.80 0.60	0.00 %	0.00 %	0.00 %	0.00 %	0.00 %
P_TFT 1.00 0.60	0.00 %	0.00 %	0.00 %	0.00 %	0.00 %
P_TFT 0.00 0.20	0.00 %	0.00 %	0.00 %	0.00 %	0.00 %
P_TFT 0.60 0.60	0.00 %	0.00 %	0.00 %	0.00 %	0.00 %
P_TFT 0.40 0.60	0.00 %	0.00 %	0.00 %	0.00 %	0.00 %
P_TFT 0.20 0.60	0.00 %	0.00 %	0.00 %	0.00 %	0.00 %
P_TFT 0.80 0.80	0.00 %	0.00 %	0.00 %	0.00 %	0.00 %
P_TFT 0.20 0.80	0.00 %	0.00 %	0.00 %	0.00 %	0.00 %
P_TFT 0.60 0.80	0.00 %	0.00 %	0.00 %	0.00 %	0.00 %
P_TFT 0.40 0.80	0.00 %	0.00 %	0.00 %	0.00 %	0.00 %
P_TFT 1.00 0.80	0.00 %	0.00 %	0.00 %	0.00 %	0.00 %

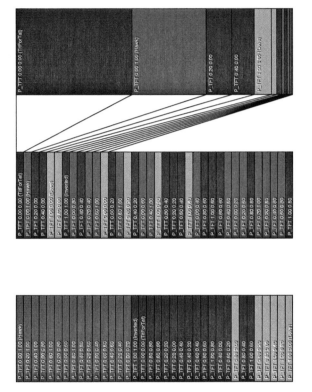

Figure 8.21: The aggregated results of those simulations of the "big series" for which the evolutionary noise was 0%.

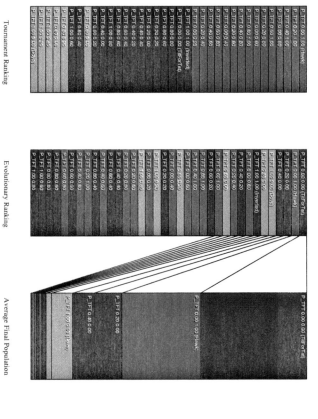

Figure 8.22: The aggregated results of those simulations of the "big series" for which the evolutionary noise was 5%.

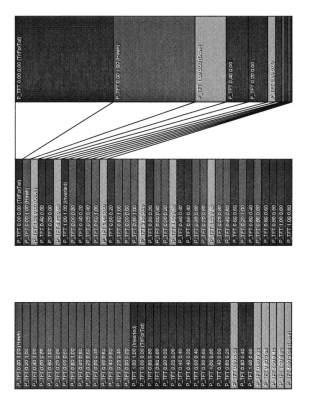

Figure 8.23: The aggregated results of those simulations of the "big series" for which the evolutionary noise was 10%.

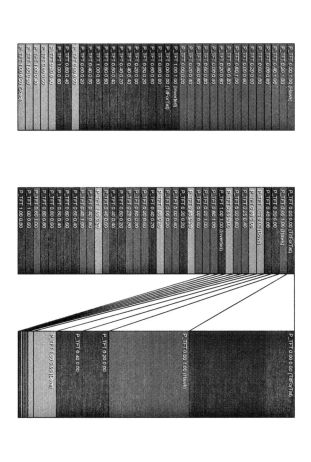

Figure 8.24: The aggregated results of those simulations of the "big series" for which the evolutionary noise was 15%.

8.3.5 The influence of degenerative mutations

The mutation rate is a probability with which after each generation of the population dynamical process, the population of each strategy mutates into a simpler strategy. See page 91 for a more comprehensive description.

Automata

Strategy	overall	m = 0.0	m = 0.01	m = 0.05
	Average Final Population Share			
AM: HHHHH (HAWK)	34.61 %	10.70 %	34.95 %	58.17 %
AM: DDHHH (GRIM)	17.28 %	27.46 %	13.95 %	10.43 %
AM: DDHDH (TIT FOR TAT)	10.22 %	14.70 %	9.70 %	6.27 %
AM: HDHHD (PAVLOV)	10.01 %	13.19 %	11.58 %	5.24 %
AM: DDDDD (DOVE)	9.27 %	1.67 %	13.58 %	12.57 %
AM: DDHHD (TWEEDLEDUM)	7.12 %	17.49 %	3.20 %	0.65 %
AM: DDHDD (TWEEDLEDEE)	2.91 %	6.84 %	1.30 %	0.60 %
AM: HDHDH (TAT FOR TIT)	1.73 %	0.69 %	3.99 %	0.52 %
AM: DHHHH	1.56 %	2.31 %	2.39 %	0.00 %
AM: DHHDH	1.39 %	0.44 %	1.67 %	2.06 %
AM: HDHDD (SIMPLETON)	1.28 %	1.38 %	1.36 %	1.10 %
AM: HHHDH	1.09 %	0.56 %	0.52 %	2.21 %
AM: HHHHD	0.52 %	1.41 %	0.17 %	0.00 %
AM: DHHDD	0.39 %	0.35 %	0.72 %	0.11 %
AM: HHHDD	0.36 %	0.29 %	0.75 %	0.06 %
AM: DHHHD	0.13 %	0.23 %	0.18 %	0.00 %
AM: DHDHH	0.10 %	0.29 %	0.00 %	0.00 %
AM: HDDHD (TWEETYPIE)	0.00 %	0.00 %	0.00 %	0.00 %
AM: HHDHD (INVERTED)	0.00 %	0.00 %	0.00 %	0.00 %
AM: DHDHD	0.00 %	0.00 %	0.00 %	0.00 %
AM: HDDDD	0.00 %	0.00 %	0.00 %	0.00 %
AM: HHDDD	0.00 %	0.00 %	0.00 %	0.00 %
AM: DHDDD	0.00 %	0.00 %	0.00 %	0.00 %
AM: HDDDH	0.00 %	0.00 %	0.00 %	0.00 %
AM: HHDDH	0.00 %	0.00 %	0.00 %	0.00 %
AM: DHDDH	0.00 %	0.00 %	0.00 %	0.00 %

Results for strategy set: "Automata"

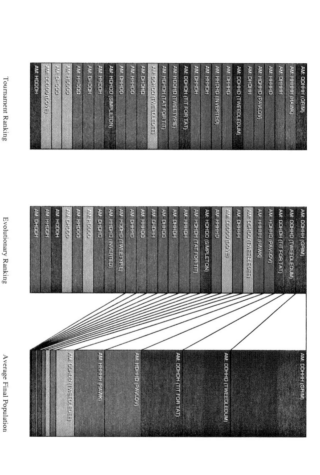

Figure 8.25: The aggregated results of those simulations of the "big series" for which degenerative mutations were turned off.

Results for strategy set: "Automata"

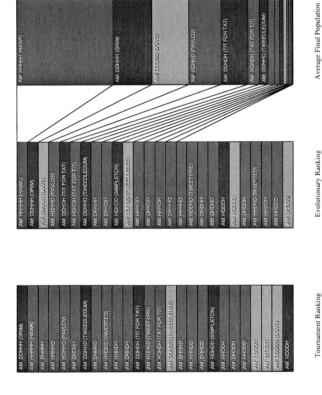

Figure 8.26: The aggregated results of those simulations of the "big series" for which 1% of the strategies degenerated in every new generation either to *Dove* or to *Hawk* (depending on whether the strategy was more cooperative or more defective before).

Figure 8.27: The aggregated results of those simulations of the "big series" for which 5% of the strategies degenerated in every new generation either to *Dove* or to *Hawk* (depending on whether the strategy was more cooperative or more defective before).

Results for strategy set: "Automata"

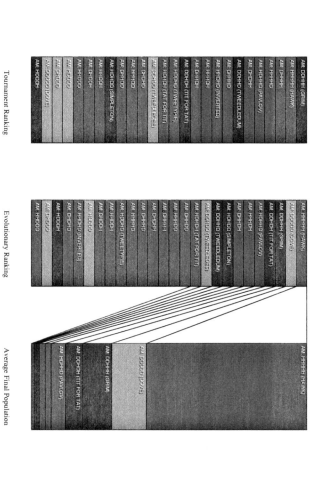

Parameterized Tit for Tats

Strategy	Average Final Population Share			
	overall	m = 0.0	m = 0.01	m = 0.05
P_TFT 0.00 0.00 (TitForTat)	38.54 %	22.22 %	39.67 %	53.74 %
P_TFT 0.00 1.00 (Hawk)	28.50 %	28.08 %	31.25 %	26.17 %
P_TFT 0.20 0.00	8.98 %	18.79 %	5.84 %	2.30 %
P_TFT 1.00 0.00 (Dove)	8.30 %	1.48 %	10.84 %	12.59 %
P_TFT 0.40 0.00	8.27 %	13.93 %	9.95 %	0.92 %
P_TFT 0.80 0.00	2.16 %	6.48 %	0.00 %	0.00 %
P_TFT 1.00 1.00 (Inverted)	1.55 %	0.00 %	1.20 %	3.46 %
P_TFT 0.00 0.80	1.06 %	3.17 %	0.00 %	0.00 %
P_TFT 0.20 0.40	0.93 %	2.78 %	0.00 %	0.00 %
P_TFT 0.60 0.00	0.51 %	0.98 %	0.54 %	0.00 %
P_TFT 0.40 0.20	0.46 %	1.39 %	0.00 %	0.00 %
P_TFT 0.60 1.00	0.38 %	0.00 %	0.33 %	0.82 %
P_TFT 0.40 0.40	0.23 %	0.69 %	0.00 %	0.00 %
P_TFT 0.60 0.20	0.12 %	0.00 %	0.36 %	0.00 %
P_TFT 0.80 1.00	0.01 %	0.00 %	0.03 %	0.00 %
P_TFT 0.40 1.00	0.00 %	0.00 %	0.00 %	0.00 %
P_TFT 0.20 1.00	0.00 %	0.00 %	0.00 %	0.00 %
P_TFT 0.00 0.60	0.00 %	0.00 %	0.00 %	0.00 %
P_TFT 0.80 0.20	0.00 %	0.00 %	0.00 %	0.00 %
P_TFT 1.00 0.20	0.00 %	0.00 %	0.00 %	0.00 %
P_TFT 0.80 0.40	0.00 %	0.00 %	0.00 %	0.00 %
P_TFT 0.20 0.20	0.00 %	0.00 %	0.00 %	0.00 %
P_TFT 0.60 0.40	0.00 %	0.00 %	0.00 %	0.00 %
P_TFT 1.00 0.40	0.00 %	0.00 %	0.00 %	0.00 %
P_TFT 0.00 0.40	0.00 %	0.00 %	0.00 %	0.00 %
P_TFT 0.80 0.60	0.00 %	0.00 %	0.00 %	0.00 %
P_TFT 1.00 0.60	0.00 %	0.00 %	0.00 %	0.00 %
P_TFT 0.00 0.20	0.00 %	0.00 %	0.00 %	0.00 %
P_TFT 0.60 0.60	0.00 %	0.00 %	0.00 %	0.00 %
P_TFT 0.40 0.60	0.00 %	0.00 %	0.00 %	0.00 %
P_TFT 0.20 0.60	0.00 %	0.00 %	0.00 %	0.00 %
P_TFT 0.80 0.80	0.00 %	0.00 %	0.00 %	0.00 %
P_TFT 0.20 0.80	0.00 %	0.00 %	0.00 %	0.00 %
P_TFT 0.60 0.80	0.00 %	0.00 %	0.00 %	0.00 %
P_TFT 0.40 0.80	0.00 %	0.00 %	0.00 %	0.00 %
P_TFT 1.00 0.80	0.00 %	0.00 %	0.00 %	0.00 %

266

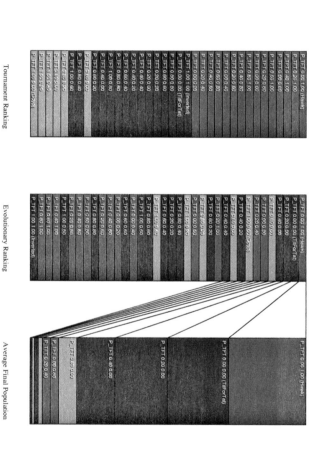

Figure 8.28: The aggregated results of those simulations of the "big series" for which degenerative mutations were turned off.

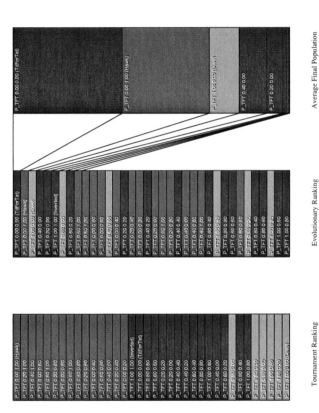

Figure 8.29: The aggregated results of those simulations of the "big series" for which 1% of the strategies degenerated in every new generation either to *Dove* or to *Hawk* (depending on whether the strategy was more cooperative or more defective before).

Results for strategy set: "TFTs"

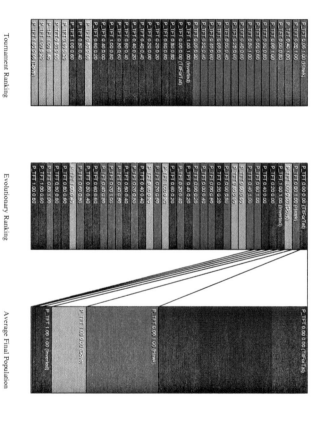

Tournament Ranking   Evolutionary Ranking   Average Final Population

Figure 8.30: The aggregated results of those simulations of the "big series" for which 5% of the strategies degenerated in every new generation either to *Dove* or to *Hawk* (depending on whether the strategy was more cooperative or more defective before).

8.3.6 The influence of different payoffs

The payoff parameters define the payoff each player gets depending on the choice of the player's own move and the opponent's move. See chapter 4.1.1 for an explanation of the Prisoner's Dilemma game.

Automata

Strategy	overall	T = 3.5	T = 5	T = 5.5	P = 2
		Average Final Population Share			
AM: HHHHH (HAWK)	34.61 %	32.00 %	27.27 %	23.77 %	55.39 %
AM: DDHHH (GRIM)	17.28 %	7.00 %	20.33 %	15.23 %	26.56 %
AM: DDHDH (TIT FOR TAT)	10.22 %	3.90 %	15.63 %	12.90 %	8.47 %
AM: HDHHD (PAVLOV)	10.01 %	32.15 %	1.07 %	6.81 %	0.00 %
AM: DDDDD (DOVE)	9.27 %	11.78 %	11.73 %	9.76 %	3.81 %
AM: DDHHD (TWEEDLEDUM)	7.12 %	7.35 %	13.12 %	5.95 %	2.04 %
AM: DDHDD (TWEEDLEDEE)	2.91 %	2.22 %	1.90 %	7.23 %	0.30 %
AM: HDHDH (TAT FOR TIT)	1.73 %	0.00 %	3.52 %	0.00 %	3.42 %
AM: DHHHH	1.56 %	3.41 %	0.00 %	2.85 %	0.00 %
AM: DHHDH	1.39 %	0.00 %	2.29 %	3.27 %	0.00 %
AM: HDHDD (SIMPLETON)	1.28 %	0.00 %	0.36 %	4.77 %	0.00 %
AM: HHHDH	1.09 %	0.00 %	2.03 %	2.34 %	0.00 %
AM: HHHHD	0.52 %	0.00 %	0.09 %	2.01 %	0.00 %
AM: DHHDD	0.39 %	0.00 %	0.41 %	1.16 %	0.00 %
AM: HHHDD	0.36 %	0.00 %	0.24 %	1.22 %	0.00 %
AM: DHHHD	0.13 %	0.00 %	0.00 %	0.54 %	0.00 %
AM: DHDHH	0.10 %	0.19 %	0.00 %	0.20 %	0.00 %
AM: HDDHD (TWEETYPIE)	0.00 %	0.00 %	0.00 %	0.00 %	0.00 %
AM: HHDHD (INVERTED)	0.00 %	0.00 %	0.00 %	0.00 %	0.00 %
AM: DHDHD	0.00 %	0.00 %	0.00 %	0.00 %	0.00 %
AM: HDDDD	0.00 %	0.00 %	0.00 %	0.00 %	0.00 %
AM: HHDDD	0.00 %	0.00 %	0.00 %	0.00 %	0.00 %
AM: DHDDD	0.00 %	0.00 %	0.00 %	0.00 %	0.00 %
AM: HDDDH	0.00 %	0.00 %	0.00 %	0.00 %	0.00 %
AM: HHDDH	0.00 %	0.00 %	0.00 %	0.00 %	0.00 %
AM: DHDDH	0.00 %	0.00 %	0.00 %	0.00 %	0.00 %

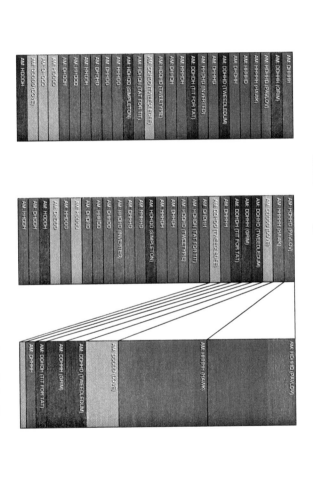

Figure 8.31: The aggregated results of the simulations of the "big series" with the payoff parameters T=3.5, R=3, P=1, S=0.

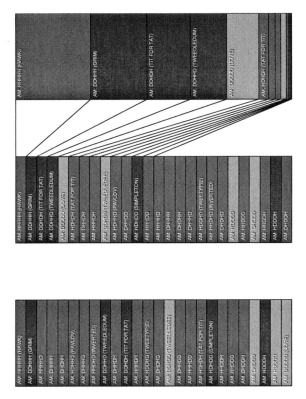

Results for strategy set: "Automata"

Figure 8.32: The aggregated results of the simulations of the "big series" with the payoff parameters T=5, R=3, P=1, S=0.

Results for strategy set: "Automata"

| Tournament Ranking | Evolutionary Ranking | Average Final Population |

Figure 8.33: The aggregated results of the simulations of the "big series" with the payoff parameters T=5.5, R=3, P=1, S=0.

273

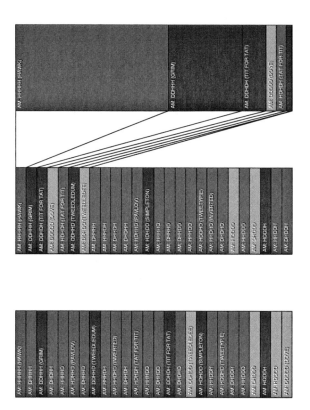

Results for strategy set: "Automata"

Tournament Ranking   Evolutionary Ranking   Average Final Population

Figure 8.34: The aggregated results of the simulations of the "big series" with the payoff parameters T=5, R=3, P=2, S=0.

Parameterized Tit for Tats

Strategy	Average Final Population Share				
	overall	T = 3.5	T = 5	T = 5.5	P = 2
P_TFT 0.00 0.00 (TitForTat)	38.54 %	19.03 %	44.75 %	47.91 %	42.49 %
P_TFT 0.00 1.00 (Hawk)	28.50 %	35.19 %	18.52 %	16.37 %	43.92 %
P_TFT 0.20 0.00	8.98 %	6.30 %	7.13 %	14.25 %	8.23 %
P_TFT 1.00 0.00 (Dove)	8.30 %	27.86 %	3.28 %	1.64 %	0.43 %
P_TFT 0.40 0.00	8.27 %	2.16 %	22.38 %	8.29 %	0.23 %
P_TFT 0.80 0.00	2.16 %	8.64 %	0.00 %	0.00 %	0.00 %
P_TFT 1.00 1.00 (Inverted)	1.55 %	0.00 %	2.68 %	3.10 %	0.44 %
P_TFT 0.00 0.80	1.06 %	0.00 %	0.00 %	0.00 %	4.23 %
P_TFT 0.20 0.40	0.93 %	0.00 %	0.00 %	3.70 %	0.00 %
P_TFT 0.60 0.00	0.51 %	0.82 %	1.00 %	0.19 %	0.03 %
P_TFT 0.40 0.20	0.46 %	0.00 %	0.00 %	1.85 %	0.00 %
P_TFT 0.60 1.00	0.38 %	0.00 %	0.27 %	1.26 %	0.00 %
P_TFT 0.40 0.40	0.23 %	0.00 %	0.00 %	0.93 %	0.00 %
P_TFT 0.60 0.20	0.12 %	0.00 %	0.00 %	0.48 %	0.00 %
P_TFT 0.80 1.00	0.01 %	0.00 %	0.00 %	0.04 %	0.00 %
P_TFT 0.40 1.00	0.00 %	0.00 %	0.00 %	0.00 %	0.00 %
P_TFT 0.20 1.00	0.00 %	0.00 %	0.00 %	0.00 %	0.00 %
P_TFT 0.00 0.60	0.00 %	0.00 %	0.00 %	0.00 %	0.00 %
P_TFT 0.80 0.20	0.00 %	0.00 %	0.00 %	0.00 %	0.00 %
P_TFT 1.00 0.20	0.00 %	0.00 %	0.00 %	0.00 %	0.00 %
P_TFT 0.80 0.40	0.00 %	0.00 %	0.00 %	0.00 %	0.00 %
P_TFT 0.20 0.20	0.00 %	0.00 %	0.00 %	0.00 %	0.00 %
P_TFT 0.60 0.40	0.00 %	0.00 %	0.00 %	0.00 %	0.00 %
P_TFT 1.00 0.40	0.00 %	0.00 %	0.00 %	0.00 %	0.00 %
P_TFT 0.00 0.40	0.00 %	0.00 %	0.00 %	0.00 %	0.00 %
P_TFT 0.80 0.60	0.00 %	0.00 %	0.00 %	0.00 %	0.00 %
P_TFT 1.00 0.60	0.00 %	0.00 %	0.00 %	0.00 %	0.00 %
P_TFT 0.00 0.20	0.00 %	0.00 %	0.00 %	0.00 %	0.00 %
P_TFT 0.60 0.60	0.00 %	0.00 %	0.00 %	0.00 %	0.00 %
P_TFT 0.40 0.60	0.00 %	0.00 %	0.00 %	0.00 %	0.00 %
P_TFT 0.20 0.60	0.00 %	0.00 %	0.00 %	0.00 %	0.00 %
P_TFT 0.80 0.80	0.00 %	0.00 %	0.00 %	0.00 %	0.00 %
P_TFT 0.20 0.80	0.00 %	0.00 %	0.00 %	0.00 %	0.00 %
P_TFT 0.60 0.80	0.00 %	0.00 %	0.00 %	0.00 %	0.00 %
P_TFT 0.40 0.80	0.00 %	0.00 %	0.00 %	0.00 %	0.00 %
P_TFT 1.00 0.80	0.00 %	0.00 %	0.00 %	0.00 %	0.00 %

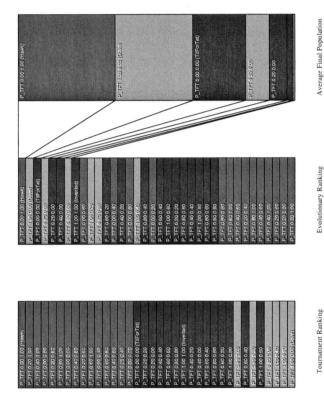

Figure 8.35: The aggregated results of the simulations of the "big series" with the payoff parameters T=3.5, R=3, P=1, S=0.

Figure 8.36: The aggregated results of the simulations of the "big series" with the payoff parameters T=5, R=3, P=1, S=0.

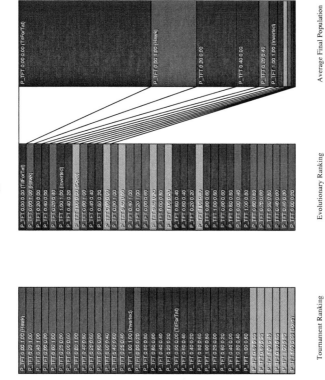

Figure 8.37: The aggregated results of the simulations of the "big series" with the payoff parameters T=5.5, R=3, P=1, S=0.

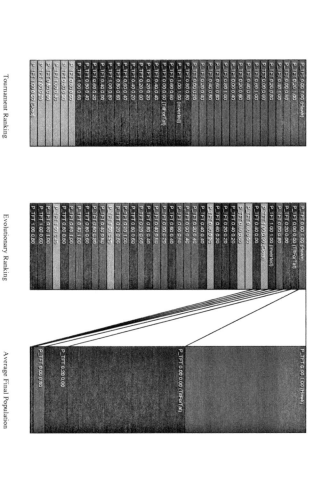

278

Figure 8.38: The aggregated results of the simulations of the "big series" with the payoff parameters T=5, R=3, P=2, S=0.

8.3.7 "Monte Carlo series" results

Strategy	Average Final Population Share overall results
AM: HHHHH (HAWK)	45.56 %
AM: DDHHD (TWEEDLEDUM)	9.29 %
AM: DDHDH (TIT FOR TAT)	8.43 %
AM: DDDDD (DOVE)	7.80 %
AM: HDHHD (PAVLOV)	6.83 %
AM: DDHHH (GRIM)	5.61 %
AM: HHHDH	2.82 %
AM: DDHDD (TWEEDLEDEE)	2.70 %
AM: HDHDH (TAT FOR TIT)	2.60 %
AM: DHHDH	2.57 %
AM: HDHDD (SIMPLETON)	2.42 %
AM: DHHHH	0.84 %
AM: DHHDD	0.76 %
AM: HHHDD	0.61 %
AM: HHHHD	0.56 %
AM: DHHHD	0.49 %
AM: HHDHD (INVERTED)	0.07 %
AM: HDDHD (TWEETYPIE)	0.02 %
AM: DHDHH	0.00 %
AM: HHDDH	0.00 %
AM: DHDDH	0.00 %
AM: HDDDH	0.00 %
AM: HDDDD	0.00 %
AM: DHDDD	0.00 %
AM: HHDDD	0.00 %
AM: DHDHD	0.00 %

	Average Final Population Share
Strategy	overall results
P_TFT 0.00 1.00 (Hawk)	25.06 %
P_TFT 0.00 0.00 (TitForTat)	24.59 %
P_TFT 1.00 0.00 (Dove)	22.29 %
P_TFT 0.20 0.00	14.01 %
P_TFT 0.40 0.00	9.94 %
P_TFT 1.00 1.00 (Inverted)	2.60 %
P_TFT 0.80 1.00	0.52 %
P_TFT 0.60 0.00	0.51 %
P_TFT 0.60 1.00	0.32 %
P_TFT 0.60 0.20	0.05 %
P_TFT 0.40 1.00	0.04 %
P_TFT 0.60 0.40	0.03 %
P_TFT 0.80 0.00	0.02 %
P_TFT 1.00 0.60	0.01 %
P_TFT 0.80 0.80	0.01 %
P_TFT 1.00 0.80	0.01 %
P_TFT 0.80 0.40	0.00 %
P_TFT 0.20 1.00	0.00 %
P_TFT 1.00 0.40	0.00 %
P_TFT 0.00 0.80	0.00 %
P_TFT 0.80 0.20	0.00 %
P_TFT 0.00 0.60	0.00 %
P_TFT 0.00 0.40	0.00 %
P_TFT 0.00 0.20	0.00 %
P_TFT 0.20 0.20	0.00 %
P_TFT 0.40 0.60	0.00 %
P_TFT 0.20 0.40	0.00 %
P_TFT 0.40 0.20	0.00 %
P_TFT 0.20 0.60	0.00 %
P_TFT 0.20 0.80	0.00 %
P_TFT 0.80 0.60	0.00 %
P_TFT 0.60 0.60	0.00 %
P_TFT 0.40 0.40	0.00 %
P_TFT 1.00 0.20	0.00 %
P_TFT 0.60 0.80	0.00 %
P_TFT 0.40 0.80	0.00 %

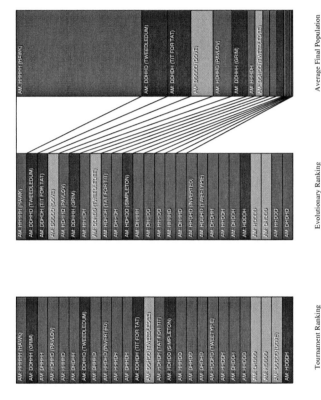

Figure 8.39: The aggregated results of all simulations of the "Monte Carlo series" using *Automata* strategies.

Figure 8.40: The aggregated results of all simulations of the "Monte Carlo series" using *Parameterized Tit for Tat* strategies.

8.4 Implementation details of the group selection model

A Computer model can be specified by describing its data structures and the algorithms that operate upon these data structures. In the following, the data structures and algorithms of the group selection model from chapter 4.3.1 are first described in general terms. Following is the Python implementation of this model.

The model of group selection is an extension of the model of reciprocal altruism. It rests on a simple type of replicator dynamics, where generational cycles are assumed to be discrete and non overlapping. The replicating entities are a fixed number species, each of which occupies a certain share of an assumed whole population of infinite (or rather undetermined) size. Replication leads to changes in the relative population shares that the species occupy, but never – save for the limits of arithmetic precision of the computer – does a species die out and never do new species emerge.

In group selection processes two kinds of entities are involved: groups of individuals and groups of groups. Therefore, it is just natural to define two types of objects in our computer model, one for groups of individuals and another one for groups of groups. The objects that describe groups of individuals will be called *deme* objects, the objects that describe groups of groups (of individuals) are termed *super demes*.

Each *deme* object contains an ordered list of *species* that are present in the deme and a *distribution* vector (of the dimension of the number of species) of population shares. What these species are, is, for the time being, completely left open. The most important property of a deme is that inside the deme replication takes place. Therefore, a *replication* function is associated with every deme object. The replication algorithm is very simple: The population share of each strategy is multiplied with its fitness value (which must always be some real number greater than zero). (See appendix 8.2 for the details.)

The fitness values themselves are determined by another function of the deme object, the *fitness* function. The fitness function is located in the deme object rather than in any object describing the species, because the fitness of a species may depend on the other species present as well as their relative sizes. Fitness is thus not a local property of a species alone. The algorithm that determines the fitness values does of course depend on the kind of species that make up the deme. As this has been left open, the concrete definition of the fitness function is also left open for the time being.[5] Only when using the deme object in a concrete simulation, we will, for example, assume that the species are strategies in a repeated Prisoner's Dilemma, and define the fitness function accordingly.

While the deme object models a population of species, the *super deme* object[6] models a population of demes. The super deme object can be thought of as a deme object itself, only with extended properties. Just as the deme object, the super deme object contains a list of species and a vector of population shares. Only this time the species are deme objects (which with respect to the super deme may be called "sub demes"). The deme objects occupy shares of a global population. Just as the ordinary deme objects, the super deme object has a fitness and a replication function. The replication algorithm is the same as that of an ordinary deme only that before replication takes place in the super deme the replicated population in the sub demes is determined. The order of calculation is important since the relative fitness of a sub deme with respect to the other sub demes may depend on the distribution of species inside the sub deme. The most distinguishing feature of a super deme is that its sub demes may be reshaped. Therefore a *reshaping* function is associated with the super deme object. The reshaping algorithm[7] proceeds in two steps:

1. Aggregate the population of all sub demes.

2. Distribute the population randomly to a new set sub demes.

As has been mentioned earlier, the choice of this algorithm represents an arbitrary modeling decision. The aggregation of demes in the first step is done by multiplying the population share of the species within the sub demes with the population share of the respective sub demes within the super deme and then adding up the populations of the same species. The distribution of the aggregated population to new sub demes is a little more difficult, because we want to make sure that the deme structure (defined by the number and the sizes of the newly created

---

[5]In the terminology of object orientated programming a function without an implementation is called an "abstract method" and objects that contain abstract methods are called "abstract objects" accordingly. The `Deme` class is therefore an abstract class. It cannot be instanced itself. In order to use it another class must be derived from the `Deme` class that implements the abstract methods. The `class PDDeme` in the program listing in appendix 8.4.3 is a derived class of `class Deme` that implements the method `_fitness`. (For technical reasons the fitness function is split into the two methods `fitness` and `_fitness` and only the latter is an abstract method.)

[6]For the implementation details see `class SuperDeme` in Appendix 8.4.2

[7]See the `reshape` method of the `SuperDeme` class in Appendix 8.4.2 for the implementation details. The full algorithm is spread over three functions, however. In addition to the `reshape` method of `SuperDeme` class these are the methods `merged` and `spawn` of `class Deme`.

demes) is more or less the same as before. The distribution algorithm[8] proceeds in three steps:

1. Create a new set of sub demes with the same structure. (The structure of the set of sub demes is defined by the number of sub demes and the minimum and maximum number of species each deme may contain.)

2. For each sub deme, determine which species will be present in the sub deme.

3. Distribute the population share of each species in the aggregated population randomly over the demes where the species appears.

Each of these steps needs a little explanation: In the first step, two assumptions enter into our algorithm: 1) the deme structure is not fixed, but may change every time the super deme is reshaped 2) The deme structure is expressed by the three parameters number of demes, minimum number of species per deme, maximum number of species per deme. (The actual numbers of species per deme is a random number within the bounds of the latter two values.) Both of these assumptions do again represent (arbitrary) modeling decisions. As to the first assumption, both the model and the algorithm would of course be simpler, if we used the same fixed deme structure every time the super deme is reshaped. But then the flexibility and therefore also the generality of the model would be much more limited. Instead of using the three parameters mentioned above, we could also use a different parametrization of the deme structure. For example, we could define the deme structure by the average number of demes and the average size of a deme and then pick random numbers in the normal distribution of these parameters for the actual number of demes and the actual sizes the demes. It is just a matter of choice to do it the one way or the other.

In the second step of the algorithm, some care must be taken to make sure that every species is represented in at least one deme. Therefore, all species are assigned one after another to the first few demes and only after all species have been assigned the remaining demes draw their species at random from the set of species. Constructing the algorithm for the assignment of species to demes this way does mean that the assignment is not fully randomized, but this restriction can be accepted for the sake of simplicity.

---

[8]For the implementation see method `spawn` of `class Deme` in Appendix 8.4.1. Out of reasons of technical convenience this algorithm is located in `class Deme` instead of `class SuperDeme`.

The last step of the algorithm hardly needs an explanation any more. It should be observed that by randomly distributing the population shares of each species, it is assured that the newly distributed population matches the previously aggregated population.

One question that is still open is how the fitness function of the super deme object (the function that determines the fitness values of all sub demes of the super deme) is to be defined. This again depends on the selection mechanism one desires to model. Without a particular empirical application of the model in mind any choice of a fitness function is arbitrary. However, instead of leaving the function open as in the case of the deme object, an arbitrary "standard" algorithm for the fitness function is proposed with the caveat that when actually applying the model this algorithm should be replaced by an algorithm that reflects the particular group selection mechanism of the application case of the model.

The proposed "standard" algorithm for "group" fitness is very simple: We assume that the fitness of a deme with respect to the other demes is the sum of the products of the fitnesses of the species within the deme with their respective population shares. (Mathematically this is expressed as the matrix multiplication of the fitness vector with the vector of population shares.) This means that the fitness of the deme is assumed to be the average fitness of its members.

Now, this algorithm for determining group fitness may look suspiciously like committing a similar mistake as the one Price's equation has been accused of (Okasha, 2005, p. 713): If the the fitness value of the species inside the demes is used again to determine the fitness of the demes themselves, does that not mean that the species' fitness is counted twice while it should only be counted once? The answer is that it is legitimate to use the fitness value of the species twice, if the fitness of the species has an independent causal effect on group selection.

For the sake of illustration one may think of the following scenario, where a group selection model might be applied: Imagine that the groups (or "demes") are insurance companies competing on a common market for customers with whom they want to place insurance contracts. Now, think of the individual agents inside the companies and assume that the better an agent performs the more new customers will be assigned to him by the management. Then there is also competition between the insurance agents inside the company. One could plausibly assume that the competition between the agents of a company is of the nature of a Prisoner's Dilemma: All agents have an incentive to out compete their colleagues, but if there is too little cooperation between the agents, they will all perform very badly which in turn means that their company will perform badly on the insurance market. Obviously, how well the agents play the Prisoner's Dilemma has an independent causal influence on both their standing inside the company and the success of the company on the market. Our "standard" group fitness algorithm then just expresses that the higher the average success of the companies' agents is in the Prisoner's Dilemma game that is played inside the company the greater is the company's success on the market.[9] Thus, this little story shows that our choice of a "standard" algorithm for group selection is by no means unsound, although no claim is made about the empirical adequacy of this particular algorithm in any realistic scenario.

8.4.1 Listing 1: The deme class

```
class Deme(object):
    """Represents a deme, i.e. a (sub-)population that is defined
    by the species in the deme as well as their distribution.
    Deme populations are not usually normalized. They need to be
    normalized explicitly by call to the 'normalize' method.
    (A species can be any object that can be identified by str(species).
    Species are always identified by str(species) and never by references,
    i.e. two different objects returning the same name for str(obj) are
    considered one and the same species. When merging (see method merged) one
    of these objects may be dropped arbitrarily. Or to put it another way:
    If the species change their characteristics, i.e. if they evolve, they
    should change their names two. For genetic species the genome should
    therefore always be encoded in the name of the species.)

    Attributes (read only!):
        name          - name of the deme
        species       - list of species
        distribution  - distribution of the strategies
        fitnessCache  - cache for the fitness values
    """
    def __str__(self):
        return self.name

    def __setattr__(self, name, value):
        """If the distribution value change the fitnessChache is cleared."""
        if name == "distribution":
            object.__setattr__(self, "fitnessCache", None)
        object.__setattr__(self, name, value)

    def __init__(self, species, distribution = None, name=""):
        """Initializes the Deme with the list of species, the distribution
        vector and a name (if desired). The list of species is always
        deep-copied into the meme to allow for independet evolution of the
        species. However, species with the same name in different demes may
        be merged back, when demes are merged.
        """
        assert len(species) > 0, "Too few species (%i)!"%len(species)
        assert distribution == None or len(species) == len(distribution), \
            "Species list and distribution array are of unequal size!"
        self.fitnessCache = None
        if distribution != None: self.__distribution = asarray(distribution)
        else: self.__distribution = UniformDistribution(len(species))
        if name: self.name = name
        else: self.name = GenericIdentifier()
        self.species = copy.deepcopy(species)
```

---

[9]Strictly speaking, there are no individual agents represented in our model. But one might think of the species as strategies in the Prisoner's Dilemma. Their population shares then represent the relative numbers of agents adopting a certain strategy.

```python
    def getDistribution(self):
        return self.__distribution
    def setDistribution(self, d):
        self.__distribution = d
        self.fitnessCache = None
    distribution = property(getDistribution, setDistribution)

    def new(self, species, distribution = None, name=""):
        """Create a deme object of the same type."""
        return self.__class__(species, distribution, name)

    def container(self, demes, distribution, name=""):
        """Create a super deme that is a suitable container for
        demes of the type of this deme."""
        return SuperDeme(demes, distribution, name)

    def merged(self, *others):
        """Returns a copy of the deme that is merged with a sequence of
        other demes. The order of species in the merged deme is arbitrary!"""
        species_dict = {};  share_dict = {}
        for deme in (self,)+others:
            for i in xrange(len(deme.species)):
                species = deme.species[i]
                name = str(species)
                if species_dict.has_key(name):
                    share_dict[name] += deme.distribution[i]
                else:
                    species_dict[name] = species
                    share_dict[name] = deme.distribution[i]
        species = species_dict.values()
        dist = array([share_dict[s.name] for s in species])
        return self.new(species, dist)

    def __add__(self, other):
        """Returns a copy of the deme that is merged with another"""
        return self.merged(other)

    def __mul__(self, faktor):
        """Returns a deme where all population shares are multiplied
        with 'faktor'"""
        ndist = self.distribution * faktor
        return self.new(self.species, ndist)

    def normalized(self):
        """Returns a normalized (population shares add up to 1.0)
        copy of the deme."""
        return self.new(self.species, norm(self.distribution))

    def normalize(self):
        """Normalizes the population share in place."""
        self.distribution = norm(self.distribution)

    def _fitness(self):
        """Determines the fitness values for the species of the
        deme."""
        raise NotImplementedError

    def fitness(self):
        """Returns the fitnesses of the species (as Numeric.array)."""
        if self.fitnessCache == None: self.fitnessCache = self._fitness()
        return self.fitnessCache

    def replicate(self):
        """Updates the distribution to the next generation."""
        self.distribution = norm(self.distribution * self.fitness())

    def aggregate(self, weighted = True):
        """Returns a new deme where all species of all subdemes are
        recursively aggregated. If 'weighted' is false the
        distribution (relative size) of the demes will not be taken
        into account. If there are no subdemes, 'self' is returned.
```

```
        Warning: If a new deme is created, the order of the species
        in this new deme arbitrary!"""
        return self

    def spawn(self, N, minSize, maxSize):
        """Returns a super deme of N demes with sizes varying between
        'minSize' and 'maxSize' and populations randomly picked from
        this deme."""
        pool = self.distribution #.copy() # don't need a copy!
        sizes = [random.randint(minSize, maxSize) for i in xrange(N)]
        assert sum(sizes) >= len(pool), "Too few or too small demes to spawn!"
        rng = range(len(pool))
        sg = [[] for i in rng];  l = 0
        for count in xrange(N):
            s = sizes[count]
            if l < len(pool):
                g = range(l, min(l+s, len(pool)))
                g.extend(random.sample(rng, max(0,l+s-len(pool))))
                l += s
            else:  g = random.sample(rng, s)
            for st in g:  sg[st].append(count)
        species = [[] for i in xrange(N)]
        distribution = [[] for i in xrange(N)]
        for i in xrange(len(sg)):
            chunks = list(RandomDistribution(len(sg[i])) * pool[i])
            for g in sg[i]:
                species[g].append(self.species[i])
                distribution[g].append(chunks.pop())
        demes = []
        for i in xrange(N): demes.append(self.new(species[i], distribution[i]))
        #assert almostEqual(sum([sum(d.distribution) for d in demes]), 1.0), \
        #    "self test failed %f"%sum([sum(d.distribution) for d in demes])
        distribution = norm(array([sum(d.distribution) for d in demes]))
        for d in demes: d.normalize()
        return self.container(demes, distribution)

    def ranking(self):
        """-> list of (rank, species name, population share) tuples."""
        l = zip(self.distribution,[str(s) for s in self.species])
        l.sort(); l.reverse()
        ranking = [(r+1, l[r][1], l[r][0]) for r in xrange(len(l))]
        return ranking
```

8.4.2   Listing 2: The super deme class

```
class SuperDeme(Deme):
    """A Deme that contains other demes as species.

    In order to determine the fitness of the (Sub-)Demes the
    simplemost model of a group selection process is implemented:
    The fitness of the (Sub-)Demes is the dot product of the vector of
    the fitness values of the species with the vector of population
    shares. As this is not generally true, but depends on the concrete
    group selection mechanism to be modeled, method '_fitness' should
    usually be overloaded with a method implementing the right fitness
    algorithm.
    """
    def _fitness(self):
        return array([matrixmultiply(d.fitness(), d.distribution) \
                    for d in self.species])

    def replicate(self):
        for d in self.species:
            if isinstance(d, Deme):  d.replicate()
        Deme.replicate(self)

    def aggregate(self, weighted = True):
        l = []
        for i in xrange(len(self.species)):
            d = self.species[i]
```

```
            if isinstance(d, SuperDeme): d = d.aggregate(weighted)
            if weighted:
                l.append(d * self.distribution[i])
            else:
                l.append(d)
        d = l[0].merged(*l[1:])
        d.normalize()
        return d

    def reshaped(self, N=-1, minSize=-1, maxSize=-1):
        """Returns a superdeme with the same population but a
        reshaped deme structure."""
        pool = self.aggregate(weighted = True);  n = len(pool.species)
        if N <= 0: N = len(self.species)
        if minSize <= 0: minSize = max(1, N/7)
        if maxSize <= 0: maxSize = min(1, max(2, N/4))
        superdeme = pool.spawn(N, minSize, maxSize)
        return superdeme

    def reshape(self, N=-1, minSize=-1, maxSize=-1):
        """Reshape the deme structure of this deme."""
        sd = self.reshaped(N, minSize, maxSize)
        self.species = sd.species
        self.distribution = sd.distribution
```

8.4.3   Listing 3: A deme class for Prisoner's Dilemma players

The Prisoner's Dilemma class relies on another module that defines classes and functions for Prisoner's Dilemma matches and tournaments, similar to those in Axelrod (1984). The module is not listed here. (It can be downloaded as a part of another simulation package under http://www.eckhartarnold.de/apppages/coopsim.html)

```
PD_PAYOFF = array([[[1.0, 1.0], [3.5, 0.0]],\
                   [[0.0, 3.5], [3.0, 3.0]]])

def check_instances(lst, cls):
    """-> True if all objects in the list are instances of class 'cls'.
    """
    for obj in lst:
        if not isinstance(obj, cls):  return False
    return True


class PDDeme(Deme):
    """A Deme where the species represent strategies in the reiterated
    two person Prisoner's Dilemma.

    Attributes:
        payoff  - the payoff matrix of the deme (due to lazy
                  creation payoff is 'None' until _fitness is
                  called for the first time.
    """
    def __init__(self, strategies, distribution=None, name=""):
        assert check_instances(strategies, Strategy),\
            "All species must be Prisoner's Dilemma strategies!"
        Deme.__init__(self, strategies, distribution, name)
        self.payoff = None

    def _fitness(self):
        if self.payoff == None:
            self.payoff = PD.GenPayoffMatrix(self.species, payoffs=PD_PAYOFF)
        return matrixmultiply(self.payoff, self.distribution)
```

8.5 Cooperation on anonymous markets: A simplified version of Schüßler's model

One of the crucial requirements of the evolution of reciprocal altruism in most of the theoretical models of this type of altruism (see chapter 4.1.5) is the (enforced) reiteration of the game. If players could cheat and then stop the interaction with the cheated opponent there would be no way the opponent could punish the cheating player by reciprocating the defection. The obvious conclusion seems to be that the evolution of reciprocal altruism is not possible any more, if the requirement of repeated interaction is relaxed or dropped altogether. However, Schüßler was able to construct a simulation where the requirement of repeated interaction is dropped and still reciprocal altruism does evolve (within a certain range of parameter values) (Schüßler, 1990, p. 61ff.). The following describes a simplified variant of Schüßler's simulation, just complicated enough to bring out the point:

We assume a population of players of two strategy types *CONCO* and *ALL_D*. *CONCO* players cooperate, *ALL_D* players defect. All players are engaged in a pairwise Prisoner's Dilemma which is repeated for a certain number of rounds. The sequence of iterations can be broken off at any time by one of two possible causes: Either by one player breaking off the interaction at will or by a chance event. If the interaction is broken off (for whatever reason) the players have to choose a new partner from "pool" of free players to start a new sequence of interactions beginning with the nest round. (The "pool" of free players is the set of players, whose interaction has been broken off after the last round.) The *CONCO* players never break off the interaction by themselves, while the *ALL_D* players voluntarily break off the interaction right after the first round, which means that if they have hit upon a *CONCO* player they run off the revenue of one round of successful cheating in order to find a new victim. After the number of rounds has run out, the population shares of each strategy are updated, taking the average payoff for the players of each strategy as the fitness value for the strategy. (The fitness determines how the shares of the strategy *change*; see page 227 for a description of the updating process.) The details of the model and its implementation can be grasped from the listing below.

As can be seen in figure 8.41, for certain parameter values, the system evolves into a polymorphic equilibrium with a strong majority of altruists. As usual, if the parameter values are changed the phenomenon may disappear. For example, if the chance for a random breakup of interaction is increased from 5% to 20%, then altruism will disappear. Still the simulation proves the logical possibility of the evolution of altruism, even if there is no continued interaction. How much impact or scientific importance the proof of this logical possibility has, is – as with most computer simulations in this field – another question. Schüßler sees his computer simulations as a contribution to the discussion about sociological normativism. Sociological normativism, of which the classical exponents are Emile Durkheim and Ferdinand Tönnies with his distinction of "Gesellschaft" (society) and "Gemeinschaft" (community) and which has had a recent revival in communitarism, asserts that strong group ties and social norms are a necessary prerequisite for social order. Now, Schüßler's simulations do in some sense show that it is conceivable that order may evolve even without the assumption of binding social norms. However, he is very cautious not to attribute any decisive role to his simulations in this dispute (Schüßler, 1990, p. 91f.) – thereby displaying a prudent modesty and intellectual honesty that unfortunately does not seem too common in the simulation business. And he was right not to do so, because the claim of sociological normativists that social norms and social ties are necessary to keep up social order and individual welfare hardly rests on any assumptions about "logical possibilities" but on theoretical considerations as well as empirical evidence. The normativist position that social order requires norms is quite compatible with the logical possibility that some type of order (or cooperation) can evolve without norms, for what they deny is only the *empirical possibility* of order without norms, not the logical possibility. A computer simulation can have any impact on the normativist hypotheses only if it adequately models some empirical process, which brings us to the question of the empirical validation of simulations that is discussed in chapter 6.

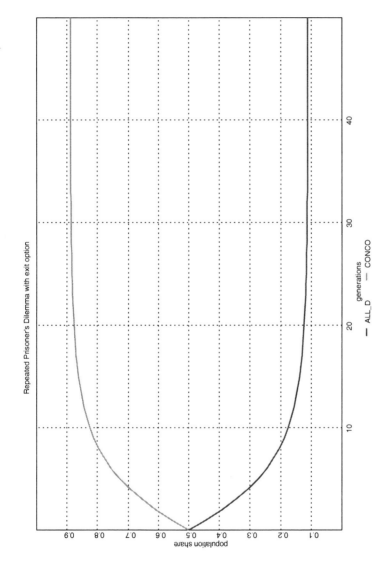

Figure 8.41: As this simulation following Schüßler (Schüßler, 1990) shows, cooperation may even evolve an "anonymous markets".

294

8.5.1 Listing: Beispiel_Schuessler_1.py

```
import Graph, Gfx
from Compatibility import *
GfxDriver = GetDriver()

# Definition of the Game

T, R, P, S = 6,4,2,1   # payoff parameters for the Prisoner's Dilemma

forced_exit = 0.05    # Chance that cooperation is terminated
                      # by external factors
initial_distribution = (0.5, 0.5)
rounds = 200
generations = 50


def OneGeneration(distribution, rounds):
    """Calculate one generation of the reiterated PD-simulation
    with exit option. 'distribution' is a 2-tuple that contains
    the population shares of CONO and ALL_D player's. 'rounds'
    is the number of rounds that are played until the strategy
    distribution is updated through replicator dynamics. The
    return value is a 2-tuple of the average score for each
    strategy.
    """
    account = [0.0, 0.0]
    cc = distribution[0]**2 / 2
    dd = distribution[1]**2 / 2
    cd = distribution[0] * distribution[1]

    for i in xrange(rounds):
        account[0] += (2*cc*R + cd*S) / distribution[0]
        account[1] += (2*dd*P + cd*T) / distribution[1]

        poolC = cc * forced_exit * 2 + cd
        poolD = dd * 2 + cd
        pool = poolC + poolD

        cc += poolC**2 / (2 * pool) - cc*forced_exit
        dd = poolD**2 / (2 * pool)
        cd = poolC * poolD / pool

    account[0] /= rounds
    account[1] /= rounds
    return tuple(account)


def PopulationDynamics(population, fitness):
    """Determines the distribution of species in the next generation."""
    n = list(population)
    L = len(population)
    f = fitness(population)
    for i in xrange(L): n[i] *= f[i]
    N = sum(n)
    if N == 0.0: return population
    for i in xrange(L): n[i] /= N
    return tuple(n)


def Schuessler():
    """A simulation of the repeated PD with exit option.
    """

    # Open a window for graphics output.

    gfx = GfxDriver.Window(title = "Repeated PD with exit option")

    # Generate a dynamics function from the payoff table.
    # dynFunc = Dynamics.GenDynamicsFunction(payoff_table, e=0.0,noise=0.0)
```

```
# Set the graph for plotting the plotting dynamics.

graph = Graph.Cartesian(gfx, 0., 0., float(generations), 1.,
    "Repeated Prisoner's Dilemma with exit option",
    "generations", "population share")
graph.addPen("CONCO", Gfx.Pen(color = Gfx.GREEN, lineWidth = Gfx.MEDIUM))
graph.addPen("ALL_D", Gfx.Pen(color = Gfx.RED, lineWidth = Gfx.MEDIUM))

# Calculate the population dynamics and plot the graph.

population = initial_distribution
graph.addValue("CONCO", 0, population[0])
graph.addValue("ALL_D", 0, population[1])
fitness = lambda p: OneGeneration(p, rounds)
for g in range(1, generations+1):
    population = PopulationDynamics(population, fitness)
    graph.addValue("CONCO", g, population[0])
    graph.addValue("ALL_D", g, population[1])
    if g % (generations/10) == 0:  gfx.refresh()

# To save the graphics in eps uncomment the following line
graph.dumpPostscript("schuessler1.eps")

# Wait until the user closes the window.

gfx.waitUntilClosed()


if __name__ == "__main__":
    print __doc__
    Schuessler()
```

8.6   Backward induction as an evolutionary process

According to the argument of backward induction, there exits one rational solution to the repeated Prisoner's Dilemma, if the number of rounds is fixed and known to the players. And this solution is never to cooperate right from the first round. The argument goes as follows: Assume both players play some arbitrary strategy. Then, unless they do not already do so, either player can get a higher payoff in the last round if he or she does not cooperate in the last round. But if both players do not cooperate in the last round for sure, then the same applies for the second but last round, and so on. Therefore the players will not cooperate during any round of the repeated game.

While the argument is mathematically sound, there exist two objections with regards to its potential empirical impact: First of all, this sort of argument only applies, if full rationality is assumed on both sides. If either of the players is not fully rational then the other might be better off with cooperating for during least some rounds. Assume, for example, that one of the players plays *Tit for Tat* without any deviations. To be sure, this is a bit irrational, because the player will then cooperate in the last round if the other player cooperated in the second but last round even though by cheating in the last round the *Tit for Tat* player would be better off. But, given this tiny bit if irrationality, the opponent would certainly do better not to cheat throughout the game right from the first round.

Still, the opponent would do best, if he or she played *Tit for Tat* with the deviation of cheating in the last round. In an evolutionary setting this would entail that all *Tit for Tat* players would in the long run be outcompeted by players that cheated only in the last round. But once the *Tit for Tat* players have given way to the *End Game Cheaters*, as we may call them, the *End Game Cheaters* are in danger of being superseded by another type of *End Game Cheater* that starts cheating in the second last round, just like the argument from backward induction suggests. (This comes as no surprise, because under standard conditions evolutionary systems typically converge to the rational equilibrium solution.)

The second objection arises from the fact that it may take the evolutionary process extremely long to reach this point, so long that it is much more likely that the process will change its directions due to some other influence or disturbance than that it will reach the equilibrium where all players play *Hawk* all the time. That the argument from backward induction may indeed be liable to this objection can easily be demonstrated by a few tentative simulations.

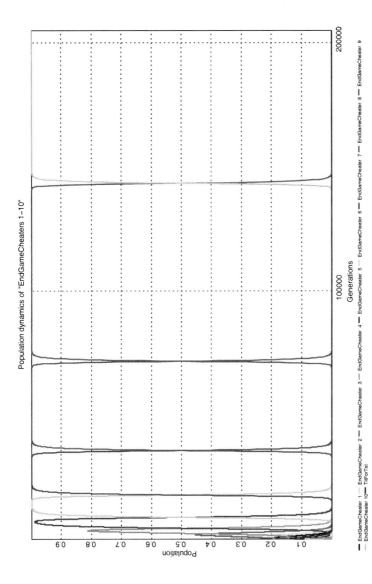

Figure 8.42: End game cheating as an evolutionary process: It takes more than 100,000 generations until it pays to cheat in the last ten rounds of a 200 round reiterated Prisoner's Dilemma.

Figure 8.42 shows a simulation where a number of end game cheaters subsequently supersede each other until finally the end game cheater that starts the earliest to cheat has taken over the whole simulation. As can clearly be seen, cheating in the last ten rounds of the repeated Prisoner's Dilemma starts to pay only after the population has firmly been taken over by cheaters that cheat during the last nine rounds. The same is true for the "nine rounds cheaters" with respect to the "eight rounds cheaters" and so on. There are no short cuts. At the same time, if we only allow for 1% of game noise the whole process stops at a much earlier point as can be seen on figure 8.43.

The obvious conclusion to be drawn is this: Even though the argument of backwards induction is true as a mathematical argument, its practical impact remains doubtful.

299

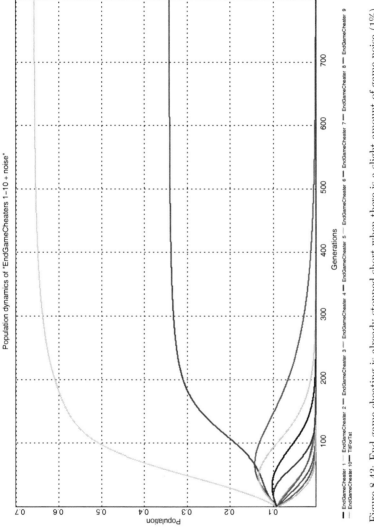

Figure 8.43: End game cheating is already stopped short when there is a slight amount of game noise (1%).

8.7 The simulation software and the full simulation results on DVD.

Both the software for the computer simulations, the results of which are described in chapter 4, and the simulation results for simulation series described in chapter 4.1.4 can be obtained on DVD for free by writing an E-Mail to eckhart_arnold@hotmail.com. Newer versions of the simulation software can also be downloaded from www.eckhartarnold.de/apppages/coopsim.html. On the DVD, the simulation software is found in the subdirectory "Software/CoopSim". This directory contains an application for simulations of the repeated Prisoner's Dilemma with a graphical user interface (CoopSim.py), with which simulations like in chapter 4.1.1 can be conducted, and two command line programs (Series.py) and (GroupSelection_test.py), which run the simulations series in chapter 4.1.4 and the group selection simulations in chapter 4.3 respectively. All simulations programs make use of the same core logic, which is concentrated in the Python-modules Simulation.py, GroupSelection.py and Strategies.py. The results of the simulation series are found in the several subdirectories (one for each series) of directors "Results" on the DVD.

8.7.1 The simulation programs

The application CoopSim.py, when started by a double click or by invoking "python CoopSim.py" from the command line, opens up an application window. Via the menu Simulation -> New Simulation... a new simulation can be configured in a dialog window. Upon clicking the "OK" button of the dialog window, the simulation is run and the simulation results are displayed in the main window. CoopSim.py comes with a complete documentation, which is browsable by selecting Help... from the Help menu. The graphical user interface was added to the simulation, because I wanted to use it with my students in class. Also, a graphical user interface greatly increases the ease of experimenting with the simulation in comparison with editing configuration files.

The simulation series from chapter 4.1.4 can be run by calling "python Series.py" from the command line after changing to the directory of CoopSim. The program runs five simulation series and stores the detailed results of each single simulation of each series as well as the aggregated data (see chapter 4.1.4 for an explanation) in a newly created directory Simulations in the user's home directory. Running all series can take several days and the data produced requires several gigabytes of hard disk space. If the program is interrupted by the user and restarted then it starts at the point where it was stopped. In order to restart the whole series over again, the subdirectories of directory `Simulations` must either be deleted or moved manually to another location.

The group selection simulations can be run by invoking "`python GroupSelection_test.py`" from the command line (after changing to directory "CoopSim" of course). In sequence seven simulations will be run and the results displayed in a window, from where they can be saved by right-clicking into the window and selecting a file name. If one or more simulations from this sequence should be suppressed, it suffices to comment out the respective lines at the end of file `GroupSelection_test.py`.

8.7.2 Browsing the results of the simulation series

Browsing the results of the simulation series from chapter 4.1.4 is easy. For each simulation series, there exists a subdirectory in the directory "Results" on the accompanying DVD. Not all of these series were described in chapter 4.1.4, because some of them served merely experimental purposes. Yet, for the sake of completeness, they have been included on the DVD, too. The most important series is the "BigSeries" in the subdirectory with the same name. In order to browse it, the file "index_frames.html" should be opened with a browser (not the file "index.html"!). The browser window is then divided into two halves. In the upper window, different parameter values can be selected and in the lower half the simulation results for the selected parameters are displayed in detail. This includes the tournament result, all of the match results and the results of the evolutionary simulation which are displayed in different steps from 50 up to maximally 25600 generations. The aggregated results of the simulation cannot be browsed via the "index.html" or "index_frames.html" files. They are instead found in the subdirectories the name of which starts with "Statistics". The aggregated results for the whole series are found in the "Statistics" subdirectory without a suffix. The suffixes of the other "Statistics"-directories indicate which parameter was kept fixed when gathering the aggregated data (this was used in chapter 4.1.4).

The other subdirectories for the the other simulation series contain similar subdirectories for the aggregated data. Unfortunately, the other results of the other series cannot be browsed so comfortably. Here, the results can only be accessed via the "index.html" file, which basically is a long list of all simulations in the respective series.

Bibliography

[Arnold 2002] ARNOLD, Eckhart: Der Einsatz evolutionärer Computermodelle bei der Untersuchung historischer und politischer Fragestellungen. in: ARNOLD, Eckhart (Ed.): *Homepage Eckhart Arnold*. Eckhart Arnold, 2002. – URL http://www.eckhartarnold.de/papers/evolution/index.html

[Arnold 2005a] ARNOLD, Eckhart: Kann die evolutionäre Spieltheorie die Entstehung von Kooperation erklären? (Studie über die schwächen eines formalen Ansatzes). in: ARNOLD, Eckhart (Ed.): *Homepage Eckhart Arnold*. Eckhart Arnold, 2005. – URL http://www.eckhartarnold.de/papers/spieltheorie-/Kritik_der_Spieltheorie.html

[Arnold 2005b] ARNOLD, Eckhart: Mehr als nur Analogien? Zur Beziehung von kultureller und biologischer Evolution. in: *Erwägen Wissen Ethik* 16 / 3 (2005), p. 372–374

[Ashworth 1980] ASHWORTH, Tony: *Trench Warfare 1914-1918. The Live and Let Live System*. MacMillan Press Ltd., 1980

[Axelrod 1984] AXELROD, Robert: *Die Evolution der Kooperation*. deutsche Übersetzung, 5. Auflage (2000). R. Oldenbourg Verlag, 1984

[Axelrod and D'Ambrosio 1994] AXELROD, Robert ; D'AMBROSIO, Lisa: Annotated Bibliography on the Evolution of Cooperation. Center for the Study of Complex Systems; University of Michigan, 1994. – URL http://www.cscs.umich.edu/research/-Evol_of_Coop_Bibliography.html

[Axelrod and Hamilton 1981] AXELROD, Robert ; HAMILTON, William D.: The evolution of cooperation. in: *Science* 211 (1981), p. 1390–1396

[Bernhard et al. 2006] BERNHARD, Helen ; FISCHBACHER, Urs ; FEHR, Ernst: Parochial altruism in humans. in: *nature* 442 (2006), August, p. 912–915

[Binmore 1994]   BINMORE, Ken: *Game Theory and the Social Contract I. Playing Fair.* Fourth printing (2000). Cambridge, Massachusetts / London, England : MIT Press, 1994

[Binmore 1998]   BINMORE, Ken: *Game Theory and the Social Contract II. Just Playing.* Cambridge, Massachusetts / London, England : MIT Press, 1998

[Blackmore 2000]   BLACKMORE, Susan: *Die Macht der Meme oder die Evolution von Kultur und Geist.* deutsche Übersetzung (2000), Ausgabe der Wissenschaftlichen Buchgesellschaft Darmstadt. Spektrum Akademischer Verlag GmbH, 2000

[Bolton et al. 2004]   BOLTON, Gary E. ; KATOK, Elena ; OCKENFELS, Axel: Trust among Internet Traders: A Behavioural Economics Approach. in: *Analyse und Kritik* 26 (2004), p. 185–202

[Boorman and Levitt 1980]   BOORMAN, Scott A. ; LEVITT, Paul R.: *The Genetics of Altruism.* Academic Press (Harcourt Brace Jovanovich, 1980

[Boyd and Richerson 1985]   BOYD, Richard ; RICHERSON, Peter J.: *Culture and the Evolutionary Process.* Chicago and London : University of Chicago Press, 1985

[Boyd and Richerson 1992]   BOYD, Robert ; RICHERSON, Peter J.: Punishment Allows the Evolution of Cooperation (or Anything Else) in Sizable Groups. in: *Ethology and Sociobiology* 13 (1992), p. 171–195

[Bryant 2004]   BRYANT, Joseph M.: An Evolutionary Social Science? A Skeptic's Brief, Theoretical and Substantive. in: *Philosophy of the Social Sciences* 34 (2004), p. 451–492

[Bshary and Grutter 2006]   BSHARY, Redouan ; GRUTTER, Alexandra S.: Image scoring and cooperation in a cleaner fish mutualism. in: *nature* 441 (2006), p. 975–978

[Cartwright 1999]   CARTWRIGHT, Nancy: *The Dappled World. A Study of the Boundaries of Science.* reprint 2003. Cambridge : Cambridge University Press, 1999

[Cavalli-Sforza and M.Feldman 1981]   CAVALLI-SFORZA, L.L. ; M.FELDMAN: *Cultural Transmission and Evolution.* Princeton / New Jersey : Princeton University Press, 1981

[Darwin 1859]   DARWIN, Charles: *The Origin of Species.* Herfordshire : Wordsworth Classics of World Literature, 1859

[Dawkins 1976] DAWKINS, Richard: *Das egoistische Gen.* deutsche Übersetzung, 4. Auflage (2002). Rowohlt, 1976

[Dawkins 1982] DAWKINS, Richard: *The Extended Phenotype. The Gene as the Unit of Selection.* Oxford and San Francisco : Oxford University Press, 1982

[Dennett 1996] DENNETT, Daniel: *Darwin's Dangerous Idea: Evolution and the Meaning of Life.* New York : Simon and Schuster Paperbacks, 1996

[Dennett 2006] DENNETT, Daniel: *Breaking the Spell: Religion as a Natrual Phenomenon.* London, England : Penguin, 2006

[Depew 2003] DEPEW, David J.: Baldwin and His Many Effects. in: WEBER, Bruce H. (Ed.) ; DEPEW, David J. (Ed.): *Evolution and Learning. The Baldwin Effect Reconsidered.* Cambridge, Massachusetts / London, England : MIT Press, 2003, Chap. 1, p. 3–31

[Diamond 1998] DIAMOND, Jarred: *Guns, Germs and Steel. A Short History of Everybody for the last 13,000 Years.* Vintage, Random House, 1998

[Diamond 2005] DIAMOND, Jarred: *Collaps. How Societies Choose to Fail or Succeed.* New York : Viking (Penguin Group), 2005

[Dugatkin 1996] DUGATKIN, Lee A.: Tit for Tat, by-product mutualism and predator inspection: a reply to Connor. in: *Animal Behaviour* 51 (1996), p. 455–457

[Dugatkin 1997] DUGATKIN, Lee A.: *Cooperation among Animals.* Oxford University Press, 1997

[Dugatkin 1998] DUGATKIN, Lee A.: Game Theory and Cooperation. in: DUGATKIN, Lee A. (Ed.) ; REEVE, Hudson K. (Ed.): *Game Theory & Animal Behaviour.* Oxford / New York : Oxford University Press, 1998, Chap. 3, p. 38–63

[Dugatkin and Wilson 1991] DUGATKIN, Lee A. ; WILSON, David S.: Rover: A Strategy for Exploiting Cooperators in a Patchy Environment. in: *The American Naturalist* 138 (1991), p. 687–701

[Dupré 1996] DUPRÉ, John: *The Disorder of Things. Metaphysical Foundations of the Disunity of Science.* Cambridge, Massachusetts and London, England : Harvard University Press, 1996

306

[Dupré 2001]   DUPRÉ, John: *Human Nature and the Limits of Science.*
Oxford : Oxford University Press, 2001

[Dupré 2003]   DUPRÉ, John: *Darwin's Legacy.* Oxford : Oxford University Press, 2003

[Engels 1998]   ENGELS, Friedrich: Philosophie von Platon bis Nietzsche.   in: HANSEN, Frank P. (Ed.):   *Herrn Eugen Dührings Umwälzung der Wissenschaften* Vol. 2.   Berlin : Directmedia Publishing GmbH, 1998, p. 50179–50789

[Fehr and Fischbacher 2003]   FEHR, Ernst ; FISCHBACHER, Urs: The nature of human altruism. in: *nature* 425 (2003), October, p. 785–791

[Ferriere and Michod 1996]   FERRIERE, Regis ; MICHOD, Richard E.: The Evolution of Cooperation in Spatially Heterogeneous Populations. in: *The American Naturalist* 147 (1996), p. 692–717

[Frean and Abraham 2001]   FREAN, Marcus R. ; ABRAHAM, Edward R.: A Voter Model of the Spatial Prisoner's Dilemma. in: *IEEE Transations on Evolutionary Computation* 5 (2001), p. 117–121

[Gehlen 1983]   GEHLEN, Arnold: *Ein Bild vom Menschen.* Vol. Arnold Gehlen. Gesamtausgabe. Band 4. Philosophische Anthropologie und Handlungslehre. p. 50–62. Frankfurt am Main : Vittorio Klostermann, 1983

[Gilbert and Troitzsch 2005]   GILBERT, Nigel ; TROITZSCH, Klaus: *Simulation for the Social Scientist.* New York : Open University Press, 2005

[Green and Shapiro 1994]   GREEN, Donald P. ; SHAPIRO, Ian: *Pathologies of Rational Choice Theory. A Critique of Applications in Political Science.* New Haven and London : Yale University Press, 1994

[Özgür Gürerk et al. 2006]   GÜRERK Özgür ; IRLENBUSCH, Bernd ; ROCKENBACH, Bettina: The Competitive Advantage of Sanctioning Insitutions. in: *Science* 312 (2006), p. 108–111

[Hamilton 1964]   HAMILTON, W.D.: The Genetical Evolution of Social Behaviour. II. in: *Journal of Theoretical Biology* 7 (1964), p. 17–52

[Hammerstein 1998]   HAMMERSTEIN, Peter: What is Evolutionary Game Theory?   in: DUGATKIN, Lee A. (Ed.) ; REEVE, Hudson K. (Ed.): *Game Theory & Animal Behaviour.* Oxford / New York : Oxford University Press, 1998, Chap. 1, p. 3–15

[Hammerstein 2003a] HAMMERSTEIN, Peter (Ed.): *Genetic and Cultural Evolution*. Cambridge, Massachusetts / London, England : MIT Press in cooperation with Dahlem University Press, 2003

[Hammerstein 2003b] HAMMERSTEIN, Peter: Why Is Reciprocity So Rare in Social Animals? A Protestant Appeal. in: HAMMERSTEIN, Peter (Ed.): *Genetic and Cultural Evolution*. Cambridge, Massachusetts / London, England : MIT Press in cooperation with Dahlem University Press, 2003, Chap. 5, p. 83–94

[Heath 2005] HEATH, Joseph: Methodological Individualism. in: ZALTA, Edward N. (Ed.): *The Stanford Encyclopedia of Philosophy*. The Metaphysics Research Lab; Center for the Study of Language and Information Stanford University, 2005. – URL http://plato.stanford.edu/archives/spr2005/entries/-methodological-individualism/

[Hegel 1998] HEGEL, Georg Wilhelm F.: Philosophie von Platon bis Nietzsche. in: HANSEN, Frank P. (Ed.): *Enzyklopädie der philosophischen Wissenschaften im Grundrisse* Vol. 2. Berlin : Directmedia Publishing GmbH, 1998, p. 41242–42195

[Hegselmann et al. 1996] HEGSELMANN, Rainer (Ed.) ; MUELLER, Ulrich (Ed.) ; TROITZSCH, Klaus G. (Ed.): *Modelling and Simulation in the Social Sciences from the Philosophy of Science Point of View (Mathematics and its Applications)*. Dordrecht / Boston /London : Kluwer Academic Publishers, 1996

[Hempel 1965] HEMPEL, Carl G.: *General Laws in History*. Chap. 9, p. 231–243. in: *Aspects of Scientific Explanation and Other Essays in the Philosophy of Science*, Collier-Macmillan Ltd. London, 1965

[Hoffmann 2000] HOFFMANN, Robert: Twenty Years on: The Evolution of Cooperation Revisited. in: *Journal of Artificial Societies and Social Simulation* Volume 3, No. 2 (2000). – URL http://jasss.soc.surrey.ac.uk/3/2/forum/1.html

[Huberman and Glance 1993] HUBERMAN, Bernado A. ; GLANCE, Natalie S.: Evolutionary games and computer simulations. in: *Proceedings of the National Academy of Sciences of the United States of America* 90 (1993), p. 7716–7718

[Humphreys 2004] HUMPHREYS, Paul: *Extending Ourselves. Computational Science, Errmpiricism, and Scientific Method*. Oxford University Press, 2004

[Huxley 1993]   HUXLEY, Thomas H.: Evolution und Ethik. in: BAY-
ERTZ, Kurt (Ed.): *Evolution und Ethik*. Stuttgart : Philipp Reclam
jun., 1993, p. 67–74

[James 2003]   JAMES, Harold: *Europe Reborn. A History, 1914-2000*.
Pearson Longman, 2003

[Kirchkamp 2000]   KIRCHKAMP, Oliver: Spatial evolution of automata
in the prisoner's dilemma. in: *Journal of Economic Behaviour &
Organiszation* 43 (2000), p. 239–262

[Kliemt 1996]   KLIEMT, Hartmut: *Simulation and Rational Parctice*.
Chap. 1, p. 13–27. in: HEGSELMANN, Rainer (Ed.) ; MUELLER, Ul-
rich (Ed.) ; TROITZSCH, Klaus G. (Ed.): *Modelling and Simulation
in the Social Sciences from the Philosophy of Science Point of View
(Mathematics and Its Applications)*. Dordrecht / Boston /London :
Kluwer Academic Publishers, 1996

[Laland and Brown 2004]   LALAND, Kevin N. ; BROWN, Gilian R.:
Sense & Nonsense. Evolutionary Perspectives on Human Behaviour.
Oxford : Oxford University Press, 2004

[Machiavelli 1980]   MACHIAVELLI, Niccolò ; BAHNER, Werner (Ed.):
Der Fürst. Wiesbaden : VMA-Verlag, 1980

[Mayr 2001]   MAYR, Ernst: *What Evolution Is*. New York : Perseus
Books Group, 2001

[Mesoudi et al. 2006]   MESOUDI, Alex ; WHITEN, Andrew ; LALAND,
Kevil N.: Towards a unified science of cultural evolution. in: *Behavioural and Brain Sciences* 29 (2006), p. 329–383

[Milinski 1987]   MILINSKI, Manfred: TIT FOR TAT in sticklebacks
and the evolution of cooperation. in: *nature* 325, January (1987),
p. 433–435

[Milinski and Parker 1997]   MILINSKI, Manfred ; PARKER, Geoffrey A.:
Cooperation under predation risk: a data-based ESS analysis. in:
Proceedings of the Royal Society 264 (1997), p. 1239–1247

[N.M.Gotts et al. 2003]   N.M.GOTTS ; POLHILL, J.G. ; LAW, A.N.R.:
Agent-Based Simulation in the Study of Social Dilemmas. in: *Artificial
Intelligence Review* 19 (2003), p. 3–92

[Nowak 1990]   NOWAK, Martin: Stochastic Strategies in the Prisoner's
Dilemma. in: *Theoretical Population Biology* 38 (1990), p. 93–112

[Nowak and Sigmund 1994] NOWAK, Martin A. ; SIGMUND, Karl: The Alternating Prisoner's Dilemma. in: *Journal of Theoretical Biology* 168 (1994), p. 219–226

[Okasha 2005] OKASHA, Samir: Altruism, Group Selection and Correlated Interaction. in: *British Journal for the Philosophy of Science* 56 (2005), p. 703–725

[Richerson et al. 2003] RICHERSON, Peter J. ; BOYD, Robert T. ; HENRICH, Joseph: Cultural Evolution of Human Cooperation. in: HAMMERSTEIN, Peter (Ed.): *Genetic and Cultural Evolution.* dahlem university press, 2003, Chap. 19, p. 357–388

[Rosenberg 2005] ROSENBERG, Alex: Lessons from Biology for Philosophy of the Human Sciences. in: *Philosophy of the Social Sciences* 35 (2005), p. 3–19

[Runciman 1990] RUNCIMAN, Walter G.: Doomed to Extinction: The Polis as an Evolutionary Dead-End. in: MURRAY, Oswyn (Ed.) ; PRICE, Simon (Ed.): *The Greek City. From Homer to Alexander.* Oxford : Oxford Clarendon Press, 1990, Chap. 14, p. 347–367

[Salwiczek 2001] SALWICZEK, Lucie: Grundzüge der Memtheorie. in: WICKLER, Wolfgang (Ed.) ; SALWICZEK, Lucie (Ed.): *Wie wir die Welt erkennen. Erkenntnisweisen im interdisziplinären Diskurs.* Freiburg / München : Verlag Karl Alber, 2001, p. 119–201

[Schopenhauer 1977] SCHOPENHAUER, Arthur: *Die Welt als Wille und Vorstellung I. Zweiter Teilband.* Zürich : Diogenes Verlag, 1977

[Schurz 2001] SCHURZ, Gerhard: Natürliche und kulturelle Evolution: Skizze einer verallgemeinerten Evolutionstheorie. in: WICKLER, Wolfgang (Ed.) ; SALWICZEK, Lucie (Ed.): *Wie wir die Welt erkennen. Erkenntnisweisen im interdisziplinären Diskurs.* Freiburg / München : Verlag Karl Alber, 2001, p. 329–376

[Schüßler 1990] SCHÜSSLER, Rudolf: *Kooperation unter Egoisten: Vier Dilemmata.* 2. Auflage (1997). München : R. Oldenbourg Verlag, 1990

[Shapiro 2005] SHAPIRO, Ian: *The Flight from Reality in the Human Sciences.* Princeton and Oxford : Princeton University Press, 2005

[Silk 2003] SILK, Joan B.: Cooperation without Counting. The Puzzle of Friendship. in: HAMMERSTEIN, Peter (Ed.): *Genetic and Cultural*

Evolution. Cambridge, Massachusetts / London, England : MIT Press in cooperation with Dahlem University Press, 2003, Chap. 3, p. 37–54

[Skyrms 1996] SKYRMS, Brian: *Evolution of the Social Contract*. Cambridge University Press, 1996

[Skyrms 2004] SKYRMS, Brian: *The Stag Hunt Game and the Evolution of Social Structure*. Cambridge University Press, 2004

[Sober and Wilson 1998] SOBER, Elliott ; WILSON, David S.: *Unto Others. The Evolution and Psychology of Unselfish Behaviour*. Harvard University Press, 1998

[Spencer 1993] SPENCER, Herbert: Evolutionäre Ethik. in: BAYERTZ, Kurt (Ed.): *Evolution und Ethik*. Stuttgart : Philipp Reclam jun., 1993, p. 75–83

[Taylor 1997] TAYLOR, Michael: *The Possibility of Cooperation. Studies in Rationality and Social Change*. reprint (first edition:1987). Cambridge : Cambridge University Press, 1997

[Tooby and Cosmides 1992] TOOBY, John ; COSMIDES, Leda: *The Psychological Foundations of Culture*. Chap. 1, p. 19–136. in: BARKOW, Jerome H. (Ed.) ; COSMIDES, Leda (Ed.) ; TOOBY, John (Ed.): *The Adapted Mind. Evolutionary. Evolutionary Psychology and the Generation of Culture*. Oxford / New York : Oxford University Press, 1992

[Trivers 1971] TRIVERS, Robert L.: The Evolution of Reciprocal Altruism. in: *The Quarterly Review of Biology* 46 (1971), p. 35–57

[Wilson 2002] WILSON, David S.: *Darwin's Cathedral. Evolution, Religion and the Nature of Society*. Chicago / London : The University of Chicago Press, 2002

ontos **PracticalPhilosophy**
verlag HerlindePauer-Studer NeilRoughley PeterSchaber RalfStoecker

Vol. 1 Peter Schaber / Rafael Hüntelmann
Grundlagen der Ethik
Normativität und Objektivität
ISBN 10: 3-937202-26-9
2. Aufl., 194 Seiten • Paperback €27,00

Vol. 2 David McNaughton
Moralisches Sehen
Eine Einführung in die Ethik
ISBN 3-937202-16-1
246 Seiten, • Hardcover € 30,00

Vol. 3 Dunja Jaber
**Über den mehrfachen Sinn von
Menschenwürde-Garantien**
Mit besonderer Berücksichtigung von
Art. 1 Abs. 1 Grundgesetz
ISBN 10: 3-937202-20-X
373 Seiten • Paperback € 24,00

Vol. 4 Kirsten B. Endres
Praktische Gründe
Ein Vergleich dreier paradigmatischer
Theorien
ISBN 10: 3-937202-22-6
231 Seiten • Paperback € 21,00

Vol. 5 Peter Schaber (Ed.)
Normativity and Naturalism
ISBN 10: 3-937202-41-2
177 pp. • Hardcover € 42,00

Vol. 6 Hans Kelsen
A New Science of Politics
*Hans Kelsen's Reply to Eric Voegelin's
"New Science of Politics". A Contribution
to the Critique of Ideology*
Edited by Eckhart Arnold
ISBN 10: 3-937202-50-1
ca. 150 pp. • Hardcover € 69,00

Vol. 7 Georg Meggle (Ed.)
Ethics of Humanitarian Interventions
ISBN 10: 3-937202-58-7
372 pp. • Hardcover € 94,00

Vol. 8 Nicholas Rescher
Value Matters
Studies in Axiology
ISBN 10: 3-937202-67-6
140 pp. • Hardcover € 58,00

Vol. 9 Raffael Iturrizaga
**David Gauthiers moralischer
Kontraktualismus**
Eine kritische Analyse
ISBN 13: 978-3-938793-60-2
367 Seiten, Hardcover, EUR 98,00

Vol.10 Diana Abad
Keeping Balance
On Desert and Propriety
ISBN 13: 978-3-938793-18-3
202 Seiten, Hardcover, EUR 79,00

ontos
verlag
Frankfurt • Paris • Lancaster • New Brunswick
P.O. Box 1541 • D-63133 Heusenstamm bei Frankfurt
www.ontosverlag.com • info@ontosverlag.com
Tel. ++49-6104-66 57 33 • Fax ++49-6104-66 57 34

ontos verlag
International Publisher
P.O. Box 15 41
63133 Heusenstamm
Tel. ++49 6104 66 57 33
Fax ++49 6104 66 57 34
info@ontosverlag.com
www.ontosverlag.com